THE COMPLETE
ENCYCLOPEDIA OF
TROPICAL
FISH

THE COMPLETE
ENCYCLOPEDIA OF

TROPICAL
FISH

How to keep,
feed and care for your Tropical Fish

ESTHER J. J. VERHOEF-VERHALLEN

REBO
PUBLISHERS

© 1997 Rebo International b.v., Lisse, The Netherlands

This 2nd edition reprinted 2004

Text: Esther J. J. Verhoef-Verhallen
Cover design: Minkowsky Graphics, Enkhuizen, The Netherlands
Coordination and production: TextCase, Groningen, The Netherlands
Typesetting: Hof&Land Typografie, Maarssen, The Netherlands

ISBN 90 366 1516 X

Contents

Introduction

The dwarf rasbora (Rasbora maculata) *can easily be kept in a small aquarium*

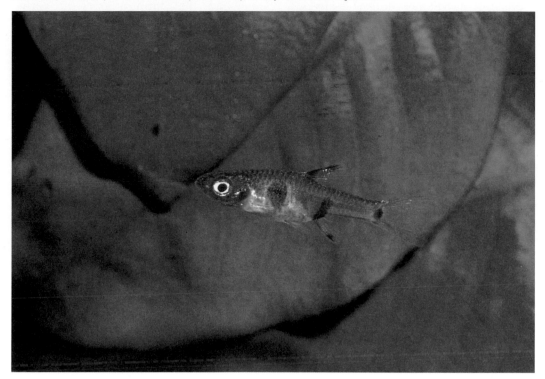

1. The aquarium

The size of the aquarium

One of the first decisions you must make when you want to buy an aquarium, is how big it should be. Obviously, financial considerations will have some part to play in your decision. Small aquaria are not only cheaper, but the equipment is also cheaper and you will quickly notice a difference in energy consumption.

The size of the aquarium also depends on its position. Not everyone wants their living room to be dominated by a large aquarium, or even has the room for one. If you own an older house with a wooden floor, you will also have to make some concessions due to the weight of the aquarium that will rest on the beams.

Left: angelfish belong in a deep aquarium

Whatever considerations you take into account, do not lose sight of the fact that the aquarium is home for your fish. In the wild some species live in enormous lakes or large rivers and like to swim large distances in them.

Clearly, an aquarium that we would call "big" can still lead to claustrophobic reactions in these fish.

There are also fish which live in small pools of water in the dry season; puddles of water that are sometimes no bigger than the hoofprint of an ox. These types of fish feel much more at home in aquaria about 30 cm wide.

Choose the size of the aquarium depending on the requirements of the fish, or vice versa. In this encyclopaedia you will find, for almost every species, a description of how large the aquarium should be to give the fish what they need.

The shape of the aquarium

There are not only many different sizes of aquaria, there is also a lot of choice as regards shapes. Originally there were only the rectangular aquaria for the living room, but nowadays there is a virtually unlimited number of possible shapes. Square, triangular, column-shaped and pyramid-shaped – even spherical aquaria on pedestals – these are just a small selection of what you can find at a well stocked aquarium dealer. The shape of the aquarium is primarily a question of taste and budget; for example traditional rectangular aquaria are much cheaper than pyramid-shaped ones. All the same, it should still be remembered that not every fish can be kept in every type of aquarium. Labyrinth fish, for example, regularly breathe above water. They have an organ called the labyrinth which enables them to absorb oxygen directly from the atmosphere. For these fish, respiration through the gills does not even provide enough oxygen, so they must take in some air

A goldfish bowl

Shoaling fish need an elongated aquarium

from above the water from time to time. If the water level is too high they will suffocate. Fish which swim fast and swim a lot (most shoaling fish have this characteristic), will only feel at home in elongated aquaria. In a narrow column-shaped aquarium, they cannot "mark out paths" and are prevented from exhibiting their natural behaviour. Remember that an aquarium must also be practical. Aquaria which are narrower at the top than at the bottom are more difficult to keep clean.

The shape of the aquarium and oxygen requirements

Aquaria with a small water surface must definitely be aerated. Fish use up the oxygen in the water. The water makes up for this shortage by taking oxygen from the atmosphere. This can only happen in places where the water is in direct contact with the atmosphere: i.e. at the water surface. If the ratio of water surface to the total contents of the aquarium is too small, the fish use up more oxygen than the water can replenish in the same period of time. The fish then "hang" just below the surface, where the first exchange of oxygen takes place and where the oxygen concentration in the water is therefore highest. If there are too many fish, the weakest will die due to lack of oxygen.

Using a simple air filter pump, with the outflow tube placed as low as possible in the aquarium, all the different zones can be supplied with oxygen.

Position

Moving an aquarium around is not good for the fish or for the aquarium itself. You should therefore choose a position where you know the aquarium can be left for several years. You should take a number of factors into account:

Direct sunlight always results in algae formation. Sometimes the algae only grow on the aquarium sides, but it is more probable that floating algae will develop, which will turn your aquarium into a green, turbid mass of water in a very short space of time. A dark location is therefore best. You can control the lighting with artificial light; this is preferable to natural light in most cases. Remember that an attractive aquarium will make a

a standard aquarium measuring 60 x 30 x 30 cm

must always be on the level, so you should start by checking whether the surface on which you want to position your aquarium is level. Always insert a layer of polystyrene foam between the base and the aquarium, even when using smaller aquaria. This will ensure that the pressure is distributed as evenly as possible and the chance that the aquarium will shatter one day because of a change in pressure can be minimised.

The material

In the past we sometimes used to find aquaria whose sides and backs were made of specially treated wood, but today's aquaria are always made of plastic or glass. A glass aquarium is always a better investment than a plastic tank. Glass is heavier, often more expensive and also more fragile than plastic, but its great advantage is that it lasts longer. Plastic is easily damaged; removing algae from the sides with a razor blade or a soft scourer

a column aquarium

dark, perhaps rather boring corner of your house much more attractive.

Aquaria should never be positioned near doors or windows. Fish are frequently shocked by the slamming of doors (some varieties of fish may die instantly from fright) and cold from outside (open windows) has a negative effect on the constant temperature of the aquarium water.

Check that the surface is strong enough. Aquaria are heavy. An empty glass aquarium weighs quite a lot on its own, but once it is filled with water and gravel it becomes even heavier. There are aquarium bases for sale which are specially designed to take this weight for years on end. A large solid oak sideboard, an ottoman or a brick plinth will also do. Do not forget that the wiring, pump(s) and food also need storage space. An aquarium

Catfish are remarkable aquarium dwellers which can be kept in all kinds of aquaria.

need thick foliage in which to hide. If they are kept in an aquarium with little or no vegetation they will rarely display their splendid colours and some fish will even gradually pine away. There are other varieties of fish which do not like bright light, for example, so it is important to create shadowy spots in the aquarium. With the help of floating plants, or strong plants with large leaves, you can create some shade for these fish. Finally, there are also varieties of fish which thrive best of all in an aquarium with a dark base or an aquarium with a sandy bottom.

Not all fish have the same requirements. So-called "beginner's fish" are well known for their adaptability. They feel at home in virtually any aquarium, irrespective of whether there is vegetation or not, whether the light is strong or moderate, and whether there is a strong current in the water or none at all. These fish are ideal for people who have just taken up the hobby.

The various requirements with regard to

always leaves ugly scratches. If you want to enjoy your aquarium for longer, then a glass aquarium is simply the best choice. Find out at the time of purchase whether the aquarium has a cover. This is a pane of glass that is placed on the aquarium below the lighting. Covers not only keep the most active fish in the aquarium, but they also lead to slower water evaporation and better heat retention. Furthermore, a cover of this type protects the light switch from water splashes. Most equipment which is intended for use with or inside aquaria is designed to cope with splashes of water, but the combination of electricity and water is still dangerous. You should always take great care here.

2. Setting up your aquarium

Setting up your aquarium

When setting up the aquarium the same applies as when choosing its size and shape; it is a question of taste and budget but the accommodation must above all be suitable for the species of fish that will live in the aquarium.

It is better not to put plants in an aquarium with plant-eating fish, or fish which sometimes burrow in the bottom and damage the roots of the plants as a result. If you still want some "greenery" in your aquarium, use plastic plants. Good quality plastic plants will last for years, and high quality ones look like the real thing. There are some shy species of fish which

Synthetic plants provide variety in an aquarium containing plant eating fish.

accommodation are described as clearly as possible for all the varieties of fish in this book. You may find a rocky aquarium particularly attractive and keep fish suitable for it, or you may keep a certain variety of fish and adjust your aquarium accommodation accordingly – it makes no difference. What is important is that the aquarium should be set up in such a way that its inhabitants feel at ease. Only then will you be able to enjoy their natural behaviours and splendid colouring. Perhaps you will even be surprised to find some baby fish: a sign that the fish feel very much at home.

The necessity of filtration

With the exception of a number of very robust varieties of fish, most of them do very badly indeed in a dirty aquarium. In fact contamination is so dangerous that it can very quickly cause the death of some or all of the fish. Aquarium water usually gets contaminated quite quickly by food remains, fish excrement and rotting plant leaves. Even in the wild, water constantly gets contaminated but because there is usually a current and the dirty water is diluted by heavy rainfall or fresh water from mountain streams, the fishes' health rarely comes under threat. In the aquarium there is no natural exchange of water and no natural current. If you do not artificially filter and regularly replace (some of) the water, waste materials will constantly accumulate and will develop into a very unhealthy, and even deadly,

You will only be blessed with baby fish if the fish feel at home in your aquarium.

environment in which poisonous ammonia and nitrates become predominant. An effective filter is therefore essential in nearly all aquaria.

Exceptions to this rule are medium to large-sized aquaria with abundant vegetation in which relatively few fish are kept. The maximum is four to five centimetres of fish per 10 litres of water. That means that in an aquarium measuring 60 x 30 x 30 cm, you can keep approximately 21 to 27 cm of mature fish; provided that the fish are only given moderate amounts of food.

In aquaria with less abundant vegetation the number falls sharply to 1 centimetre of fish per 10 litres of water. Obviously this is not an option for most people. An effective filter and regular (partial) changing of water are therefore definitely necessary if you want to keep more fish.

DIFFERENT TYPES OF FILTERS

There are various ways of filtering the aquarium. Powerful motorised filters, where the filter component is located outside the aquarium, and corner filters, in which the small filter is actually inside the aquarium and the motor is outside, are the most popular filter types.

Filters are filled with materials that retain the dirt and release the water. After some time, useful bacteria begin to grow inside the filter. These bacteria convert harmful nitrates and ammonia in the water into harmless substances and therefore play an important role in the development of a biological equilibrium. If you replace the filter material with new filter material whenever it is saturated with dirt, you are throwing away not only the dirty filter contents, but also these useful bacteria. It is therefore a good idea to introduce ceramic air stones into the filter as well as filter wadding. These air stones have a porous surface which retains the bacteria, even if you rinse them under running water. You can put the air stones back in the filter again once you have cleaned the filter and changed the filter wadding, so that the bacteria can continue their useful activity immediately.

You should always ensure that the filter that you buy has sufficient capacity. Get advice on this from your specialist dealer, since the capacity depends not only on the contents of the aquarium and the number of fish that live in it, but also on the type of filter itself.

Labyrinth fish can absorb oxygen directly from the atmosphere and can therefore survive in water with low oxygen levels.

A small corner filter has sufficient capacity for a small aquarium.

An airstone ensures a steady stream of air bubbles through the aquarium.

Heating

If you keep fish which are used to temperatures from 22 to 30°C in their natural environment, then you cannot avoid – especially in colder seasons – heating the aquarium artificially. he best way of doing this is using elements which combine a heater and thermostat in a single unit. You will notice that there are heating elements with different wattages. Which wattage you need depends on the capacity of the aquarium, the extent to which the aquarium is insulated (cover) and the room in which the aquarium is situated. In cold, unheated rooms, about 1 watt per litre of water is needed. In heated rooms, half a watt per litre will be more than enough. If you have an aquarium measuring 60 x 30 x 30 cm (54 litres capacity) in your heated living room, you will need a 25 to 30 watt heating element. If the same aquarium is in a cold, unheated room, then a wattage of 50 to 55 is better. If the wattage is too high or too low this will almost always lead to problems. If the temperature outside the aquarium rises too high, for example during a very warm summer, it is sensible to switch off the heating temporarily. This is because few fish can stand temperatures above 30°C over a long period of time. Check the water temperature every day, since fluctuating water temperatures cause stress, which can make the fish ill. Most heating combinations should not project above the water when switched on. The best place for a heating element is a few centimetres above the bottom, preferably in a horizontal position, because this distributes the rising heat better. A heating ele-

Some varieties of fish need very warm conditions, such as these discus fish.

Macropodus occelatus *can also be kept in unheated aquaria.*

ment should never come into contact with plants, decorations or material on the bottom.

Lighting

Every aquarium needs to be lit, especially if you keep tropical fish. These fish are used to twelve to fourteen hours of light per day. Outside the tropics, the sun will only shines for that long during certain seasons, and its intensity is much lower. If the aquarium is not artificially lit, ugly brown algae will grow, the fish will feel uncomfortable and they will be susceptible to disease. What is more, plants will not grow and they will gradually wither away.

There are various ways of lighting your

Floating plants filter the bright neon light and provide shaded spots in the aquarium.

aquarium, but neon lighting is by far the best method. Neon tubes are cheapest in terms of energy consumption and they give off the most light in relative terms. A single neon tube will often be adequate in smaller aquaria, but if the aquarium is wider than 60 cm, or deeper than 30 cm it will be necessary to install one or more neon tubes to achieve optimal lighting. A neon tube must always be placed at the front of the aquarium so that its shadow, from your perspective, falls behind the fish and plants. There are special neon tubes which stimulate plant growth and others which bring out the colours of the fish much better (fluorescent tubes). Various types of neon tubes can easily be placed next to one another. If you connect each neon tube to a separate switch, you can also create an artificial twilight, so that you will be able to observe the nocturnal fish in your aquarium better in the evening. In aquaria without plants, a simple fluorescent tube will be enough to make the fish feel at home. The colours of the fish also look much more attractive in this light than when a "normal" neon tube is used.

The wattage which you need depends largely on the size and the depth of the aquarium. It is better to use too high a wattage than too low; you can use floating plants to create spots of shade for fish which are less suited to this . For a standard aquarium measuring 30 to 40 cm high, 0.25 to 0.5 watts per litre will be plenty. If the aquarium is deeper, you can also adjust the wattage to 0.75 or 1 watt per litre of aquarium water. A standard aquar-ium measuring 60 x 30 x 30 cm can therefore be illuminated by a neon tube of approximately 27 watts. A neon tube will give off less and less light during its lifetime until it finally goes out completely. It is therefore sensible to replace all neon tubes with new ones about once a year.

The back wall

A back wall is used to make the aquarium "opaque". A back wall makes the aquarium look "complete" – it is simply more attractive. There are many different types of back walls. Some, in the form of dyed Styrofoam boards with contours, are placed in the aquarium itself. Others can be attached to the back of the aquarium.

These might consist of coloured or printed paper with pictures of rocks or plants. You can also paint the back of the aquarium (obviously on the outside!) with black-board paint. Which option you choose will depend on your own personal preference. In any case, do not use normal paint, because it leaves ugly brush-strokes on the glass. Avoid using any material inside the aquarium that could harm the plants and fish.

Nutrient base

Plants need nutrients in order to grow. Gravel and washed sand do not contain any nutrients for the plants. Therefore, a nutrient base, which you can purchase ready for use from an aquarium centre, is necessary to keep the plants looking attractive and to give them a chance to grow. The nutrient base should not be placed right on the bottom, but on top of a layer of gravel. Do not use too much nutrient base: a 2cm layer is usually more than enough. If you use more the plants will get too much food, which results in excessive root growth. The plant itself does not grow as much, which defeats the objective. You should also add a thick layer of gravel on top of the nutrient base to prevent the soil from rising up and making the water cloudy. Of course, you need only apply this kind of fertiliser in the places where plants will later be growing.

Gravel and sand

The material covering the bottom in the vast majority of aquaria consists of gravel. Gravel comes in all shapes, colours and sizes. The type of gravel you use will depend not only on your personal prefer-ence, but also on the preferences of the fish that you will be keeping in the aquar-ium.

Some fish like to burrow or dig around in the bottom, so they must be given the chance to do this. If you use sharp gravel, their mouths may be injured. With these species of fish, you should always use smooth, fine gravel or well washed sand. Of course mixtures of fine gravel and sand are also good. There are also fish – the Corydoras varieties, for example, which enjoy rooting in the ground in search of food, and there are those which some-

Fish like Corydoras aeneus *need a soft (sandy) substrate.*

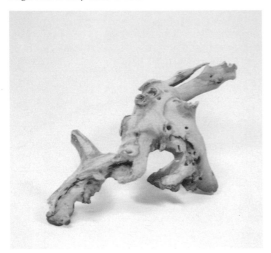

Bogwood is very decorative.

times like to bury themselves in the bottom. You must definitely create a thick sandy base for these fish. If you don't want to do this, you can set aside part of the aquarium with well-washed sand especially for these fish. Never use ordinary sand, but only use sand that you have bought from your aquarium centre. Only then can you be sure that the sand contains no heavy metals or other harmful substances.

The colour of the sand or the gravel is also important. Most fish are accustomed to dark substrates. This makes them feel more secure then and their colours come out much better. The gravel should rise towards the back for best effect. The gravel should not be up against the glass at the front of the aquarium, but at the back it can be 7 cm thick or even more. The advantage of this is that the aquarium is given more visual depth and the dirt, which tends to accumulate at the lowest level in the aquarium, ends up at the front. No plants are growing there and it is more easily accessible to siphon out the dirt.

Often the gravel does not stay as you would like it. One solution is to create borders. These borders also have the advantage of giving more depth and variation. An aquarium with borders is also much more attractive for the fish than an aquarium with a flat bottom. You can make borders from pieces of slate or petrified wood. Place these in specific areas and fill up the space behind them with gravel.

Both the gravel and sand that you buy at the specialist dealer have been washed already, but that doesn't mean that it is ready for immediate use in the aquarium. Gravel and sand should be thoroughly cleaned first. This is not as difficult as it looks. If you put a small amount of gravel at a time in a bucket and let it stand under running water for a time, very soon the water in the bucket will no longer be cloudy. You can speed up the process by stirring around in the sand or the gravel with your hand. Only when the water remains crystal clear is the sand or gravel clean enough to be used in the aquarium.

Decorative materials

STONES AND ROCKS

Stones and rocks are best bought from your aquarium centre. Some (calcareous) stones react to water and make it too hard. Other stones contain metals, which is bad for the health of the fish. The stones – such as lava – which you will find at an aquarium centre, are definitely safe for the fish and do not affect the composition of the water.

Some fish like to hide. If you have such fish, you must arrange the stones in such a way that there are cavities for the fish to hide in and under. Very strong and large fish species, particularly the larger cichlids, can create real havoc if they start digging around in the gravel and this can cause the structures to collapse. Most aquarium glass is not strong enough to withstand this. It is advisable to glue the

Purple cichlid (Pelvicachromis pulcher)

Many cichlids thrive well in an aquarium without plants.

Most varieties of fish like a living environment with dense vegetation.

stones together beforehand if you keep strong fish. Do this with an adhesive that is suitable for use in aquaria. In any case you will have to be patient before you can use stones in the aquarium: the poisonous substances must be removed from the glue first. The glue packaging will tell you how long this takes.

BOGWOOD
Root wood, which is sold as bogwood or mopane wood, is very decorative. It comes in convoluted shapes and therefore offers ideal refuges for smaller fish. One very common problem with this wood is that it can turn the water an orange colour after a time. You can avoid this by treating the wood first with a thin coat of transparent polyurethane lacquer. Obviously, once it has set, this lacquer should give off no (more) poisonous substances into the aquarium water. Exactly

The aquarium should ideally be densely planted for killifish

how long it takes to set will vary   seek advice from your aquarium centre.

OTHER DECORATIVE MATERIALS
There are many ready-made decorative materials for sale. Some look very natural, others are rejected by many people as kitsch. The choice is entirely up to you. Flower pots, and by these we mean only orange-coloured earthenware pots, are ideal hiding and brooding places for some fish. You should actually always give Pelvicachromis varieties, including the well-known purple cichlids, such a pot as a hiding place. You can lie the pot on its side, half buried in the gravel, or enlarge the hole in the bottom (file down any sharp edges!) and press the pot upside down into the gravel. If you do not like the colour and shape of these pots you could use a half coconut shell.

Plants

There are some aquaria without plants, but most people prefer an aquarium with plenty of vegetation. Before buying plants that look nice at first glance, it is best to draw up a plan. Ask yourself what fish are going to populate your aquarium. Some fish varieties are plant eaters and will see your aquarium full of vegetation as a huge banquet. Within a very short time your expensive aquatic plants will be reduced to a few pitiful gnawed sprouts. Other fish like feathery-leafed plants or floating plants because they can hide among the thick leaves.

Your choice of plants should not be based exclusively on the preference of the fish, but also on the water composition that you need to keep your chosen fish in tip-top condition. Some plants require a low pH, and others prefer a high pH. If these do not correspond, either the plants or the fish will not do as well. You should also ask how big the plants will grow. The small plants which you buy at an aquarium centre may grow into giants which dominate your whole aquarium in a very short space of time.

MARSH PLANTS

There are also some plants which are sold as aquatic plants but are actually marsh plants. You will recognise a number of these plants as house plants. These are attractive to look at, but they are only partially suitable for underwater life. They are frequently found growing in jungles. They live on what is virtually dry land outside the rainy season, but the high humidity in the jungle ensures that they do not dry out. Whole areas of the jungle are flooded during heavy rainfall and the plants have to adjust to living under water for a few

months. Despite this high natural adaptability, these plants cannot survive in the aquarium for years on end. Marsh plants are generally easy to recognise: if they keep the same shape when they are taken out of the water, then they are not true aquatic plants.

AQUATIC PLANTS IN THE AQUARIUM

Aquatic plants are not always cheap and that is why many people only buy a few plants. However it is not sensible to skimp on the number of plants you buy. Algae, and particularly the algae which turn the water green and turbid, are disliked by most hobbyists. By ensuring that the aquarium is not too sparsely planted when newly set up, algae can be given less opportunity to multiply quickly and make their presence felt. This is because in that case the scarce nutrients which are present in the aquarium are consumed by the plants, leaving fewer nutrients for the algae.

What is more, an aquarium with plenty of vegetation is also much more attractive to look at. The more plants, the more attractive the final effect will be, as long as the plants are arranged in an aesthetically

Mussel plant

pleasing manner. There are certain rules of thumb for this. Plants which stay small should be placed in the foreground, larger plants in the middle and the largest plants at the back. Remember that it looks better if you put larger groups of plants of the same variety together and let these grow in the aquarium, rather than buying just one of each type of plant. Never position the one or at the most two real "eye-catchers", so-called solitary plants, which grow to a large size and are conspicuous in their colours or leaf shapes, right in the middle. An asymmetric arrangement which gives the impression of depth, will create a better effect.

Less demanding plant varieties, such as the various cabombas, most cryptocorynes, Samolus parviflorus (lettuce plant), vallisnerias, Lysimachia numularia, Cardamine lirata and Lobelia cardinalis are recommended for new aquarists. These plants do very well in varying water compositions and are not as sensitive to water temperature. Vesicularia dubyana (Java moss) is an eminently suitable plant, which is very decorative if attached to the back wall of the aquarium or to a piece of petrified wood, and also offers refuge for fry. Crystalwort is often used as a floating plant. Mussel plants develop huge roots and therefore provide an ideal refuge for small and young fish. The disadvantage of these plants is that they are really designed for outside ponds and do not cope well with neon light.

3. Water composition
Correct water composition

As an aquarist you will need to become familiar with different chemical concepts, such as pH and gH. If you want to keep varieties of fish which are not as easy to care for, or if you want to breed fish, then you must at least have an understanding of these two concepts.

The acidity of the water (pH value)

The pH indicates whether the water is acidic (less than pH 7), basic (more than

Most African cichlids do well in hard water.

Wild-caught guppies hardly makes any demands on the water composition.

pH 7) or neutral (pH 7). Mixtures of all these values occur in nature. Some fish are accustomed to living in highly acidic waters (with a low pH), while others are accustomed to a basic environment (and therefore a high pH). There are various species of fish which can survive in waters with both high and low pH values, irrespective of the levels in their natural environments. There are also some which die if they are kept in water where the pH value is too different from the pH in their natural habitat.

There are various additives on the market which can decrease or increase the pH value. However it is advisable, particularly if you do not have much experience, either to keep fish which are not very demanding in this respect, or fish which are used to the same pH value as your tap water. You can always contact your water company to find this out, but you can also test the water yourself using the various pH testers which are available from specialist outlets. The pH values mentioned in this encyclopaedia are only guidelines; they are ideal values. So you do not always need to adhere to these values precisely. If the precise pH value is really essential for the health of a certain species of fish, this will be specifically mentioned when discussing that species.

Water hardness (gH)

There are various terms used to indicate water hardness, but the only one which is important for the new aquarist is gH (average hardness).

The gH value is measured in degrees. 0° to 4° gH denotes very soft water, 4 to 8° gH is soft water, 8 to 12° gH is slightly hard water, 12 to 18° gH is fairly hard water and 18 to 30° gH means hard water. The gH value actually expresses the amount of magnesium salts and calcium sulphates dissolved in the water. Hard water contains a large quantity of dissolved calcium. It is mainly found in lakes and streams with rocky bottoms in mountainous areas. Soft water is found mainly in tropical rainforests. The hardness of the water is very easy to adjust in accordance with what your fish are accustomed to. There are various preparations which you can use. If you are not familiar with this area, however, it is better to ask your water company first how hard the tap water is in your home, or to measure it yourself using a simple water test. If you buy fish varieties which feel comfortable with the composition of your tap water at home, you will save yourself a great deal of trouble.

Preparing the water

Tap water has to be prepared before you put it in the aquarium, because tap water is not intended for use as aquarium water, but as drinking water. This means that there should definitely not be any substances in the water which are harmful to

Hepsetus odoe *is a real predator*

Shoaling fish do not feel happy if they are kept individually.

people. Chlorine is added in small quantities to keep the water free from bacteria and make it drinkable for people. Metals are also present in drinking water; tiny quantities are given off by (copper) water pipes. These substances, especially in such tiny quantities, are not harmful to people, but they are to fish. Fish have a protective, slimy coating over their scales which, amongst other things, protects them from harmful bacteria and other pathogenic organisms. This layer cannot withstand aggressive chlorine and metals and it is seriously affected by them. If you place your fish in water taken straight from the tap, they will react to this almost immediately by spreading their fins and breathing with jerky movements – a sign that something is wrong. Robust fish can survive in tap water, but they will certainly be destined for a shorter life than those kept in prepared water.

There are special chemicals for sale

which you can use to convert tap water into aquarium water. There is also a method of treating the water which does not involve any chemicals – if you let the tap water stand in a bucket for some time (about a week), most of the harmful substances will disappear. It is important that the bucket should only be used for this purpose and not for washing the windows, or for other purposes where soap and other substances may be used. That is because if so these substances may find their way into the aquarium, and they are definitely harmful to the fish. The same applies to all the tools used to maintain the aquarium, such as sponges. It is best to buy a few extra items and to use them exclusively for the aquarium.

Since the "bucket method" is time-consuming, it is more practical to have a bottle of water preparation at home all the time, for example, for when you change some of the water. Previously rainwater was widely used by aquarists, but nowadays rainwater is only suitable for aquarium water if it is collected in an area without exhaust fumes and industrial estates nearby. Otherwise the rainwater may contain just as many harmful substances as tap water.

4. Fish

Not all varieties can be combined

There are many different varieties of fish, and they all have their own lifestyle. Among others we can differentiate be-

Shoaling fish like to be together.

tween shoaling fish, solitary fish and fish which live in pairs. The temperament and nutritional requirements of the fish also differ from one species to another. It is quite an art to find fish which can live together harmoniously in an aquarium. Of course small fish do not belong in an aquarium with fish-eating predators and robust, fast swimmers will upset slower, more fragile fish too much. You should also remember that different fish occupy different zones. Some fish prefer the middle zone, while others prefer to live on the bottom, or just below the surface. Obviously you will achieve the most attractive effect if you choose fish which live in different zones. If you only keep fish which occupy the middle zone, the overall effect will not be harmonious. The fish will also get in each other's way when they are swimming around.

You should therefore try to match the

The neon tetra is a real shoaling fish.

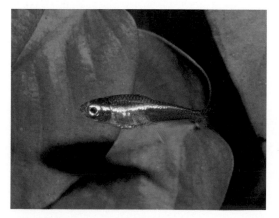

This Epalzeorhynchus bicolor is a solitary fish.

Sturisoma aureum

Synodontis schoutedeni

shadow. A single shoaling fish is always searching for other similar specimens. The larger the shoal, the more secure the fish feel. Many types of shoaling fish are among the most popular aquarium fish.

People who know no better sometimes keep shoaling fish as individuals, or in groups which are too small. Since there are so many different varieties of shoaling fish, with as many different colours and markings, and varying shapes and sizes, most people find it difficult to make a choice. They therefore decide to buy four or five small shoals of different shoaling fish, in the hope that they will be able to enjoy several varieties of fish. Unfortunately it does not work out that way in practice. The small fish usually operate in the same zone and are constantly getting in each other's way. The many different colours and shapes give a cluttered appearance and, because the shoals are too small, the fish do not feel at their best. This is immediately evident from their coloration, behaviour and health. On the other hand one, or if there is enough space perhaps two, good shoals of at least twenty fish will make any aquarium look attractive, particularly if the fish differ considerably in colour, shape and swimming technique. You may need to dig deeper in your wallet, but the end result will be much more attractive and the fish will feel much more at ease in your aquarium.

fish populations in the aquarium. To make it easier to identify which fish can live together without any problem, we have classified them below by living habits. If you want a harmonious aquarium in which all the fish feel comfortable, you will have to take the wishes and requirements of the fish into account.

Shoaling Fish

Shoaling fish live in large groups in the wild. In their natural biotopes, fish of this type are often encountered in shoals containing thousands of similar specimens. In many cases these are smaller fish which are not very well equipped to defend themselves against predators. When they crowd together in a single mass, they look like one large fish to their predators. These types of fish have a natural instinct to swim very close to one another. If the front fish turns, the whole group will follow as close as his

Solitary fish

Solitary fish, perhaps because of their intolerant or aggressive behaviour towards similar specimens, are best living on their own. In the wild these fish can avoid each other – there is always enough space to keep out of the way. The fish seek each

Many cichlids like to live in pairs.

Pseudotropheus lombardoi

other out again during the mating season. In the aquarium, however, the fish are forced to live together in a relatively small space. They have no way of avoiding one another and the struggles can be so violent that the weakest will eventually die. One characteristic of these solitary fish is that they generally leave other species of fish alone; the aggression of most varieties is mainly directed at their own kind. Most solitary fish thrive well in a community aquarium.

Fish which live in pairs

Many cichlids belong to this group. In the wild, fry that hatch out from eggs often swim together and form a kind of small shoal. Young fish of the same kind from different parents also join such a group. As the fish mature, they develop a preference for a certain fish in the group. They then break off from the group and retreat to a territory of their own together with this partner. In this territory they make a nest, lay eggs and care for their young until they are old enough to look after themselves. After that the parent fish simply see them as intruders or tasty morsels. The fry swim off in a small shoal and the whole process starts again from the beginning.

Fish which live in pairs have an interesting method of reproduction and the way in which they protect and care for their eggs and young is a very special sight.

Territorial fish

Most territorial fish are either solitary or pairing varieties. Most cichlids, for example, are territorial. This term refers to fish which lay claim to a certain part of the aquarium, often close to an artificial cavity. Usually no other fish are tolerated in this territory and certainly no other fish of the same variety. In the case of cichlids the territory is occupied by a pair, but the solitary Labeo bicolor establishes a territory entirely by himself.

If you want to keep fish of this type in your aquarium (and most of them are really worth keeping), then you must make sure that there are enough refuges. Rocky

Most cichlids are territorial.

Most cichlids are territorial.

Hatchet fish are surface fish.

areas, plenty of vegetation, petrified wood in convoluted shapes and miscellaneous upside-down flower pots are ideal refuges which will appeal to many territorial fish. Due to the aggression that the fish display if other fish "invade" their territory, the aquarium must definitely be large. Also it should not contain too many fish. There is more jostling in an overpopulated aquarium, and the other aquarium dwellers are left with no other choice but occasionally to enter another's territory, with all the ensuing consequences. If you have a spacious aquarium with plenty of refuges, it is usually quite possible to keep several territorial fish together.

Surface fish

Surface fish are, as the name implies, fish which prefer to live just below the surface in the top zone. The fish are easily recognisable. The mouth opening is usually on the upper side of the body, so that they can easily take food from the surface of the water. Their backs are usually straight and these fish usually do not have large fins on the upper side of the body. A robust dorsal fin would protrude above the water, giving prey – usually small insects – an early warning system. The natural diet of surface fish consists of small insects (fruit flies or mosquitoes) and their larvae, such as mosquito larvae.

This type of fish includes both shoaling fish and solitary fish. Well-known surface fish include, for example, hatchet fish, butterfly fish and a number of killifish. Another feature that these fish have in common is that they like to jump. There are some examples of fish which can jump several metres in the wild. If you want to keep these fish in an aquarium, a cover is absolutely essential.

Inhabitants of the middle zone

Many shoaling fish are included in the large group of fish which mainly occupy the middle zone. Examples of these are neon tetras (Paracheirodon innesi), cardinal tetras (Paracheirodon axelrodi) and Buenos Aires tetras (Hemigrammus caudovittatus). They take their food almost entirely from the middle zone, although some species will swim to the top zone occasionally if there is food to be found there. They are rarely or never found on the bottom. Most fish which come into this category are particularly fast swimmers and are always on the move.

Bottom dwellers

Bottom dwellers have the opposite body design to that of the surface fish. In these fish the mouth is situated on the underside of the body, so that they do not have to manoeuvre themselves into difficult positions in order to eat. The dorsal fin is often prominent, while most have a flat lower body. The fish are therefore perfectly equipped for life on the bottom, which is where they prefer to live.

Bottom dwellers are frequently excellent "vacuum cleaners" in the aquarium. Everything that is not eaten by the other inhabitants of the aquarium and falls to the bottom, is found and eaten by these fish. They are found in most aquaria, not only because they perform a very useful task, but also because they often have a striking appearance. Most are quiet by day, or do not show themselves at all, but become active at dusk. Most bottom dwellers are solitary fish, but there are some varieties which prefer to live in small shoals.

Fish which occupy the whole aquarium

Among the fish which make their home throughout the aquarium are, amongst others, the live-bearing tooth carps such as the guppy (Poecilia reticulata) and the variegated platy (Xiphophorus variatus), but also many barbs, minnows and carp varieties. These fish take food from the surface of the water, from the bottom and from in between. They are boisterous, busy swimmers, which feel most at home

Synodontis angelicus *is a real bottom dweller.*

Arius seemani

Papiliochromis ramirezi *or butterfly cichlid*

in a shoal or small group. They can displace shyer fish because of their active lifestyle.

5. Buying fish

Releasing the fish

Patience is one of the most important characteristics which an aquarist must possess. If you don't have it, the whole undertaking will rarely be successful. We can do a lot ourselves; the water composition can be adjusted, the water can be heated, lit, filtered, and so on and so forth. But biological equilibrium is something that appears over time and there is little you can do to speed it up.

Once the aquarium is set up, including the plants, you should leave it alone for a week or two. Turn the lighting on and off at the appropriate times (or install a timer to do this), make sure that the filter works and keep the water at the desired temperature. After a few weeks you can release the first inhabitants into the aquarium. Start with two or three strong fish and do not buy the rest until a few weeks later. One of the most common "beginner's mistakes" is not just to buy the fish much too quickly, but also to introduce too many at once. The carefully constructed and very fragile balance within the aquarium is therefore destroyed at a single stroke, with the result that many fish very soon become fatally ill and die. In the United States, this huge fish mortality is known as "New Tank Syndrome", and the fact that a term has been devised for it

At an aquarium centre you will find a huge range of fish and plants.

shows that this problem does not just arise occasionally. You can easily avoid large scale fish mortality by building up the fish environment carefully and with a great deal of patience.

Buying fish

If you want to buy fish, it is best to go to an aquarium centre. Most pet shops sell fish, but an aquarium centre will sell a full range of aquarium equipment and fish and the staff will be properly trained in this area. There is also a much larger choice at specialist outlets. Here you will not only find the most popular fish, but also less well known species, some of which are very suitable for new aquarists. Obviously you should check when choosing the fish that they are healthy. If they are squeezing their fins, if they have prominent scales, if their gills are moving up and down very rapidly or if they are rubbing against stones and plants, this is not a good sign. The same applies if there are dead fish floating in the water, or if there are fish with damaged fins, fin rot or incomplete fins, if the fish are very thin or listless, or swim around in a haphazard manner.

Even if there is only one fish in the aquarium which clearly gives the impression of being sick and the rest are perfectly healthy, it is still not sensible to buy one or more fish from this aquarium. You may be taking bacteria home with you on these fish. The fish may not have shown any signs of sickness in the store, but under the influence of stress

Fish need time to acclimatise to the aquarium.

(transportation and their new surroundings) they will become more susceptible and there is a good chance that the aquarium you have just set up so beautifully will be full of terminally ill fish within a few weeks. You should therefore always choose fish from an aquarium in which all the fish look lively and healthy, and it goes without saying that you should not be tempted into buying a fish which is deformed in any way.

Transport

Fish are very sensitive to stress. Among other things, stress makes the fish more susceptible to disease and sick fish are not always easy to nurse back to health. It is quite a difficult task to keep this process under control. Transporting fish always causes stress.

The best way to transport fish is in a strong plastic bag. Contrary to what most people believe, fish do not require large quantities of water in the bag used for transport – just the opposite. It is important that there should be plenty of oxygen (air) in the bag, particularly if the fish are to remain in the transport bag for a long time. The transport water only keeps the fish wet; the oxygen in the bag enables them to breathe.

Changes in temperature should be avoided as far as possible. For this reason most aquarium centres will wrap the transport bag in several layers of newspaper. If it is very cold outside, and if it will take more than an hour to get home, ask for a transport box made of polystyrene foam, which is better at retaining the heat in the water. The fish should be kept in the dark during transportation; sudden flashes of light will give them an unnecessary shock.

When you get home, lay the transport bag on the aquarium water for at least a quarter of an hour. The water in the bag will gradually adjust to the temperature of the aquarium water and the fish will become acclimatised to it. Then open the transport bag and pour some water from the aquarium into the transport bag, so that the fish can become at least slightly accustomed to the water composition, which is always slightly different from what they are accustomed to. After about five minutes you can remove the fish from the transport bag using a fine mesh net and release them into the aquarium. Always throw the transport water away, since it is quite often full of excreta. The fish will not swim about very energetically at first. That is not so very strange, since they have been through quite an unusual experience. Never knock against the aquarium to make the fish move, since this will only make them more stressed than they already are. What is more, there are some varieties of fish which are so terrified by this that they die on the spot, and that cannot be your intention. Do not feed the fish on the first day – give them a chance to acclimatise first.

Other water dwellers

At the aquarium centre you will not only find fish but there will usually be other water dwellers as well. By this we mean snails, freshwater shrimps and terrapins, for example. It is good to know about the advantages and disadvantages of these creatures, as many people enjoy keeping such creatures in the aquarium alongside their fish.

Snails are kept out of the aquarium by most people. That is not surprising, since in many cases snails will damage plants. Only the post-horn snail (*Planorbarius corneus*) and the striped viviparid (*Viviparus fasciatus*) do not touch the vegetation. Snails do clear up surplus food, but they also produce excreta, so you do not need them to keep the aquarium water clean. Quite the opposite. Nevertheless snails, particularly the larger varieties

apple slug

shrimps

Red-eared terrapins do not belong in an aquarium with fish.

such as the apple snail (*Ampullarius scalaris*) in particular, are interesting water dwellers. Feed them regularly on blanched lettuce leaves or food tablets for bottom dwellers, because they will start nibbling the aquatic plants when these run out. Small snails reproduce at lightning speed and can very quickly become a plague. This is no problem if you have fish which like eating snails. If you do not have any snail eaters, however, it is advisable to remove the surplus snails from the aquarium regularly.

Freshwater shrimps are also useful little creatures. They live on the bottom, where they eat food residues with relish. What is not so well known is that some varieties will not hesitate to attack smaller fish, so take note of this.

Terrapins, and more specifically the well-known red-eared terrapin, do not belong in an aquarium which is populated with fish. They are certainly small and amusing to look at when you buy them, but they grow rapidly in tropical water temperatures with plenty of food, and they start to look around for more satisfying nutrition – your fish! Red-eared terrapins can grow to 30 cm long and produce huge quantities of excrement. These creatures must also be allowed to dry out regularly and can sunbathe on an artificially created bank. This is obviously not possible in a completely full aquarium. These creatures therefore should be kept in a large glass tank set up especially for them.

Origin

The fish which you will see at the aquarium centre come from various areas. Some varieties of fish, particularly those which do not, or hardly ever, reproduce in the aquarium, are caught in their native habitat by local people and sold to tropical fish exporters. The fish are then

Tropical fish are caught in their natural habitat using primitive methods.

Hemigrammopetersius caudalis

Variant of Pterophyllum scalare

exported to tropical fish wholesalers throughout the world.

Fish which are caught in the land of origin are called wild-caught. They only make up a small proportion of the total range at the aquarium centre. Contrary to what the media would sometimes have us believe, catching poses no threat to the natural population of tropical fish. The methods which are used to catch the fish are still extremely primitive and the numbers caught cannot be compared with the fish caught at sea for human consumption. Some fish are bred in the aquarium by enthusiastic aquarists. Most of the fish which you will come across at the aquarium centre actually come from Asia, where they are specially grown in large tanks for export.

Since the temperatures are always very

The demand for tropical fish in western countries provides a living for many people who live near the equator.

favourable in these areas, tropical fish varieties can be reared without excessive energy costs.

6. Maintenance

Maintenance

If you do not keep too many fish and you feed them moderately, if the aquarium is large enough and if you have carefully followed all the other instructions (positioning, filters, lighting, etc.), you should not have to spend too much time maintaining your aquarium.

Every day you must feed the fish, check the temperature and look to make sure all the fish are healthy and not displaying any deviant behaviour. Once a week you should carefully remove overgrown plants, remove loose leaves from the aquarium and siphon out dirt and excreta from the bottom. This is best done with a piece of garden hose, and the part outside the aquarium must always be lower than that inside. Start off the process by sucking some aquarium water through the hose, and you can leave the rest to the law of communicating vessels. Make sure no small fish are dragged through the hose by the considerable suction power of the water. After siphoning, the water level will have fallen by a few centimetres. You can replenish it with normal tap water to which a water preparation has been added (TetraSafe). Part of the aquarium water must be changed regularly. You can

If the aquarium is neglected, the fish react by falling sick.

change a small amount of water weekly when you siphon the dirt from the bottom. It is also good to know that you should leave the aquarium alone as much as possible. Every time you adjust a plant, scrape some algae off the sides or connect the hose for the air filter pump, for example, this is a major event for the fish, which can cause them a lot of stress. You know that stress can cause diseases in fish; also, an aquarium which is tampered with too often never has a chance to establish an equilibrium. So do everything which needs to be done in one go, rather than spreading it over several days.

7. Feeding

Dry food

Once dry food was only used for aquarium fish in emergencies, because its quality could not always be guaranteed, but that time is now long gone.

Dry food, such as food tablets, sticks, flakes and granules, form an excellent basic staple for nearly every type of fish. It has been found that many, if not most varieties of fish can remain healthy for a lifetime without any problems on a diet of varied, high quality dry food. The advantage of dry food is that you always have it available. You do not need to keep it in a deep freeze, and you do not have to go out regularly to buy it. Another advantage is that dry food is absolutely free from parasites and other causes of disease.

You should, however, remember that not all fish thrive on food of the same composition. Some species of fish need more vegetable food, while others never eat vegetarian fare. If you buy different sorts of food you can provide a varied diet for your fish, which will do them good. It is known that bottom dwellers seldom or never absorb food from the middle or top zone, so special tablets have been developed which sink straight to the bottom. Most bottom dwellers only become active at dusk, so these should not be given tablets until later in the day.

Live food

By live food we mean various types of live food organisms. The best-known live food

food flakes

food tablets for plant eaters

food tablets

cichlid sticks

organisms are white, black and red mosquito larvae, cyclops, daphnia (water fleas), tubifex and artemia (brine shrimps). You can catch many of these small creatures yourself using a fine mesh net, for example in a shallow lake near your house, or buy them from an aquarium centre. You can

Granules

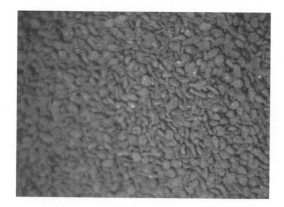

also breed some of them yourself. Live food is difficult or impossible to find out doors in the winter, but it is plentiful in the summer. Catching live food yourself has one disadvantage. You may also introduce unwelcome bacteria or beetle larvae into your aquarium along with the live food organisms. Breeding live food organisms yourself is safer in this respect. Various publications have appeared which describe the best ways of doing this. You can also buy live food organisms such as shrimps, mosquito larvae and water fleas in dry or frozen form. Always take care with frozen food – you should never give it to the fish while still frozen. Let the creatures thaw out well beforehand and always give them at room temperature. Obviously they should never be refrozen once they have thawed out.

The live food organisms mentioned above are all quite small and are suitable for most aquarium fish. Larger live food organisms, such as earthworms, make excellent food for large South American cichlids. You cannot buy these in dry or frozen form but it is not difficult to collect them outside after heavy rain. Never feed earthworms directly to the fish, but put them in a box first until their intestinal tract, which is full of sand, is empty.

Vegetable food

You regularly come across fish in this encyclopaedia which only, or mainly, eat vegetable food. Many catfish belong to this category, as well as many livebearing fish and some carps and minnows. These types of fish particularly like algae. Algae are usually already growing on the glass, plants and stones in an aquarium which has already been in use for some time – this is quite normal. As long as it is not out of control, it shows that the aquarium is healthy. If there is not enough algae you must give the fish a supplement.

Possibilities include watercress, lettuce and spinach. Place these vegetables briefly in boiling water (blanching), before you give them to the fish. There are also dry vegetable foods, which are readily eaten by most plant-eating fish and contain all the nutrients they need.

There are some fish which only accept live food.

Mastacembelus

Other food types

Other types of food do exist which cannot be categorised as vegetarian, frozen, live or dry food – for example pieces of meat, fish and crustaceans. Some fish, particularly the large cichlids, need solid food. You can give them both suitable dry food and larger pieces of live food, but most will very much enjoy a small piece of beef heart, fish or mussel from time to time. You can also give your fish some egg yolk (boiled) from time to time, but not too much, since it makes the water cloudy and the fish can quickly get

fat. Never give your fish bread; this expands in their stomach and can cause problems.

How much food

A common beginner's mistake is to overfeed the fish. Fish do not need as much food as is commonly thought. As a result they are usually given far too much food. That has several disadvantages. Everything that the fish do not eat ends up on the bottom of the aquarium, where it rots and adversely affects the water composition. Fish which eat too much also produce more excrement because they do not need a large part of the food. All this also ends up on the bottom. The pieces of rotting food and excrement form an ideal nutrient base for organisms

Algae eaters are useful aquarium dwellers, but when the algae runs out you must give them extra food.

Most cichlids boast splendid colours.

Shoaling fish usually live in the middle zone.

that cause disease, which is not conducive to clear aquarium water and healthy fish. The waste also contributes towards a larger concentration of poisonous substances, which most fish are completely unable to tolerate.

It is best to feed the fish several times a day, but make sure that you really do not give them any more than they will eat in a short time. You will see that there are some real gluttons amongst these fish and also fish which are naturally not great eaters. Some cichlids, and also some ovoviparids, for example, eat proportionally more than small shoaling fish. It is a matter of experimenting to find out how much your fish need, but remember that fish will do much better if they get no food for a day than if you constantly overfeed them.

Tropical Aquarium Fish from A to Z

Acanthophtalmus kuhlii
(syn. Pangio kuhlii*)*

KUHLI LOACH

FAMILY
Cobitidae (loaches)

SUB FAMILY
Cobitinae

HABITAT
South East Asia, in stagnant and slow-flowing shallow waters

GESLACHTSONDERSCHEID
It is not always easy to tell the difference between the sexes. The male often has larger pectoral fins than the female.

LENGTH
Up to about 10 centimetres

ACCOMMODATION
The *kuhli* loach is a peaceful fish which is well suited to both large and small community aquaria with rather subdued light

Left: Anchistrus dolichopterus, *below:* Acanthopthalmus kuhlii.

and containing plenty of vegetation, since this small loach prefers to hide by day. Because it likes to burrow, soft substrate in certain places (e.g. peat dust or sand) is advisable and sharp stones definitely should not be used as a substrate. The fish does not particularly mind whether or not there is a current in the water.

SOCIAL CHARACTERISTICS
The kuhli loach feels comfortable whether it is alone or surrounded by several of its kind and is extremely peaceful towards other aquarium dwellers.

The fish usually only becomes active at dusk when searching for food.
They usually spend the day in the soil on the bottom. However they do leave plant roots alone and do not burrow. Kuhli loaches can be kept in an aquarium with plentiful vegetation without any problem.

TEMPERATURE AND WATER COMPOSITION
22-28°C. This fish does not make great demands on the water composition, although a pH below 10 is ideal.

FOOD
A. kuhlii cheerfully polishes off all the food which has not been eaten by the other aquarium dwellers. It also likes small live food, mainly tubifex, and also greatly appreciates food tablets for bottom dwellers (Sera Viformo).

BREEDING
Not much is known so far about the reproductive system of this fish. But there are occasional reports of "accidental breeding."

VARIANTS
No variants of this fish are known, but there are different species which look very similar to one another. They differ from each other mainly in colour and markings, but are frequently sold under the same name at specialist outlets.

SPECIAL REMARKS
Since these fish breathe through their intestines and are very tough, they can also survive in less clean water with low oxygen levels.

Aequidens rivulatus
(syn. Acara rivulata*)*

FAMILY
Cichlidae (cichlids)

HABITAT
South America

SEXUAL DIFFERENCES
The females are darker in colour than the males and slightly smaller. Full-grown males have a protruding forehead.

LENGTH
Up to about 20 centimetres

ACCOMMODATION
A. rivulatus is only suitable for larger aquaria (at least 1 metre long). Rocks and pieces of petrified wood are suitable for decoration, and also to offer protection to the fish.

These strong and robust fish nibble plants and dig up roots, so only very strong and large-leafed plants are suitable. Always plant these in a pot and bury them in the gravel. Always use smooth gravel, because sharp gravel can cause mouth injuries.

SOCIAL CHARACTERISTICS
This cichlid species should best be kept as a pair. They can be somewhat bad-tempered towards other fish once fully grown. For that reason they are usually only kept with other strong cichlid species. There must be sufficient space and refuges for all the fish in the aquarium, because these fish are territorial.

Aequidens rivulatus

20-24°C, 20-30°gH, pH 7-8. Above all the water must be clear and preferably constantly moving. A powerful motorised filter is definitely necessary in order to keep the water clear.

FOOD

These cichlids are gluttons. Special flake food or cichlid sticks can be used as the basic staple, but the fish also need more solid live food such as small fish and earthworms. Small pieces of beef heart and mussels are very popular.

BREEDING

If the temperature is raised by a few degrees and other conditions are optimal, a well-suited breeding pair should begin to lay eggs on stones or wood. The parent fish guard and care for both the eggs and the fry for a long time. The young brood can be raised on artemia and fine powdered food (Sera Micron).

Ancistrus dolichopterus
(syn. Ancistrus temminckii)

FAMILY

Loricariidae (armoured catfish)

SUB FAMILY

Ancistrinae

HABITAT

Amazon region, in fast-flowing streams

SEXUAL DIFFERENCES

The males can be recognised by the larger and thicker spines on the head.

LENGTH

Up to 13 centimetres

ACCOMMODATION

A. dolichopterus prefers a larger community aquarium with sufficient refuges in the form of rocks and pieces of petrified wood. The fish are accustomed to fast-flowing water in their natural biotope and also appreciate this in the aquarium. You can successfully re-create the natural conditions of their biotope by using a very powerful motorised filter. The fish scrape algae from the aquarium walls, stones and

Anchistrus dolichopterus

plants and will feel much better in an aquarium which has become rather "algae-fied", than in an aquarium which has only just come into use.

SOCIAL CHARACTERISTICS

These algae eaters do very well as solitary fish and keep themselves to themselves. They will leave even the smallest fish in the aquarium alone. They are mainly quiet by day and like to stay hidden under petrified wood or in the vegetation. They become rather more active around dusk.

TEMPERATURE AND WATER COMPOSITION

23-27°C. The hardness and acidity of the water are not very important, but the water must have plenty of oxygen.

FOOD

A. dolichopterus is mainly an algae eater. If there is a shortage of algae, you should ensure that you provide the fish with enough vegetable food as a substitute. You can use food tablets for bottom dwellers as basic staple (Sera Viformo/Sera Premium) and also give them (blanched) watercress and spinach leaves occasionally.

BREEDING

The parent fish lay their eggs in a small hollow between stones or petrified wood. The male takes complete responsibility for the eggs.

Anostomus ternezi

Anostomus ternezi

Anostomidae (headstanders)

SUB FAMILY
Anostominae

HABITAT
Brazil, in large rivers

SEXUAL DIFFERENCES
So far, no external differences between the sexes have been found.

LENGTH
Up to 12 centimetres

ACCOMMODATION
This variety of fish belongs to the group of headstanders, fish which constantly swim with their heads pointing downwards. Since they are quite large and are generally kept in a shoal, these fish need a spacious aquarium with plenty of open space for swimming. They should be kept amidst dense peripheral vegetation and need quite a sunny location.

SOCIAL CHARACTERISTICS
Headstanders are best kept in large shoals. They are good-natured towards other fish, as long as these are not too small and fragile. Never put them with very obtrusive or aggressive fish, since this kind of company will send them fleeing into the vegetation, never to be seen again. If you only keep one or two ternezis, the fish frequently develop deviant, aggressive behaviour towards the other occupants. They prefer to live in the bottom zone.

TEMPERATURE AND WATER COMPOSITION
24-27°C. The pH can be neutral (pH 7) or slightly acidic. The fish like soft to medium-hard water (6-12° gH is ideal).

FOOD
These headstanders mainly eat vegetable food, so there certainly should be algae in the aquarium. They also like dry food (Sera Flora) and small live food. Since these fish prefer to pick up their food from the bottom, it is also a good idea to feed them vegetable food tablets for bottom dwellers.

BREEDING
So far the fish have never been bred in the aquarium.

Aphyocharax anisitsi
(syn. A. rubropinnis*)*

BLOODFIN

Aphyocharax anisitsi

FAMILY
Characidae (characins)

SUB FAMILY
Aphycocharacinae

HABITAT
Argentina, mainly in clear water

The difference between the sexes can be seen clearly in the body shape – the males are thinner than the females.

LENGTH

Up to five centimetres

ACCOMMODATION

This peaceful and robust shoaling fish needs space and therefore belongs in aquaria with plenty of space for swimming. It does appreciate some vegetation. If light gravel is used as a substrate you will barely see any colour on this fish; a dark substrate will bring out the colours much better.

SOCIAL CHARACTERISTICS

This lively fish lives in a shoal with at least seven others of its kind.
This species is extremely peaceful and is therefore perfectly suited to a community aquarium with fish with a similarly tolerant disposition. A shoal of these fish is not the best company for aquarium dwellers which like peace and quiet, since the blood fin is quite an active swimmer.

TEMPERATURE AND WATER COMPOSITION

18 27°C. This fish is not very demanding as regards water hardness and acidity. It prefers very clear water. A few hours of sunlight (in the morning) are also appreciated.

FOOD

These fish are good eaters. The blood fin likes small live food, but dry food is also readily taken.

Aphyocharax anisitsi

BREEDING

This fish is quite easy to breed, but unfortunately the colours of fish bred in captivity are less intense that those of fish caught in the wild. The fish soon begin spawning eggs in a separate breeding tank where the temperature is gradually increased to around 24°C. Blood fins are free layers, which means that the eggs are scattered throughout the aquarium.

Unfortunately they are also formidable egg predators and just as happily eat up all the eggs which they have laid. The parent fish should therefore be removed as soon as the eggs are laid. The fry can be raised without any problems on fairly small (young) artemia and fine powdered food (Sera Micron).

Aphyosemion australe

CAPE LOPEZ LYRETAIL

Aphyosemion australe, *variant*

FAMILY
Cyprinodontidae (egg-laying tooth carps)

SUB FAMILY
Rivulinae

HABITAT
West Africa, in shallow flooded areas in the rainforest

SEXUAL DIFFERENCES
The males are much more colourful than the females. The tail, back and anal fin taper to a point in the males, while the females have rounded fins.

LENGTH
Up to about 5.5 centimetres

Aphyosemion australe, *variant*

ACCOMMODATION

The Cape Lopez lyretail is best kept in smaller special aquaria with a fairly low water level, plenty of floating plants, a moderate amount of light and plenty of vegetation. Make sure that you buy plants which, like this fish, do well in a rather shadowy environment (Java fern, Java moss and anubias). A dark substrate consisting largely or entirely of peat dust is necessary. The fish also appreciates refuges, which you can make out of pieces of petrified wood.

SOCIAL CHARACTERISTICS

As a rule, this killifish will leave other aquarium dwellers in peace and can be kept both as a pair and with several of its kind. The males of this species are not always very friendly to one another. In a small aquarium (40 centimetres wide) it is therefore best to keep one male with two or three females. You can keep a larger group in an aquarium 60 centimetres long, for example five males and ten females. If the aquarium is populated by only two or three males, this will usually result in fights.

TEMPERATURE AND WATER COMPOSITION

22-25°C, 6-10° gH, pH 5.5 to 6.5. Filter over peat if the bottom does not already consist of peat.

FOOD

These fish mainly need small live food such as red mosquito larvae, artemia and fruit flies. They also eat dry food (Sera San).

BREEDING

Breeding these interesting and colourful fish is best left to specialists. The water level should be no more than 20 centimetres and the pH no higher than 6.5. Adding some sea salt is advisable. Make sure that no direct sunlight shines into the aquarium and that at least 60% of the surface is covered by floating plants. The female lays eggs at constant intervals among feathery-leafed plants or Java moss. For reasons of hygiene breeders also use plastic breeding substrata, which can be used several times without becoming dirty or collecting too much bacteria (wash out regularly). The fry can be raised on fine powdered food and small brine shrimps (artemia).

VARIANTS

There is one known variant of this fish, which is sold under the name "Golden" Cape Lopez lyretail.

SPECIAL REMARKS

The Cape Lopez likes to jump; a cover is necessary.

Aphyosemion bitaeniatum

Aphyosemion bitaeniatum *'Lagos'*

FAMILY

Cyprinodontidae (egg-laying tooth carps)

SUB FAMILY

Rivulinae

HABITAT

West Africa, especially in Cameroon and Nigeria. In shallow pools and small streams in the rainforest.

Aphyosemion bitaeniatum

SEXUAL DIFFERENCES
The difference between the sexes is quite easy to see. The males are more colourful than the females and also have more pointed fins.

LENGTH
Up to five centimetres

ACCOMMODATION
This fish is best kept in a special aquarium which need not be very big. Plenty of floating plants, refuges, vegetation, a moderate amount of light and dark substrate (partly peat dust) are necessary to keep these fish in good condition.

SOCIAL CHARACTERISTICS
This killifish is friendly towards others of its kind and other aquarium dwellers. It is best to keep a male and two or three females together. These fish stay mainly in the middle and top zone.

TEMPERATURE AND WATER COMPOSITION
23-24°C, 6-10° gH, pH 6-6.5. The water must be changed regularly and kept totally free of nitrates (it is therefore absolutely vital to siphon out the dirt regularly!). Add a teaspoonful of sea salt to the aquarium water regularly.

FOOD
These killifish mainly eat small live food. They only eat dry food very rarely.

BREEDING
Breeding is particularly interesting, but definitely a job for specialists. The reproductive process is comparable to that of other killifish such as A. australe, for example, with the difference that this fish

makes even more stringent demands as regards the water composition.

Aphyosemion christy

Aphyosemion christy

FAMILY
Cyprinodontidae (egg-laying tooth carps)

SUB FAMILY
Rivulinae

HABITAT
Tributaries of the River Congo (Africa) in the jungle

SEXUAL DIFFERENCES
The difference between the sexes is not too difficult to spot. The males are recognisable by their brighter colours. They also have rather more pointed fins and are larger than the females.

LENGTH
Up to five centimetres

ACCOMMODATION
This fish thrives best in a small aquarium specially designed for killifish. Make sure there are enough refuges in the form of petrified wood. Ideally, the surface should also be about half covered with floating plants, and there should also be plenty of feathery-leafed aquatic plants. Only buy plants which, like the killifish, thrive in a rather shadowy environment (e.g. Java moss and Java fern). Peat dust is the ideal substrate.

A. christy leaves other occupants in peace, but the males can be aggressive towards each another.

If you have a small aquarium (40 centimetres wide), it is best to keep one male with two or three females. You can keep several males without any problems in larger aquaria, but always keep more than five, since fights always break out in aquaria with smaller numbers of males.

TEMPERATURE AND WATER COMPOSITION
23-24°C, 4-8°gH, pH 6

FOOD
These small fish do not always accept dry food, but they prefer small and varied live food (water fleas, fruit flies).

BREEDING
Reproduction is similar to that of other *Aphyosemion* varieties.

Aphyosemion cognatum

FAMILY
Cyprinodontidae (egg-laying tooth carps)

SUB FAMILY
Rivulinae

HABITAT
Republic of Congo, in shallow waters in the rainforest

SEXUAL DIFFERENCES
The males of this species of fish are much more brightly coloured than the females.

LENGTH
Up to 5.5 centimetres

ACCOMMODATION
This fish does well in special aquaria. Floating vegetation, shelter and abundant plants are essential, as is a dark substrate and a moderate amount of light (no sunlight!). The water must be very pure.

SOCIAL CHARACTERISTICS
These are peaceful and lively fish which

Aphyosemion cognatum *'Kruge'*

do well in pairs or with several of their kind and other like-minded killifish.

TEMPERATURE AND WATER COMPOSITION
23-24°C, 7-10° gH, pH 6

FOOD
These fish mainly eat small live food, including fruit flies and mosquito larvae, and sometimes refuse to eat dry and frozen food.

BREEDING
In very soft and shallow water, these fish are sometimes prepared to lay their eggs. Unlike most other fish, killifish do not lay all their eggs at once, but they do so at intervals. The fry can be reared on miniscule morsels of live food (infusoria and microworms).

Aphyosemion elberti

Aphyosemion elberti
(syn. **Aphyosemion bualanum***)*

FAMILY
Cyprinodontidae (egg-laying tooth carps)

SUB FAMILY
Rivulinae

HABITAT
Cameroon and Central African Republic

SEXUAL DIFFERENCES
The males are much more colourful and also have pointed fins, while the females' fins are rounded.

Aphyosemion elberti

LENGTH
Up to five centimetres

ACCOMMODATION
These fish thrive best in a small special aquarium with plenty of floating plants, diffuse and moderate(!) lighting, sufficient feathery-leafed plants and floating plants, and also a dark substrate consisting (partly) of peat dust. Like most other killifish, they only really feel at home if there are enough refuges in the aquarium (petrified wood and vegetation). They can also easily be kept in community aquaria with the correct water composition.

SOCIAL CHARACTERISTICS
This lively fish can easily be kept with other, equally peaceful, varieties and does well as a pair or with several of its kind (one male with two or three females).

TEMPERATURE AND WATER COMPOSITION
22-24°C, 4-12° gH, pH 6, definitely no higher! You do not need to filter over peat if the bottom consists of peat.

FOOD
These killifish eat both small live food and dry food.

BREEDING
Breeding should be left to killi-specialists. A single mature male can be transferred to a smaller breeding tank with two or three mature females. The water composition is extremely important and the water level must not be higher than twenty centimetres. The eggs are laid among feathery-leafed plants or Java moss, but also in a special purpose-made dense bunch of syn-

thetic yarn. The fish take their time over this; spawning may last a few weeks. The fry are raised on fine dry food, small brine shrimps (artemia) and microworms.

This fish may have different colours, depending on its precise origins. It is one of the stronger killifish species.

Aphyosemion exiguum

FAMILY
Cyprinodontidae (egg-laying tooth carps)

SUB FAMILY
Rivulinae

HABITAT
West Africa, in the rainforest

SEXUAL DIFFERENCES
The males are much more colourful than the females and also have pointed fin tips.

LENGTH
Up to 4.5 centimetres

ACCOMMODATION
This attractive fish can be kept either in a smaller special aquarium or in a community aquarium with other like-minded, peaceful fish.

There must however be plenty of floating vegetation and feathery-leafed plants, and the bottom cover should consist of peat dust. *A. exiguum* cannot tolerate bright lighting and the aquarium should there-

Aphyosemion exiguum

fore be only moderately lit. Make sure that no sunlight can enter the tank and that the fish have enough refuges, otherwise they will never really feel at home.

SOCIAL CHARACTERISTICS
Extremely peaceful and lively fish, which can be kept together with several of its kind or as a pair.

TEMPERATURE AND WATER COMPOSITION
20-24°C, 7-11° gH, pH 6. Peat filtration is necessary to attain the correct water composition unless the bottom consists of peat.

FOOD
These fish mainly eat small live food but they can also be given some dry food in exceptional cases.

BREEDING
Breeding these killifish is a job for specialists. It is important for the pH to stay below 6.5 and the water level below 20 centimetres. Add a few spoonfuls of sea salt to the aquarium water. During breeding these fish mainly need peace and quiet. Cover the aquarium so that no sunlight can enter and use a low wattage light to create a dim environment.

Cover more than half of the water surface with floating plants. Java moss is eminently suitable as a breeding substrate. The fry can be raised on small live food, such as newly hatched brine shrimp, but they also eat fine powdered food (Sera Micron).

Aphyosemion gardneri

FAMILY
Cyprinodontidae (egg-laying tooth carps)

SUB FAMILY
Rivulinae

HABITAT
West Africa

SEXUAL DIFFERENCES
The male is more striking in colour and also larger than the female.

LENGTH
Up to six centimetres

Aphyosemion gardneri

Aphyosemion gardneri

ACCOMMODATION

This fish does best in a small special aquarium with plenty of feathery-leafed plants and floating plants, sufficient refuges and a dark substrate (peat dust). Also ensure that the light is never too bright and avoid direct sunlight.

SOCIAL CHARACTERISTICS

This fish is intolerant of, sometimes even aggressive towards, other fish and is therefore better kept in a separate special aquarium with others of its kind. The males do not usually tolerate one another very well, and you are sure to have problems if you keep two or three males together. If you keep a larger group of these fish, the males will get used to each other and will not fight.

TEMPERATURE AND WATER COMPOSITION

22-25°C, 6-12° gH, pH 6.5. It is preferable to add some sea salt.

FOOD

This variety mainly eats live food, such as artemia, fruit flies and mosquito larvae. They will only eat dry food in exceptional cases.

BREEDING

Similar to other *Aphyosemion* varieties, with the difference that the eggs should be kept for a few weeks in a well sealed plastic bag without(!) water, on a shallow bottom of moist peat dust and in a moderately warm environment, prior to atching. It takes two to four weeks for the eggs to hatch, depending on where the fish come from. The fry can be given microworms, and, when they are a little bigger, newly hatched artemia.

Aphyosemion sjoestedti

FAMILY
Cyprinodontidae (egg-laying tooth carps)

SUB FAMILY
Rivulinae

HABITAT
West Africa

SEXUAL DIFFERENCES
Males are larger and more colourful and have rather more pointed fins.

LENGTH
9-11 centimetres

ACCOMMODATION
A. sjoestedti can be kept in a largish special aquarium with moderately lighting, plenty of (floating) plants and sufficient refuges. It is recommended to use peat dust as substrate.

Aphyosemion sjoestedti *"Red"*

SOCIAL CHARACTERISTICS

This variety is quite aggressive towards other fish and does not belong in an aquarium with less hardy species. The males also fight each other, especially if you keep two or three in the same aquarium. If you populate the aquarium with a large group, the males will generally leave each other alone. Since the fish are not very demanding as regards the water composition (unlike some other killifish), they can be kept in a community aquarium with other (hardy!) fish which require a similar water composition.

TEMPERATURE AND WATER COMPOSITION

22-24°C, 5-12° gH, pH 6.5

FOOD

A. sjoestedti mainly eats live food, such as – amongst other things – red mosquito larvae, tubifex and artemia. The fish also eat suitable dry food.

BREEDING

Similar to *A. gardneri*

Aphyosemion striatum

FAMILY

Cyprinodontidae (egg-laying tooth carps)

SUB FAMILY

Rivulinae

HABITAT

West Africa

SEXUAL DIFFERENCES

The males stand out because of their diverse colouring. The females are much paler.

LENGTH

Up to five centimetres

ACCOMMODATION

Comparable to that of other *Aphyosemion* varieties.

SOCIAL CHARACTERISTICS

A. striatum is a peaceful fish which can be kept in an aquarium with other similar species without any problems. Difficulties with its own kind are also rare.

Aphyosemion striatum

TEMPERATURE AND WATER COMPOSITION

23°C, 6-11° gH, pH 6. Add a small amount of sea salt, but otherwise it is advisable to keep the aquarium water very clean.

FOOD

Mainly live food and also suitable dry food (Sera San).

BREEDING

Comparable to other killifish and best left to specialists.

SPECIAL REMARKS

A. striatum likes to jump out of the water, so a cover is absolutely essential.

Apistogramma agassizi

AGASSIZ'S DWARF CICHLID

FAMILY

Cichlidae (cichlids)

HABITAT

South America, in the Amazon region

SEXUAL DIFFERENCES

The difference between the two sexes is quite easy to spot, even for the layman. The males are not only much more colourful, they are also larger than the females.

LENGTH

Up to eight centimetres

ACCOMMODATION

These small cichlids can be kept in small or medium-sized aquaria in which there are enough refuges, such as plants, rocks and petrified wood. The colours of the fish stand out much better against a dark substrate. The fish very much appreciate floating plants.

SOCIAL CHARACTERISTICS
These fish form territories within in which no other fish are tolerated. It is best to keep only a few these fish and not several males alongside one another, since they can be intolerant of one another.

TEMPERATURE AND WATER COMPOSITION
23-25°C, 7-9° gH, pH 6. These fish are very sensitive towards dirt residues in the aquarium and must therefore be kept in clean and clear water. Change some of the aquarium water once a week.

FOOD
Cichlid sticks are good as basic staple, but the fish also need live food such as mosquito larvae.

BREEDING
A well suited breeding pair will – if conditions are optimal – start reproducing very quickly. The eggs are laid in a half scooped out coconut shell or an upturned flower pot. The female mainly takes care of the eggs and the fry.

Apistogramma agassizi

Apistogramma borelli

DWARF CICHLID

Apistogramma borelli

FAMILY
Cichlidae (cichlids)

HABITAT
South America (Rio Paraguay and Mato Grosso)

SEXUAL DIFFERENCES
The difference between the sexes is quite easy to see.

The male is not only conspicuously larger, but also more colourful than the female and has more protruding, pointed fins.

LENGTH
From 4 (♀) to eight centimetres (♂)

ACCOMMODATION
Due to its small size, A. borelli can easily be kept in smaller aquaria. This species is territorial, so you must provide sufficient refuges (petrified wood, rocks). A dark bottom, plenty of refuges and a wealth of dense vegetation are preferable.

SOCIAL CHARACTERISTICS
These fish form a pair that "take up residence" in a territory together and, as long as other fish keep away, everything is fine. During breeding, however, these cichlids become much more intolerant of other aquarium dwellers. If you want to keep other fish species alongside A. borelli, provide a spacious aquarium and, above all, plenty of refuges.

Apistogramma borelli

Apistogramma cacatoides

TEMPERATURE AND WATER COMPOSITION
24°C, 4-14° gH, pH 6-7. These fish cannot tolerate dirty water, so some of the water should be changed on a regular basis.

FOOD
Live food is absolutely essential, as these fish will not all eat dry food.

BREEDING
The pair hide away in their territory and lay the eggs in a hollow. Both the male and the female guard and care for both the eggs and the fry. Some accounts state that one male of this species may keep several females. They are then fertilised and protected against intruders by the same male. The fry need small live food.

Apistogramma cacatoides

FAMILY
Cichlidae (cichlids)

HABITAT
Amazon region

SEXUAL DIFFERENCES
The males are larger than the females. During the mating season, the females turn a bright yellow colour.

LENGTH
From four (♀) to eight centimetres (♂).

ACCOMMODATION
This fish can be easily kept in small aquaria, provided that there are sufficient

refuges, such as petrified wood, ample vegetation and rocks. The fish like a dark bottom.

SOCIAL CHARACTERISTICS
It is best to keep one male together with one or more females, since the males do not always get on well together. The females each form a territory in which no other females are tolerated, but the males are allowed to move freely between these territories.

TEMPERATURE AND WATER COMPOSITION
25° C, 9-12° gH, pH 7

FOOD
Mainly varied live food, but the fish also eat cichlid sticks and Sera San.

BREEDING
A male can attend to several females. The females each raise their offspring in their own territory. The male then bustles around protecting all his females and descendants.

Apistogramma cacatoides

This fish is very sensitive to dirty water, so regular changes of water are necessary. Overfeeding inevitably leads to problems because it results in surplus excrement. Furthermore, any uneaten food at the bottom turns acid. An active mailed catfish, such as *Pterygoplichthys gibbiceps*, can be kept together with these cichlids without any difficulty and can usually reduce the amount of surplus food.

Apistogramma ramirezi
(syn. **Microgeophagus/Papliochromis ramirezi***)*

BUTTERFLY CICHLID

FAMILY
Cichlidae (cichlids)

HABITAT
Colombia and Venezuela, in clear water

SEXUAL DIFFERENCES
The difference between the two sexes is not very difficult to see. The front fin ray on the dorsal fin is longer in males than in females. The females are also often smaller and more colourful.

LENGTH
About 4cm (♀) to 5.5cm (♂)

ACCOMMODATION
This small and tolerant dwarf cichlid can be very easily kept in a rather smaller

Apistogramma ramirezi

aquarium. The aquarium should ideally be well lit, as long as there are refuges in the form of rock formations, petrified wood and plenty of plants. A fairly sunny location (morning sun) is appreciated. The fish also like a current, although this must be gentle.

SOCIAL CHARACTERISTICS
These fish are usually kept in pairs, but they can also get on well with several of their own kind.

Ramirezis are good-natured and interesting fish which can be kept in a community aquarium with virtually no problems and usually leave even smaller fish in peace. They mainly live in the bottom zone and do tend to be territorial.

TEMPERATURE AND WATER COMPOSITION
24-26°C, 4-12° gH, pH 6-7. Occasional peat filtration will keep these fish in good condition and good health.

FOOD
A. ramirezi are not difficult to feed. Dry food (Sera Vipan) is very popular, but the fish are also very partial to small live food from time to time, such as mosquito larvae, tubifex and water fleas.

BREEDING
Under the right circumstances (increased temperature, very soft water (2-4° gH), correct acidity), these fish will lay eggs. Both these and the fry which emerge are carefully looked after and protected by the parent fish.

VARIANTS
There is one variant of this fish – the golden or yellow butterfly cichlid.

SPECIAL REMARKS
If your butterfly cichlids fall sick, even though you are looking after them well, it is nearly always due to incorrect water composition. To rule out other causes, first test the water values. Since it is usually water which is too hard which causes the problems, (temporary) peat filtration or the addition of a water preparation agent should bring a rapid improvement.

Aplocheilus lineatus
(syn. Panchax lineatus*)*

FAMILY
Cyprinodontidae (egg-laying tooth carps)

SUB FAMILY
Rivulinae

HABITAT
South India and Sri Lanka

SEXUAL DIFFERENCES
The most obvious difference between the males and females is that the females are darker in colour and less colourful than the males.

LENGTH
Up to about 11 centimetres

ACCOMMODATION
This killifish will feel at home in a somewhat larger aquarium around 70-90 centimetres long. Provide peripheral vegetation with feathery-leafed plants and plenty of refuges (petrified wood, stones), while still leaving enough free space for swimming.

SOCIAL CHARACTERISTICS
A. lineatus can sometimes be aggressive towards others of its kind and its behaviour towards other fish is not always exemplary either. It is therefore sensible to keep these fish alongside robust, rather

Aplocheilus lineatus

Aplocheilus lineatus

larger fish. They mainly live in the middle and top zone.

TEMPERATURE AND WATER COMPOSITION
23-25°C, 5-13° gH, pH 6-7

FOOD
A. lineatus eats both live food, with the emphasis on mosquito larvae, and various types of dry food (Sera San).

BREEDING
In a small shallow breeding tank (use a cover!), with increased water temperature, a good, constant water composition, diffuse, sparse lighting and Java moss, feathery-leafed plants and floating plants, the fish will sometimes start to lay eggs. Fry can be raised on fine artemia and fine powdered food (Sera Micron).

VARIANTS
A number of variants of this fish are known.

SPECIAL REMARKS
A cover is necessary on the aquarium, since A. lineatus likes to jump.

Arius seemani

FAMILY
Ariidae

SUB FAMILY
Ariinae

HABITAT
Southern North America and Central America

SEXUAL DIFFERENCES
Until the fish reach their adult size, the difference between the sexes is scarcely visible. In mature fish the females have a fatter stomach during the mating season.

LENGTH
A. seemani can grow to 35 centimetres or longer in the wild, but in the aquarium it does not exceed about 20 centimetres.

ACCOMMODATION
This active catfish feels most at home in a large aquarium. It requires refuges in the form of petrified wood or largish stones, rather diffuse lighting and plenty of current in the water. The fish feel more at ease with a dark bottom than if the substrate consists of light coloured gravel.

These fish like to swim a lot, so plenty of open space for swimming is more than preferable.

SOCIAL CHARACTERISTICS
A. seemani is a friendly fish which keeps itself to itself and leaves the other aquarium dwellers in peace. Despite this, its active lifestyle and size mean that it is not the ideal cohabitant for shy and reserved fish.

TEMPERATURE AND WATER COMPOSITION
22-25°C. This fish is not very demanding as regards the water composition. It thrives well in all sorts of water, as long as it is not too soft. Add some sea salt to the aquarium water now and then; these fish sometimes live in brackish water in the wild.

Arius seemani

Arius seemani

FOOD
This fish is an omnivore. It likes both dry food (Sera Vipan) and food tablets (Sera O-Nip). Make sure that the fish, especially when it grows larger, also has some live food now and then. It will normally polish off food which is not eaten by the other fish, but it is not as thorough at doing this as the Corydoras varieties.

BREEDING
Little is known so far about breeding in the aquarium. In the wild, the fish keep their eggs in their mouth to protect them until they hatch.

Astronotus ocellatus

RED OSCAR CICHLID

FAMILY
Cichlidae (cichlids)

HABITAT
Amazon region

SEXUAL DIFFERENCES
It is very difficult to recognise the difference between the sexes; outside the mating season it is completely impossible. The mature female is only recognisable by its sexual papilla during the mating season. The males sometimes display dark stripes on the base of the dorsal fin.

LENGTH
Up to 30 centimetres

Astronotus ocellatus, *a young oscar cichlid*

ACCOMMODATION

The oscar cichlid is usually only about seven centimetres or smaller when purchased, but the fish grow quickly and most aquaria soon become too small. For fully grown oscars, an aquarium at least two metres wide and 60 centimetres high will provide an ideal home. This variety likes to burrow in the bottom and usually does not leave plants and their roots alone. A thick layer of fine, smooth gravel (not sharp!), stone and petrified wood decorations, and possibly some more robust plant varieties, are advisable.

Since the oscar cichlid digs up plant roots, it is best to put the plants in earthenware pots with some heavy stones on top of them. These fish burrow, eat quite a lot and also produce a lot of excrement, so a very powerful motorised filter is necessary to keep the aquarium clean and the water constantly moving.

SOCIAL CHARACTERISTICS

This cichlid is not aggressive, although its size and appearance suggest the opposite. The fish usually get on well and you can also expect few problems with other fish. Obviously the community should consist of large cichlid varieties and one or two large catfish, since small fish will be seen as food. You can keep them as a pair, but also in a group, from which one or more pairs will spontaneously form.

TEMPERATURE AND WATER COMPOSITION

23-26°C. This fish is not very demanding as regards the water composition, as long as the water is free of waste substances. Regular partial changing of the water will help to keep the fish healthy and in good condition.

FOOD

This enormous cichlid always seems to be hungry and can take in large quantities of food. Even if has already eaten more than enough, it will seldom refuse food when offered. You should therefore be careful not to give the fish too much food. Suitable food includes cichlid sticks, earthworms, small fish, pieces of mussel and pieces of beef heart.

One reason why this species of fish, which is not always easy to keep, is so popular with hobbyists is its typical habit of

Astronotus ocellatus

"begging" for food from the carer. If you walk along the aquarium, they will follow you all the way along. They can also be trained to eat out of your hand.

BREEDING

If the fish are well fed and taken care of in suitable accommodation, you will not need to take any special precautions if you want to encourage them to breed. Oscar cichlids are very productive and good at caring for their fry. Both the eggs and the fry are cared for and defended vigorously against intruders.

VARIANTS

A number of variants of this fish are known. The "normal" oscar cichlid is illustrated here, but we also know of a variant whose flanks are almost entirely coloured orange-red without markings and an albino form.

SPECIAL REMARKS

The fish in the photograph is still young and still has its splendid colour. As the fish grow bigger, they become paler and a lot less colourful. Some oscars remain relatively attractive, but most of them gradually turn an unattractive greyish-brown colour with some pale orange and copper-coloured patches. The black spot on the tail fin remains there permanently, and indeed it is an identifying characteristic of the "oscar cichlid".

Astyanax fasciatus mexicanus
(syn. Anoptichthys jordani)

BLIND CAVE CHARACIN

FAMILY
Characidae (characins)

SUB FAMILY
Tetragonopterinae

HABITAT
Mexico and surrounding areas, but mainly in caves in the Rio Panuco area

SEXUAL DIFFERENCES
The males are usually thinner than the females. The females are characterised by rather rounder stomach contours.

LENGTH
Up to eight centimetres

ACCOMMODATION
The blind cave characin does very well in a community aquarium. They like to swim – a lot -, and therefore need plenty of room. Although they primarily live in dark caves in their natural habitat, they can be kept without any problems in an aquarium with normal lighting.

SOCIAL CHARACTERISTICS
The blind cave characin is a shoaling fish and feels particularly unhappy if it is kept with only one or two of its kind, so keep at least five and preferably more, blind cave characins together. They are fast swimmers and good-natured fish, which get on well with other fish species and

Astyanax fasciatus mexicanus

The sighted original form of the blind cave characin

leave even smaller fish alone. They stay mainly in the middle zone.

TEMPERATURE AND WATER COMPOSITION
17-25°C. These fish do not make particularly high demands on the water composition, although they do prefer harder water.

FOOD
The blind cave characin is an omnivore; the fish will eat both live food and dry food with gusto. Their blindness in no way hinders the fish from finding and eating its food.

BREEDING
The fish are free layers and also tend to eat their own eggs after spawning. It is typical for the young blind cave characin fish still to have eyes. These disappear as they get older. The species is fairly easy to breed.

SPECIAL REMARKS
This blind, flesh-coloured fish is assumed to be a natural mutation of the *Astyanax mexicanus*. Its seeming "handicap" does not cause the fish any difficulty at all.

Aulonocara hansbaenschi

AFRICAN PEACOCK

FAMILY
Cichlidae (cichlids)

HABITAT
Africa, especially in Lake Malawi

SEXUAL DIFFERENCES
The difference between the two sexes is very easy to see in mature fish. The males are bright blue in colour with an orange-yellow coloured breast. The females are much paler.

LENGTH
Up to 10 centimetres

ACCOMMODATION
You can keep this cichlid in a rather larger aquarium (at least 70 centimetres long). No vegetation is needed, and it is not recommended, because the fish burrow vigorously in the bottom and can damage the plant roots in this way. They need plenty of refuges in the form of rocks. The bottom should ideally consist of fine, and definitely not sharp, gravel and should ideally be thick to allow for the burrowing activity.

SOCIAL CHARACTERISTICS
It is best to keep one male and several females of this species together. Males can sometimes be aggressive towards one another. They can easily be kept with a number of other more hardy cichlid varieties. The fish prefer to stay near the bottom.

TEMPERATURE AND WATER COMPOSITION
23-26°C. The fish like a hard, basic environment.

FOOD
These cichlids enjoy both live food and dry food.

BREEDING
If the fish are well looked after, you need not devote any special attention to them in order for them to breed. The eggs and fry are kept in the female's mouth (mouth brooder). The young can be nurtured with very fine live food and dry food.

VARIANTS
This is a fish which does not occur in different varieties, but does come in various types with differences of appearance. The differences are in the colouring. The fish in the photograph has been given the title "Red Flash", after the Latin name.

Balantiocheilus melanopterus
(Barbus melanopterus)

BALA SHARK

FAMILY
Cyprinidae (carps and minnows)

SUB FAMILY
Cyprininae

HABITAT
South East Asia, in fast-flowing water (Thailand, Malaysia and Indonesia)

SEXUAL DIFFERENCES
The difference between the sexes can scarcely be seen in immature fish. Mature females have a fatter stomach.

LENGTH
The fish can grow to 30 centimetres or more in the wild, but are generally much smaller in the aquarium, at around 17 centimetres.

ACCOMMODATION
This boisterous and fast swimming shoaling fish with its spectacular silver scales can really only be kept in larger, preferably elongated aquaria, where it can move freely.
An aquarium 1.5 metres long is therefore the minimum. They like nibbling plants, so it is advisable to put no plants at all, or only very strong ones, in the aquarium.

SOCIAL CHARACTERISTICS
These fish can only be kept in a shoal of at least five fish. Fry tolerate other fish with no problems, but as they mature, or if they are kept as solitary fish, they develop an intolerant and even predatory character. They prefer to occupy the middle zone.

TEMPERATURE AND WATER COMPOSITION
23-27°C, 6-12° gH, pH 6-7.

FOOD
The bala shark is an omnivore. The fish eat large live food as well as frozen food and dry food (Sera Flora/Sera San) and they also like (blanched) vegetable food such as blanched spinach, lettuce leaves and watercress.

Barbus titteya

BREEDING
Occasional reports are heard of accidental breeding, but every serious attempt to breed this variety of fish so far has been a failure.

SPECIAL REMARKS
The bala shark is a fast swimmer and may also jump out of the aquarium; a well sealed cover is therefore necessary to keep the fish in the aquarium.

Balantiocheilus melanopterus

Barbus conchonius

ROSY BARB

FAMILY
Cyprinidae (carps and minnows)

SUB FAMILY
Cyprininae

HABITAT
Northern India, Assam and Bengal, both in stagnant and flowing water

Barbus conchonius *(♀), long finned variety*

SEXUAL DIFFERENCES
The difference between the sexes is easy to spot. The males are much more intensely coloured (red) than the females, which are also recognisable by their rather fuller stomachs.

LENGTH
In the aquarium, the rosy barb seldom grows to longer than six centimetres, but in the wild and in large ponds these fish can sometimes exceed 12 centimetres.

ACCOMMODATION
These undemanding shoaling fish suit every aquarium, provided that there is enough open space for swimming. This fish feels best in moving water, which you can provide by means of a powerful motorised filter, but a current is not actually necessary. The fish like to dig around in the bottom now and then, so make sure that the gravel is not sharp.

SOCIAL CHARACTERISTICS
The fish belong in a shoal with at least five others and always stay close together when swimming. Males and females are

tolerant of one another and also of other fish. Since they are boisterous and robust swimmers, they are less well suited to an aquarium with shy, fragile or very quiet fish. Rosy barbs usually swim in the middle zone, but they move throughout the aquarium in search of food.

TEMPERATURE AND WATER COMPOSITION
17-24°C. The rosy barb feels at home in almost all water conditions, as long as the water contains plenty of oxygen. In the summer months, these fish can be kept in unheated aquaria or in outdoor ponds.

FOOD
The rosy barb really is easy to feed. The species eats both dry food (Sera Viformo) and vegetable food, and also live food such as, for example, mosquito larvae, water fleas and brine shrimps (artemia).

BREEDING
It is not at all difficult to get rosy barbs to breed. The fish are sexually mature from six centimetres upwards. A breeding pair forms naturally; if you observe a shoal of barbs closely, you will see for yourself which two fish are constantly seeking one another out. Place the breeding pair in a breeding tank a grid should be inserted beforehand through which the eggs can fall and be outside the reach of the parent fish; this is because the rosy barb eats its own eggs. As the fish tend to lay their eggs among feathery leafed plants, you can attach a good piece of Java moss and some myriophyllum to the substrate spawner. A cover is also necessary because they sometimes jump out of the water during their mating ritual.

To speed up the spawning process, the breeding tank should be placed in a sunny location. Remove the parent fish, and also the grid, after spawning. The fry can be easily raised on fine powdered food (Sera Micron).

VARIANTS
There is a long finned variant of the rosy barb.

SPECIAL REMARKS
This particularly strong and undemanding shoaling fish swims about cheerfully and is very suitable for beginners.

Barbus everetti

FAMILY
Cyprinidae (carps and minnows)

SUB FAMILY
Cyprininae

HABITAT
South East Asia (Singapore, Borneo).

SEXUAL DIFFERENCES
The females are plumper than the males.

LENGTH
In the wild and in large lakes in tropical areas, these barbs may exceed 13 centimetres in length, but in the aquarium they are normally no longer than nine centimetres.

ACCOMMODATION
These barbs can be accommodated in medium-sized or large aquaria. Plenty of open space for swimming and dense peripheral vegetation is preferable.

SOCIAL CHARACTERISTICS
B. everetti is always kept in a shoal of at least five fish. The fish are peaceful and do not annoy another aquarium dwellers, although very shy and fragile fish may be intimidated by these vigorous swimmers. The fish occupy the whole aquarium.

TEMPERATURE AND WATER COMPOSITION
25-28° C. The fish can survive for a short time in water conditions which are not ideal, but a pH of 6-7 and a water hard-

Barbus everetti

ness of around 12° gH comes closest to the water in their natural habitat.

FOOD
These barbs are real omnivores and gluttons. They will enjoy plenty of vegetable food, dry food and live food.

BREEDING
It is possible to breed these fish in a well planted, roomy aquarium in a sunny location. The fish are egg predators, so a substrate spawner is an absolute necessity.

Barbus oligolepis

CHECKERED BARB

FAMILY
Cyprinidae (carps and minnows)

SUB FAMILY
Cyprininae

HABITAT
Indonesia, mainly Sumatra

SEXUAL DIFFERENCES
The male has black-edged fins and is generally redder in colour than the brownish-green coloured female.

LENGTH
Up to five centimetres

ACCOMMODATION
This small barb feels at home in various types of aquaria, as long as there is enough room to swim. It also appreciates peripheral vegetation. The fish do dig around in the ground in search of food, so the (fine) gravel should not be too sharp.

The colours of the fish stand out better against a dark substrate and lighting which is not too bright.

SOCIAL CHARACTERISTICS
This peace-loving and lively, but sometimes rather boisterous swimmer is very suitable for the community aquarium. The fish must always be kept in a shoal of at least five fish. Chequered barbs prefer to occupy the middle and bottom zone.

Barbus oligolepis

TEMPERATURE AND WATER COMPOSITION
21-24°C. The water composition is not very important, but rather soft (6-9° gH) and clear water is best.

FOOD
The chequered barb eats both dry food (Sera Flora) and live food and also needs vegetable food such as algae or vegetable food tablets (Sera Viformo/Sera Premium).

BREEDING
Breeding is similar to that of the rosy barb. A good breeding pair will form naturally if you keep a large shoal. A pair that is ready for breeding will, in a separate breeding tank under good conditions (increased water temperature, correct water composition, sunny position for the breeding tank) very quickly start to lay eggs. The parent fish must be removed quickly after spawning, since they eat their own eggs and young. A substrate spawner is essential.

SPECIAL REMARKS
The chequered barb is an undemanding and lively fish which is eminently suitable for the community aquarium. It is a very good beginner's fish because of its robust nature.

Barbus pentazona pentazona

Barbus pentazona pentazona

FAMILY
Cyprinidae (carps and minnows)

SUB FAMILY
Cyprininae

HABITAT
South East Asia, mainly Malaysia and Indonesia, in stagnant and slow-flowing water.

SEXUAL DIFFERENCES
The differences between the sexes only really become clear once the fish are mature. The males are rather smaller and more brightly coloured than the females.

LENGTH
Up to six centimetres

ACCOMMODATION
B. pentazona pentazona will thrive in a community aquarium where there is plenty of room to swim and enough refuges such as petrified wood and vegetation. Medium-sized aquaria (60-70 centimetres wide) will provide enough space.

SOCIAL CHARACTERISTICS
This friendly *Barbus* variety is quite peaceful and only really feel at ease in an aquarium where the other occupants are equally quiet. It is a shoaling fish and therefore belongs in a shoal of at least five fish.

TEMPERATURE AND WATER COMPOSITION
24-26°C. The water composition is not particularly important, although slightly acidic, soft water is preferable.

FOOD
This fish is justifiably known as an omnivore and a glutton. It enjoys food flakes, vegetable food and also live food.

BREEDING
If you want to breed this fish, then it is first of all important to find a well-suited breeding pair. In a large enough shoal, you will notice that one or more pairs form which always swim close to one another. Such a pair can be transferred to a separate breeding tank, in which the temperature is slowly raised to around 27-28°C. The pH should be around 6.5, or even lower, and the gH should definitely be no more than 11°. Remove the parent fish after spawning, as they eat their own eggs.

Barbus 'schuberti'

SCHUBERT'S BARB

FAMILY
Cyprinidae (carps and minnows)

SUB FAMILY
Cyprininae

HABITAT
This fish is not found in the wild. The original form of this fish (*B. semifasciolatus*) originates from South East China. The "Schuberti" is a popular variant bred by T. Schubert (United States).

Barbus *'schuberti'*

SEXUAL DIFFERENCES
The male fish are somewhat smaller and thinner than the female ones.

LENGTH
Up to seven centimetres

ACCOMMODATION
This sturdy barb feels at home in a very wide range of aquaria, provided there is enough space for swimming. The fish like a current in the water, so use a powerful filter or some jets.

SOCIAL CHARACTERISTICS
The Schubert barb is a fast swimming, very active and peaceful fish, which should be kept in a shoal of at least five fish.
Other fish are left in peace, but do not put them next to very shy, fragile fish or fish which are accustomed to peace and quiet, because their active swimming will put these under pressure.
They prefer to live in the middle zone, but also take food from the water surface and the bottom.

TEMPERATURE AND WATER COMPOSITION
19-24°C. The water should ideally be slightly acidic and medium-hard, but the fish are quite robust and can adapt to different water conditions.

FOOD
This barb is an omnivore. It eats both dry food and live food, and vegetable food is also well received.

BREEDING
Breeding is very simple and comparable to the method for other barbs. Make sure

A brood of Schubert's barb fry

you have a compatible breeding pair, a separate breeding tank in a sunny location and enough feathery-leafed plants. The Schubert barb, like many other free layers, eats eggs. The parent fish must be removed as soon as they have finished spawning. A substrate spawner introduced beforehand and fixed a few centimetres above the bottom will keep the eggs and parent fish apart during spawning.

SPECIAL REMARKS
Due to its strong constitution and lively behaviour this fish is a very suitable beginner's fish.

Barbus tetrazona

TIGER BARB

FAMILY
Cyprinidae (carps and minnows)

SUB FAMILY
Cyprininae

HABITAT
Indonesia

SEXUAL DIFFERENCES
When the fish are mature, the females are larger, somewhat plumper and less brightly coloured than the males.

LENGTH
Up to six centimetres

ACCOMMODATION
The tiger barb feels very comfortable in a community aquarium, as long as there is enough room to swim. It very much appreciates a current in the water. The colour of the substrate and the lighting has hardly any effect on the bright colouring of this popular and well-known variety of fish.

SOCIAL CHARACTERISTICS
Tiger barbs will only thrive in a rather large shoal with at least five fish. They then swim close together, which gives a spectacular effect. These attractive and robust fish unfortunately does have one negative trait – they have a tendency to make life difficult for other, weaker fish. They also nibble the "antennae" of labyrinth fish (gouramis) and also sometimes

A little shoal of tiger barbs

Moss green tiger barb

annoy other fish with luxurious fins, so they should only be placed alongside fish species without large fins or spines. They mainly occupy the middle zone.

TEMPERATURE AND WATER COMPOSITION
23-26°C. The water composition is not particularly important as long as the aquarium water is clear, clean and, above all, rich in oxygen.

FOOD
The tiger barb is an omnivore, and readily takes both live and dry food (Sera Flora/Sera Premium).

BREEDING
The technique for breeding these popular shoaling fish is practically identical to rosy barbs. The only difference is in the water composition. The tiger barb is much more demanding during the mating season. A gH of 5°, a pH of around 6-7 and a water temperature of 28°C are best. The species is very productive. Fry can be raised on fine powdered food (Sera Micron).

VARIANTS
There are many known variants. The golden-yellow with black bands is the best known original form, but the green and the albino tiger barbs are also very popular world-wide.

SPECIAL REMARKS
This tough, lively and colourful shoaling fish is highly suitable for new aquarists.

Barbus ticto (syn. Puntius ticto)

Barbus ticto *(syn.* Puntius ticto*)*

TWO SPOT BARB

FAMILY
Cyprinidae (carps and minnows)

SUB FAMILY
Cyprininae

HABITAT
India and Sri Lanka

SEXUAL DIFFERENCES
The difference between the sexes can only be clearly seen when the fish are mature. The females are then somewhat larger and plumper than the males. During the mating season the male has a wide red stripe along its body (see photograph).

LENGTH
Up to nine centimetres, depending on the swimming space available.

ACCOMMODATION
B. ticto is very adaptable and is an ideal inhabitant for the community aquarium,

Barbus ticto (♂ *above,* ♀ *below*)

as long as there is enough room to swim. Due to its active lifestyle it is not very suitable for keeping alongside shy or small species of fish. It never feels completely at home in small aquaria, and likes a current in the water.

SOCIAL CHARACTERISTICS
B. ticto is a shoaling fish and must be kept together with at least five others, and preferably more. Other aquarium dwellers are generally left in peace. The fish prefer to occupy the middle zone, but they also take food from the surface and the bottom.

TEMPERATURE AND WATER COMPOSITION
15-24°C. *B. ticto* feels at home in nearly all water conditions and, like the rosy barb, can be kept in the garden pond during the summer months.

FOOD
This fish is an omnivore. It likes both dry food (Sera Vipan) and live food.

BREEDING
Under ideal conditions in a breeding tank in which the water temperature is gradually increased, these fish will very quickly begin to lay eggs. You can transfer a well suited breeding pair to a breeding tank, but good results have also been obtained where a male is mated with several females at once. The fish are egg-eaters, so it makes sense to remove the parent fish from the breeding tank as soon as the eggs have been laid. The fry are reared on fine powdered food (Sera Micron).

SPECIAL REMARKS
These fish can be kept extremely well in unheated aquaria and ponds. However, the temperature should not remain lower than 15°C for any length of time.

Barbus titteya

FAMILY
Cyprinidae (carps and minnows)

SUB FAMILY
Cyprininae

HABITAT
Sri Lanka, mainly in stagnant and shallow waters

SEXUAL DIFFERENCES
Outside the mating season these fish are beige-red in colour and the females are recognisable by their plumper body. The male is also rather smaller and more elongated in form. During the mating season, the male fish are a much brighter red than the females.

LENGTH
Up to five centimetres

ACCOMMODATION
B. titteya can be kept in smaller community aquaria, with plenty of peripheral vegetation and refuges, together with very peaceful neighbours. The fish feel more at home, and are at their most attractive, in an aquarium with a dark substrate and some floating plants (shaded places).

Barbus titteya *(♂ left, ♀ right)*

These fish are best kept in a group, although they do not form such close shoals as is usually the case with shoaling fish. If there is too much turmoil and activity in the aquarium these fish will hardly show their faces at all, and their attractive dark red colour will also not be at its best. They occupy the bottom and middle zone.

TEMPFRATURE AND WATER COMPOSITION

22-26°C. These particularly hardy fish usually thrive in the most varied water compositions, though they do prefer medium to medium-hard water.

FOOD

Titteyas are not difficult to feed, and do not cause problems for the aquarist in this area. They eat dry food (Sera Flora), live food and algae.

BREEDING

Under ideal conditions, in a separate breeding tank with enough vegetation (plenty of Java moss), there is a chance that a well suited breeding pair may reproduce. The males can sometimes behave rather aggressively towards their partner during the courtship ritual. For this reason several females are often placed with one male in a breeding tank.

Cherry barbs are egg predators, so they should be removed from the breeding tank immediately after spawning. It can take some time before all the eggs are laid, so it is wise to place a substrate spawner in the breeding tank, so that the eggs remain separate from the parent fish. The fry can be raised on fine powdered food (Sera Micron).

Baryancistrus *sp.* L81

FAMILY
Loricariidae (armoured catfish)

SUB FAMILY
Ancistrinae

HABITAT
Brazil, in fast-flowing streams and rivers

SEXUAL DIFFERENCES
Unknown

Baryancistrus Spec.

Up to 14 centimetres

ACCOMMODATION
This striking bottom dweller belongs in medium-sized or large aquaria. Constantly moving water is preferable. The fish need refuges; during the day they like to lie in a quiet spot under a piece of petrified wood, among dense foliage, and only come out later, at dusk, to actively search for food. They like to scrape algae from the sides, petrified wood and plants. As we seldom encounter this in a recently set up aquarium, it is better only to buy them once sufficient algae has formed in the aquarium.

SOCIAL CHARACTERISTICS
The fish are naturally peaceful and keep to themselves. They leave other aquarium dwellers in peace and are usually kept as solitary fish.

TEMPERATURE AND WATER COMPOSITION
24-26°C. Their demands on the water composition are not too high, but crystal clear and moving water is definitely best.

FOOD
These fish eat what is left by other aquarium dwellers but in particular they need plenty of vegetable food, mainly algae. Give them food tablets (Sera Premium) or blanched water cress and lettuce leaves at dusk.

BREEDING
Nothing is known so far about breeding these fish.

VARIANTS
There are no known variants of this fish but there are some fish of the same species which have a deviant, polka-dot pattern. All these variants have been given an L number instead of a Latin name.

Beaufortia leveretti

FAMILY
Balitoridae

SUB FAMILY
Gastromyzoninae

HABITAT
China

SEXUAL DIFFERENCES
None known so far

LENGTH
Up to about 13 centimetres

ACCOMMODATION
This unusual fish will do best in larger aquaria in a sunny location, where there is sufficient algae growing in the aquarium. Also make sure that there are no rough stones or other sharp objects on which the fish can injure itself. They very much appreciate a current in the water (created with a powerful filter or several airstones).

SOCIAL CHARACTERISTICS
These remarkable fish are extremely peaceful.
They keep to themselves and leave both others of their own kind and other aquarium dwellers alone. They prefer to occupy the bottom and middle zone.

Beauforta leveretti

Beauforta leveretti

18-23°C. The hardness and acidity of the water are not very important, although a gH of around 15° and a neutral pH is be ideal. The water should always be crystal clear and rich in oxygen.

FOOD
This variety does not only eat algae, although it does have a preference for it. If there is not enough algae in the aquarium, or if the fish has eaten it all, give it some food tablets for bottom dwellers (Sera Viformo) and occasionally some blanched lettuce leaves and watercress. The fish will also clear away food that the other aquarium dwellers have not eaten. Live food is very welcome too.

BREEDING
These peculiar fish were "discovered" only quite recently by aquarium hobbyists and nothing is therefore known about breeding as yet.

Bedotia geayi

FAMILY
Atherinidae (silversides)

HABITAT
Madagascar

SEXUAL DIFFERENCES
The difference between the sexes is difficult to establish.

LENGTH
Up to about 12 centimetres

ACCOMMODATION
These fish do best in rather larger and elongated aquaria (at least 80 centimetres long). They like to swim a lot, so sufficient space for swimming is an absolute necessity. *Bedotia geayi* particularly appreciates peripheral vegetation and some current in the aquarium water, for example from a powerful filter or airstones.

SOCIAL CHARACTERISTICS
This variety is peaceful, not only towards others of its own kind but also towards other varieties of fish, and it can easily be

Bedotia geayi

Bedotia geayi

kept together with other fish which make the same demands with regard to water composition, without any problems. Shyer varieties will not feel at all comfortable in an aquarium with this species of fish as these boisterous swimmers – unintentionally – force them into the foliage. Keep the fish in shoals of at least five, but preferably more.

TEMPERATURE AND WATER COMPOSITION
20-23°C. These fish come from crystal-clear mountain streams in the wild and need clear, clean water, rich in oxygen with as few waste substances as possible. They prefer medium-hard or hard water.

FOOD
This fish is not very demanding when it comes to food. It eats both dry food and small live food. Since they live in the top and middle zone, and do not readily take anything from the bottom, a group of catfish are advisable as "food residue collectors".

BREEDING
Breeding is not very easy, but it is definitely possible. Cleanliness is very impor-

tant, as is rich planting with feathery-leafed plants and the correct water hardness and temperature (26°C). You do not need to select a breeding pair; the fish will generally mate within the shoal.

Betta imbellis

FAMILY
Anabantidae (labyrinth fish)

SUB FAMILY
Macropodinae

HABITAT
Malaysia

SEXUAL DIFFERENCES
The males of this species are easy to recognise because they are more colourful than the females and also have rather longer fins.

LENGTH
Up to about five centimetres

ACCOMMODATION
This *Betta* variety, which is much less known and in demand than its cousin, the immeasurably popular *Betta splendens*, can easily be accommodated in a smaller aquarium. The fish are not used to constantly moving water, so do not use a powerful filter. Make sure the bottom is fairly dark, with dense peripheral vegetation, feathery-leafed plants and some floating plants on the water surface. The water level should not be higher than 25 centimetres.

Betta imbellis ♀

This variety is good at jumping, so a cover is necessary to keep the fish in the aquarium.

SOCIAL CHARACTERISTICS
These fish can be kept in a community aquarium, as long as the other aquarium dwellers are not too small. A community with a number of other labyrinth fish, for example, a shoal of rasboras and *Corydoras* varieties as bottom dwellers, is ideal. The males are not always very tolerant of each other, but the "fights" between males are usually quite harmless and are no more than mock fights and bravado. Nevertheless, it is better for their peace of mind to keep only one male with two or three females.

TEMPERATURE AND WATER COMPOSITION
25-28°C. The water composition is not very important. The water should of course be very clean and clear.

FOOD
These fish are easy to feed. They will readily take dry food, but also like to eat small live food.

BREEDING
Breeding is interesting and similar to *Betta splendens*.

Betta splendens

SIAMESE FIGHTING FISH

FAMILY
Anabantidae (labyrinth fish)

SUB FAMILY
Macropodinae

HABITAT
Thailand and Vietnam

SEXUAL DIFFERENCES
The males are much larger and more colourful than the females and are also known for their long fins.

LENGTH
Up to six centimetres

ACCOMMODATION
The *Betta Splendens*, or Siamese Fighting

Betta splendens ♂

Fish, feels very much at home in both larger and smaller aquaria. Plenty of floating plants, diffuse light, plenty of refuges and not too high a water level are advisable. The fish like peace and quiet and prefer still water.

SOCIAL CHARACTERISTICS
The fish deserves the name Siamese fighting fish, since the males fight until one of them dies. Even in a large aquarium

Betta splendens ♂

you can never keep more than one male at a time. Siamese fighting fish usually live near the surface among the (floating) plants in search of food (mosquito larvae), but they also descend to the bottom zone to chase small fish down there. It is therefore not a good idea to keep them alongside less hardy or smaller fish. On the other hand, because of its enormous fins, it is itself attacked by larger, more aggressive fish species and tiger barbs. The population in the aquarium must therefore be selected carefully. Due to the particularly strong reproductive drive among the males, it is best to keep two or three females for every male, rather than a single female which will almost certainly be chased to death by an over-active lover. You can also choose to keep only one male, without females, since this usually also works well.

TEMPERATURE AND WATER COMPOSITION
25-28°C. The water composition is not so very important, but the fish do need plenty of warmth. If the water is too polluted, this fish can make use of its labyrinth, an organ behind the head which allows the fish to take oxygen from the atmosphere. A cover is definitely necessary to prevent

Betta splendens ♂

Betta splendens ♂

major fluctuations in temperature between the water and the atmosphere. This can cause the fish to become very ill and die.

FOOD
These fish likes dry food (Sera San). They also appreciate live food (mosquito larvae, tubifex).

BREEDING
Breeding these fish is very interesting. The breeding pair, and you must make sure that both the female and the male really are mature and in top condition, are transferred to a separate breeding tank. The water level should not be too high, 10 to 15 centimetres is enough, and there must also be plenty of floating plants (for example, crystalwort) to provide refuges for the female.

The substrate can be omitted, or it consist of very fine gravel or washed sand. To speed up the spawning process you can gradually raise the temperature to 30°C and filter the water over some peat.

The male builds a nest of bubbles below the surface and courts the female in the meantime – if she displays dark diagonal bands on her body when the male approaches her, she is ready to mate. If not, remove the female, or the male will chase her to death. After spawning the female must be removed in any case, since the male will then no longer tolerate her presence near the nest.

The male takes care of the eggs and the nest. Once the eggs have hatched, you must remove the male, because it no longer sees them as offspring, but as welcome additions to his diet. The fry are raised on fine powdered food (Sera Micron). Regularly change part of the water to prevent it becoming too dirty.

VARIANTS
The original variety is a fish with slightly shorter fins, but over the years Siamese fighting fish have been bred with longer and longer fins. There are many different colours of Siamese fighting fish, such as red, blue and turquoise coloured ones as well as the very rare white fish. Multi-coloured varieties do also occur. The females are less striking, though they also come in various different colours.

SPECIAL REMARKS
In Thailand "fights" have been organised between *Betta* males since time immemorial. Such fights are very popular there and large sums of money are placed on the fish. However the fish are not allowed to fight until one is dead (which is what happens in the aquarium), but the males are separated once there is a clear winner.

If you want to see how threatening a male Siamese fighting fish can be when it spots an intruder, hold a small mirror in front of him. (It is not good for the health of the fish to do this too often, and it reduces their life expectancy).

Boehlkea fredcochui

FAMILY
Characidae (characins)

SUB FAMILY
Tetragonopterinae

HABITAT
Peru

SEXUAL DIFFERENCES
The difference between the sexes is not easy to establish at a young age. It is generally true that the males are somewhat smaller and more elongated in shape than the females.

LENGTH
Up to five centimetres

ACCOMMODATION
This shoaling fish feels quite at home in a community aquarium with enough peripheral vegetation and plenty of space to swim. If the fish is kept in an aquarium with a light coloured substrate, it will remain pale. A dark substrate will allow their colours come out better.

SOCIAL CHARACTERISTICS
Boehlkea fredcochui is a friendly and peaceful fish which likes to be in a community with others of its kind and leaves other aquarium dwellers in peace. It can only be kept in a small shoal with at least five others; individuals pine away. The fish prefer to occupy the middle zone.

TEMPERATURE AND WATER COMPOSITION
23-25°C. The fish feel fine in various different water compositions, although the water should not be too hard.

FOOD
This small characin is easy to feed. It eats both dry food (Sera Vipan) and small live food.

BREEDING
Little is known so far about reproduction.

Botia lohachata

FAMILY
Cobitadae (spiny loaches)

SUB FAMILY
Botiinae

HABITAT
India

SEXUAL DIFFERENCES
Unknown

LENGTH
Up to about 10 centimetres

ACCOMMODATION
This fish likes to burrow in the bottom and does not therefore belong in an aquarium with dense vegetation. Only robust plant varieties should be used, placed in earthenware pots which are buried and covered with heavy stones. In this way the plant roots will remain intact. The fish needs a (partly) soft substrate such as washed sand, plenty of room to swim and enough refuges. It usually stays hidden by day, and you will not see it very

Boehlkea fredcochui

Botia lohachata

much. It does not like very bright lighting.

This fish lives a rather withdrawn lifestyle within its own territory and is best kept as a solitary fish. Other fish are not allowed into the territory.

TEMPERATURE AND WATER COMPOSITION
25-29°C. This *Botia* variety likes slightly acidic, soft water; a gH below 9° is ideal.

FOOD
This Botia variety eats both algae and dry and live food. It also eats food tablets for bottom dwellers (Sera Viformo). It is better not to feed these fish until dusk.

BREEDING
Nothing is known so far about breeding.

Botia macracantha

CLOWN LOACH

FAMILY
Cobitidae (loaches)

SUB FAMILY
Botiinae

HABITAT
Indonesia

SEXUAL DIFFERENCES
The difference between the sexes is not easy to spot in young fish. In mature fish, a trained eye will notice the rather more slender build of the females.

Botia macracantha

Botia macracantha

LENGTH
In an aquarium, clown loaches seldom exceed 15 cm, but in the wild – like so many other fish species – they can grow much larger because there is practically unlimited space available.

ACCOMMODATION
The clown loach belongs in larger aquaria (at least 80 centimetres). Since the fish like to swim a lot, they need plenty of space and there must be enough room to swim in the aquarium. The fish appreciate a strong current in the water, which you can create with airstones or a powerful motorised filter. This also makes them more active.

SOCIAL CHARACTERISTICS
A solitary clown loach often tends to make life difficult for other aquarium dwellers. Two loaches together will also cause problems, since the fish then attack one another. The clown loach is best kept in a shoal with at least five fish. In a shoal the fish should display their natural cheerful disposition and enjoyment of swimming, and the lively community spends almost the whole day play-fighting, which is not very brutal and gives the impression that the fish are playing. Within the shoal, they will leave the other aquarium dwellers in peace, but you should remember that due to their lively temperament they may well frighten shy and fragile fish.

Clown loaches mainly swim in the middle and bottom zone and are active both during the day and at dusk.

25-29°C. The water must be changed regularly and should be rich in oxygen (airstone). Slightly acidic, soft water is preferable.

FOOD
The clown loach eats both dry (Sera Flora) and live food and algae.

BREEDING
Little is known so far about breeding these fish in the aquarium.

SPECIAL REMARKS
This striking and popular fish is, unfortunately, very susceptible to disease, particularly whitespot. By keeping the aquarium water as clear and clean as possible and regularly changing part of the water, an environment can be created in which whitespot will find it harder to gain a hold on the fish. Test the water values because hard water can also cause disease. Stress can also lower the resistance of the fish, so make sure that the aquarium is not over-populated and that you do not intervene in the aquarium any more than necessary.

Botia striata

Botia striata

FAMILY
Cobitidae (loaches)

SUB FAMILY
Botiinae

HABITAT
South East Asia

SEXUAL DIFFERENCES
Unknown

LENGTH
In the wild these fish grow to around 10 to 12 centimetres long, but in the aquarium they usually remain smaller.

ACCOMMODATION
These loaches do well in small or medium-sized aquaria. Make sure that there are enough refuges. As this species likes to burrow in the bottom, you can give them what they want by creating certain areas in the aquarium with a thick layer of washed sand. Despite their burrowing behaviour, the fish need thick vegetation and they usually leave the roots of plants in peace, particularly if there are special "digging spots" available.

B. striata is not only striking to look at, but it is also very friendly, keeps to itself and leaves the other aquarium dwellers in peace. In the wild these fish live together in large groups and in the aquarium they also appreciate a community of several family members.

Thanks of their peaceful nature they can easily be kept in community aquaria.

TEMPERATURE AND WATER COMPOSITION
24-26°C. The water composition is not particularly important for these tough fish.

FOOD
This loach is an omnivore. It consumes everything which the other aquarium dwellers allow to sink to the bottom, but you can occasionally also give it food tablets for bottom dwellers (Sera Viformo), (blanched) lettuce, spinach and watercress, and live food.

BREEDING
Little is known so far about reproduction in the aquarium.

SPECIAL REMARKS
This striking and robust fish is a very suitable and interesting fish for beginners.

Brachydanio albinoleatus

SPOTTED DANIO

FAMILY
Cyprinidae (carps and minnows)

SUB FAMILY
Rasborinae

HABITAT
South East Asia

SEXUAL DIFFERENCES
The males are thinner and more intensely coloured than the females.

LENGTH
Maximum six centimetres

ACCOMMODATION
This lively shoaling fish does especially well in a community aquarium. Plenty of

Brachydanio albinoleatus

open space for swimming, dense peripheral vegetation and powerful aeration are advisable. Place petrified wood and rocks in the aquarium if it is large enough. (In medium-sized aquaria 60-70 centimetres wide they will form obstacles to these fast swimmers). These fish can jump out of the water, so put a cover on the aquarium.

SOCIAL CHARACTERISTICS
Spotted danios are easy and very lively fish which leave other fish in peace. They prefer to occupy the middle and top zone. Always keep the spotted danio in a shoal of at least seven specimens.

TEMPERATURE AND WATER COMPOSITION
21-24°C. The fish are tough and adapt to most water compositions, although they are not very well suited to excessively hard water.

FOOD
The spotted danio is easily satisfied. It eats both dry and live food, as well as vegetable food.

BREEDING
Breeding these fish is not particularly difficult. In order to make sure that as many eggs are fertilised as possible, you can put one female and two or three males in a breeding tank with plenty of feathery-leafed plants. Gradually increase the temperature to 26-27°C. The fish are free layers and happily devour their eggs after spawning, so remove them as quickly as

possible from the breeding tank. The fry can be reared on fine powdered food.

This fish is exceptionally suitable for beginners.

Brachydanio rerio

ZEBRA DANIO

FAMILY
Cyprinidae (carps and minnows)

SUB FAMILY
Rasborinae

HABITAT
India, mainly in the east

SEXUAL DIFFERENCES
The difference between the sexes cannot be seen until the fish are mature. Then the male fish are thinner, more elongated in shape and also more intensely coloured than the females.

LENGTH
Up to five centimetres

ACCOMMODATION
This very lively and undemanding shoaling fish feels at home both in smaller and larger aquaria. They are fast and tireless swimmers which need enough open space for swimming.
   It sometimes seems as if these fish are playing – if there is an airstone in the

Brachydanio rerio

aquarium they swim downwards against the flow of bubbles and then allow themselves to be carried back up again. The fish can do this for a long time. Many zebra danios disappear from the aquarium in this way: you definitely need a cover.

SOCIAL CHARACTERISTICS
The zebra danio must be kept in a shoal containing at least five fish. The fish are very active, even boisterous, but they are extremely peaceful towards each other and other aquarium dwellers. However these fast swimmers are definitely not suitable company for shy and calm fish. Zebra danios tend to occupy the middle and top zone.

TEMPERATURE AND WATER COMPOSITION
18-24°C. The fish adjust very well to different water compositions, but soft to medium-hard water (6-15° gH) with a neutral pH (7) is ideal.

FOOD
The zebra danio is an omnivore. The fish can easily be kept healthy on a diet of varied dry food (Sera Vipan, Sera O-Nip). They also like to eat live food, as long as it is not too raw: tubifex and water fleas provide very suitable live food for these shoaling fish.

BREEDING
These fish will very readily lay eggs in a separate breeding tank with plenty of sunlight and feathery-leafed plants, if the water composition is close to the ideal values. Zebra danios are free layers and like many other free laying fish they also eat their own eggs. Make sure there is a substrate spawner in the breeding tank so that the eggs and parent fish are separated, or remove the parent fish as quickly as possible after spawning. The fry can be raised on fine powdered food (Sera Micron).

VARIANTS
There is also an attractively patterned leopard danio *(Brachydanio "Frankei")* and long-finned variants of both types exist.

SPECIAL REMARKS
The zebra danio is very suitable for beginners.

Brachygobius xanthozona

BUMBLEBEE FISH

FAMILY
Gobiidae (gobies)

HABITAT
Indonesia, in coastal areas

SEXUAL DIFFERENCES
The sexes are not easy to differentiate, but the trained eye will observe that the female has a fatter body. During the mating season, the females are visibly paler in colour.

LENGTH
Up to about four centimetres

ACCOMMODATION
The bumblebee fish is not much of a swimmer, and therefore feels very at home in a small aquarium. Ideally, this aquarium should be specially designed for this species, so that the water composition and accommodation are perfectly suited to them.

Brachygobius xanthozona

Brachygobius xanthozona

This fish can also be kept in community aquaria, as long as a number of requirements are met. The fish like to conceal themselves amongst dense vegetation, so make sure there are enough plants in the aquarium. Petrified wood and stones are also used for this purpose, so these are also vital elements in the set-up.

SOCIAL CHARACTERISTICS
Bumblebee fish are very quiet fish. They usually "lie" somewhere amongst the plants on a large leaf, or on the bottom if there is enough shelter there. As regards contact with other fish, you do not need to expect any problems from this small black and yellow striped fish.

They are not always very friendly towards each other though; the fish occupy their own territory and no others of their kind are allowed in outside the mating season. In order to avoid problems, it is best never to keep more than two fish in the same aquarium.

TEMPERATURE AND WATER COMPOSTION
26-29°C, at least 20° gH (!), pH 8. Add a few heaped spoonfuls of sea salt to the aquarium water once a week. This fish likes brackish water (half seawater / half fresh water) and therefore thrives in brackish water aquaria.

FOOD
This fish is not easy to please when it comes to food. These fastidious fish only really eat small live food, such as tubifex and mosquito larvae, for example. They may possibly eat frozen food organisms as well, but will rarely or never accept dry food.

BREEDING
Breeding these super little fish is a complicated affair, best left to specialists. The male always cares for and defends the eggs himself.

Brycinus longipinnis
(syn. Alestes longipinnis)

FAMILY
Alestidae (African characins)

SUB FAMILY
Alestinae

HABITAT
West and Central Africa

SEXUAL DIFFERENCES
The males are recognisable by their dorsal fin, which is longer than the dorsal fin of the females.

LENGTH
In the wild these fish grow to around 16 centimetres long, but in the aquarium they do not usually exceed 10 centimetres.

ACCOMMODATION
Due to the size which these fish can reach, the fact that they always have to be kept in a group and their lively disposition, they are best kept in quite a large aquarium, at least 80 centimetres long. Plenty of room to swim is definitely necessary. In brightly lit aquaria with a light-coloured bottom the fish usually remain pale in colour. If there are some floating plants and dark substrate, the colours of the fish will stand out much better. A cover is definitely not a luxury since these fish tend to leap above the surface.

SOCIAL CHARACTERISTICS
These are shoaling fish and at least five must therefore always be kept together. Other fish are left in peace, but very shy or sensitive fish could feel threatened by these robust, active swimmers. They prefer to occupy the middle and top zone.

TEMPERATURE AND WATER COMPOSITION
22-25°C. These fish are tough and easily adjust to all types of water characteristics.

FOOD
These fish eat both dry and live food, but they rarely take food which has landed on the bottom. It is therefore sensible to keep one or more bottom dwellers in an aquarium with these fish. The fish also eat vegetable food.

BREEDING
If you want to try and breed these fish, transfer the entire shoal, or a well matched pair, to a breeding tank in a sunny location. Although the fish do not usually make any demands as regards the water composition, the water should not be too hard when it comes to breeding. The ideal level is 2-6°gH. The eggs are laid all over the aquarium and the fish then like to eat them. A substrate spawner will keep the parent fish away from their eggs.

Bunocephalus coracoideus

BANJO CATFISH

FAMILY
Aspredinidae (banjo catfish)

SUB FAMILY
Bunocephalinae

HABITAT
Amazon region

SEXUAL DIFFERENCES
The females are generally rather plumper than the males.

LENGTH
Up to about 13 centimetres

ACCOMMODATION
This fish is not very demanding, but it does like a chance to burrow in the substrate. A (partly) sandy substrate is therefore ideal. Due to this burrowing and a tendency to dig, this fish does not belong in an aquarium with dense vegeta-

Brycinus longipinnis

tion. Keep coarse gravel and other sharp protruding objects out of the aquarium as these can injure the fish.

SOCIAL CHARACTERISTICS
An easy, peaceful bottom dweller which can be kept both as a solitary fish or with several others of its kind. The fish prefer to stay on the floor and in the bottom zone. They usually remain hidden by day, and sometimes conceal themselves in the substrate. They only really come to life at dusk, when they go searching for food.

TEMPERATURE AND WATER COMPOSITION
21-27°C. These fish are virtually insensitive to the water composition.

FOOD
Omnivore. Food tablets for bottom dwellers (Sera Viformo) are preferred but these fish also like to eat live food such as tubifex and mosquito larvae. Always distribute the food when it is getting dark, otherwise it will have all been eaten by the other aquarium dwellers by the time this fish becomes active.

Bunocephalus coracoideus

BREEDING
So far little is known about how to breed these fish in the aquarium. In the wild they dig a hole in a sheltered spot in which the eggs are laid. The eggs are guarded by both parents against hungry or inquisitive fish.

Bunocephalus coracoideus

Carassius auratus

GOLDFISH

FAMILY
Cyprinidae (carps and minnows)

SUB FAMILY
Cyprininae

HABITAT
The ancestor of the goldfish is the crucian carp. The goldfish was kept and bred thousands of years ago in China, and it is now bred throughout the world. The fish is not found in the wild.

SEXUAL DIFFERENCES
The difference between the sexes can only be seen properly once the fish are sexually mature. Then the rounder and fuller body contours of the female and the so-called spawning rash on the male become visible; small white spots on the gill covers and sometimes also on the pectoral fins.

LENGTH
In large lakes the goldfish can easily reach 40 centimetres or longer. In the aquarium these fish seldom grow to longer than 15 to 20 centimetres maximum. In small bowls, in which these fish are unfortunately all too often still kept, they do not grow longer than six to eight centimetres due to shortage of space and usually poor feeding.

ACCOMMODATION
Most goldfish bowls are not suitable for the goldfish, because they are much too small. Robust specimens can survive in them for a number of years, but given that a goldfish can easily survive for fifteen to twenty years, it is obvious that the fish is doomed to a short life in too small a bowl. You can keep goldfish in a very large bowl (minimum diameter 40 centimetres), in which the water level is just above the widest point to maximise the oxygen supply, but you should definitely not keep more than two fish at once, since in this case an oxygen shortage very quickly results, which soon causes the death of one or more fish. An oxygen-rich, well aerated, spacious aquarium rich in oxygen, with a good current, sturdy plant varieties (cold-water plants) and plenty of open space for

swimming, is the ideal environment for a goldfish, apart from an outside lake. The fish like to dig around in the bottom to look for food. To give them a chance to display their natural behaviour, you should not use sharp gravel as a substrate.

SOCIAL CHARACTERISTICS
Goldfish are extremely peaceful, both towards their own kind and towards other fish. The exceptions are those fish which have spent a long time alone in too small an aquarium or too small a bowl; these sometimes develop aggressive behaviour towards newcomers. If they are transferred to a different environment, they will no longer be aggressive. Goldfish feel much more at ease with several others of their own kind.

Shubunkin comet-tail goldfish

White goldfish. A goldfish with its original colour can be seen in the background

TEMPERATURE AND WATER COMPOSITION

2 to 25°C. A water temperature of 17 to 21°C is ideal. The temperament of the fish depends on the temperature of the water. In warm water the fish are many times more active than in cold water. The fish are strong and not very sensitive to the water composition, but the water must be rich in oxygen (well aerated with airstones) and free of waste. Regular changing of the water (for example a quarter of the water once a week) will help to keep the fish in good condition and good health.

FOOD

The goldfish is an omnivore. As a basic staple give it dry food specially intended for goldfish (Sera Goldy) and no tropical fish food, since goldfish need less proteins and more carbohydrates than most tropical fish. As well as dry food, the fish like to eat small insects (fruit flies) and live food (mosquito larvae, water fleas). They also like vegetable food. If they receive too little of this, the fish will nibble feathery-leafed plants. There are dry flake foods for vegetarians, but (blanched) watercress, lettuce leaves and spinach are also popular with these fish.

BREEDING

Goldfish breed most easily in largish garden ponds, and you will notice that there are more fish swimming around in the pond than you originally put there. The goldfish will also breed easily in a spacious aquarium with plenty of oxygen and feathery-leafed vegetation, provided the aquarium is in a sunny position and the fish have already been well fed on a varied diet. If, preferably in the late spring, fish ready for breeding (one female and two or three males, in order to ensure optimal fertilisation of the eggs) are placed in the breeding tank, it is possible that they will breed on the same day (or otherwise at daybreak the next day). A substrate spawner is definitely necessary, as the parent fish eat their own eggs. For the same reason the parent fish are removed after spawning. It is not always easy to raise the fry. They are very sensitive to changes in temperature. A variation in temperature of even one degree Celsius can lead to deformities. The fry can be raised on fine powdered food (Sera Micron). Nowadays goldfish are almost never bred naturally in the larger nurseries. The spawn and milt are removed by hand and mixed together, so that as many eggs as possible are fertilised.

VARIANTS
The goldfish is bred in various colours and shapes including (almost) single-coloured white, red, yellow and black fish,

Two veiltail goldfish variants

Goldfish can grow very large in spacious aquaria and garden ponds

as well as spotted fish and fish which have blue, black, red or white spots (shubunkins). There are also some goldfish with elongated fins. These are called comets and are very popular because of their decorative appearance. All young goldfish are initially green-grey in colour and only acquire their mature colour after about three months. Some retain their original colour.

SPECIAL REMARKS
You must pay good attention to the health of the fish when purchasing goldfish, even more than with other varieties of fish. Never buy goldfish which are ailing, too thin, affected by disease or deformed.

Carassius auratus (veiltails)

VEILTAIL GOLDFISH

FAMILY
Cyprinidae (carps and minnows)

SUB FAMILY
Cyprininae

HABITAT
The veiltail goldfish is a variant of the ordinary goldfish and was originally bred by the Chinese.

SEXUAL DIFFERENCES
The difference between the sexes can only actually be spotted when the fish are mature. Mature females are then slightly plumper than males, which display small

Calico veiltail goldfish

Red Cap veiltail goldfish

white spots on their gill covers during the mating season (spawning rash).

Given sufficient space, the veiltail goldfish can grow to around 30 centimetres long. The fish seldom grow longer than fifteen centimetres in the aquarium.

ACCOMMODATION
In principle the veiltail goldfish has the same requirements as the normal goldfish, but it is not so happy with too strong a current in the aquarium because it is not such a powerful swimmer. Most veiltails are rather sensitive and are therefore less suitable as pond fish.

SOCIAL CHARACTERISTICS
The veiltail goldfish, like the ordinary goldfish, is a friendly fish which will co-exist happily both with other fish and with its own kind. Never put these veiltails with more aggressive fish species (such as sunfish), since they are slow swimmers and their luxuriant fins will be nibbled by these varieties. Fast swimmers may also frighten the veiltail; you should ideally keep these fish in a special aquarium with other veiltails. Veiltails are very quiet fish.

TEMPERATURE AND WATER COMPOSITION
12 to 24°C. The variants are less tolerant of low water temperatures than ordinary goldfish. The water should be crystal clear, definitely rich in oxygen and free of waste substances (nitrates and the like).

FOOD
The veiltail has the same food requirements as the ordinary goldfish.

BREEDING
The method for breeding veiltail goldfish is similar to the method for normal goldfish.

VARIANTS
Veiltail goldfish come in different colours and shapes, of which the best known are undoubtedly the Red Cap Oranda, Calico Goldfish, Black Telescope Fish and the Lionhead, and need little specific care. Other species such as – amongst others – the Skygazers, whose eyes are directed directly upwards, the Ranchu (with no dorsal fin) and the Bubble Eye, which has enormous bubble-shaped protrusions under its eyes, the Pearl Scale and the Pumpkin Nose are all varieties that require specific and meticulous care.

SPECIAL REMARKS
It is obviously true for all species that you should be sure to buy healthy fish with no deviations. Veiltails are rather more sensitive than normal or Comet-Tail goldfish.

Carnegiella strigata strigata

MARBLED HATCHET FISH

FAMILY
Gasteropelecidae (hatchet fish)

SUB FAMILY
Gasteropelecinae
HABITAT

Carnegiella strigata strigata

Peru, in small streams

SEXUAL DIFFERENCES
The difference between the sexes is impossible or very difficult to recognise.

LENGTH
Up to five centimetres

ACCOMMODATION
This small hatchet fish can be kept very easily in medium-sized aquaria. The fish mainly live in the top zone and need enough open space for swimming there where they are not hindered by large plants or pieces of petrified wood. Peripheral vegetation is appreciated, though. Hatchet fish do sometimes like to jump, especially if they see a small insect just above the surface. To protect the fish from themselves, always place a cover on the aquarium. Hatchet fish like a current, which can be provided by a powerful filter or an airstone.

SOCIAL CHARACTERISTICS
This shoaling fish must be kept with at least five family members, since that is the only way to make them feel at ease. They are usually quite peaceful. Particularly keen swimmers are not so suitable to keep with hatchet fish, as they turn the fish upside down as they pass. A small shoal of corydoras as bottom dwellers and another shoal of fish to occupy the middle zone of the aquarium are ideal for combining with a shoal of hatchet fish.

TEMPERATURE AND WATER COMPOSITION
23-28°C. This fish is not particularly sensitive to the water composition.
FOOD

The hatchet fish is, as its body shape perhaps already suggests, a fish that mainly takes its food from the water surface. They eat dry food quite happily, but the fish love small fruit flies and mosquito larvae and they should not be deprived of these delicacies.

BREEDING
Hatchet fish are not easy to breed. A separate breeding tank with very soft water (below 5° gH) filtered over peat and lots of feathery leafed plants will sometimes prove successful.

SPECIAL REMARKS
The hatchet fish family includes several varieties which, in their mature state, vary from around two and a half to nine centimetres in length. The marbled variety is definitely one of the most popular (See also *Thoralocharax securis*).

Cichlasoma citrinellum

MIDAS CICHLID

FAMILY
Cichlidae (cichlids)

HABITAT
Central America

SEXUAL DIFFERENCES
Mature males have an enormous bulging forehead (see photograph), while the female's head tapers to a point. Males

Cichlasoma citrinellum *with fry*

Cichlasoma citrinellum ♂

also have longer, pointed fins. The two sexes are so different that they look like two different species of fish.

LENGTH
25 to 30 centimetres

ACCOMMODATION
Midas cichlids belong in a large and spacious "cichlid aquarium" dominated by stones and rocks. The stones must always be placed on the bottom and not on the gravel, since the fish like to reconstruct the aquarium according to their own specifications. For the same reason there is little point in putting plants in the aquarium. The midas cichlid like refuges, but these can almost only be created with larger pieces of rock, which must be glued to each other securely to protect the glass aquarium. This fish likes to swim in crystal clear water which is constantly moving. The gravel and decorative materials must never be sharp as the fish can otherwise injure themselves.

SOCIAL CHARACTERISTICS
The species can be quite intolerant. It is best to keep only a single pair, together with several large cichlids. This is only possible if there are enough refuges, so that all the species can form their own territories. The fish mainly stay in and around the artificially constructed "hollow".

TEMPERATURE AND WATER COMPOSITION
22-25°C. This fish makes few demands as regards the water composition, but like most larger burrowing cichlid varieties, a very powerful motorised filter (perhaps with surplus capacity) is an absolute

necessity in order to keep the aquarium water clear.

FOOD
You can give the fish large, solid live food, such as small fish and earthworms as well as cichlid sticks. Pieces of beef heart and mussels also go down well. The midas cichlid always seems to be hungry so take care not to overfeed them.

BREEDING
If you want to breed these fish, all you actually need to do is gradually raise the temperature of the water to around 26-27°C (sometimes even that is not necessary). A breeding pair which is well cared for and has enough space will also produce offspring even an aquarium where other fish are present. The fish care for both the eggs and young. You can raise the offspring on small live food and powdered dry food.

SPECIAL REMARKS
Young midas cichlids are always greyish in colour. The fish only gradually acquire the splendid deep yellow colour after which they are named. Some fish, however, never lose their grey colour.

Cichlasoma dovii

FAMILY
Cichlidae (cichlids)

HABITAT
Central America

SEXUAL DIFFERENCES
Male fish have a bulging forehead and are larger than the females.

LENGTH
Males can grow longer than 65 centimetres, but the females remain slightly smaller. The fish do not usually reach this length in the aquarium.

ACCOMMODATION
An aquarium two metres wide or larger will soon be necessary if you want to give these fish enough space. They like to burrow in the bottom. A thick layer of gravel, which must not be too sharp, is

therefore advisable. These cichlids like to hide themselves, so you will have to build a refuge with large stones. Glue the structure together well and place it on the bottom, not on the gravel. This is because it is not inconceivable that these strong cichlids will cause the entire structure to collapse with their burrowing and digging in the gravel.

SOCIAL CHARACTERISTICS
This is not a very friendly species, and sometimes the fish are downright aggressive. Ideally you should keep an individual pair which, if there is enough space, can be kept alongside one or two other large, strong cichlid pairs or a large catfish.

TEMPERATURE AND WATER COMPOSITION
23-28°C. This species is not very demanding as regards the water composition, but a very powerful motorised filter is necessary to keep the water clear.

FOOD
The fish eat both dry food (cichlid sticks) and solid live food (earthworms and fish). You can also give it pieces of beef heart, mussel and fish.

BREEDING
A well-suited breeding pair, if kept under optimal conditions and well fed, will provide offspring without you having to do very much. If you find that you have been waiting a long time for this, you can help the process along by gradually increasing the temperature. The parent fish both care for the brood and the fry. You can feed the fry on water fleas and newly hatched brine shrimps.

Cichlasoma meeki *(syn.* **Thorichthys meeki***)*

FIREMOUTH

FAMILY
Cichlidae (cichlids)

Cichlasoma meeki *(fry)*

play their natural behaviour. Obviously the gravel should not be sharp because otherwise the fish may injure themselves. Only put sturdy plant varieties in the aquarium and cover their roots with stones and petrified wood to prevent the fish from digging them up. You can also put the plants in pots, which you should bury well in the gravel. This usually provides adequate protection for the roots.

Firemouth cichlids do not need rich vegetation in their environment and can therefore thrive very well in an aquarium without plants, in which rocks and petrified wood can be placed as decoration and refuges. It is definitely wiser to place the rocks and petrified wood directly on the bottom, or to glue them together firmly, since these cichlids can undermine them with their digging activities. A powerful filter is necessary to keep the water clear.

HABITAT
Central America, particularly on the Yucatan peninsula in still waters.

SEXUAL DIFFERENCES
The difference between the two sexes is not difficult to spot. The dorsal fin and the anal fin are more pointed in the male than in the female. The males are also conspicuous during the mating season, with their fire-red underside and neck.

LENGTH
Up to about 15 centimetres

ACCOMMODATION
This well known and popular cichlid variety belongs in a large aquarium (at least a metre) with plenty of open space for swimming. The fish like to burrow in the bottom, particularly during the mating season, and have no consideration for roots and plants. A thick layer of gravel is necessary to enable them to dis-

SOCIAL CHARACTERISTICS
Firemouth cichlids are normally kept as a pair. Outside the mating season these territorial cichlids are peaceful towards other fish, provided the aquarium is roomy enough. Despite this, it is better because of their size and eating habits, to keep them only with other robust cichlid varieties and not with smaller fish.

TEMPERATURE AND WATER COMPOSITION
21-24°C. This species is not very demanding as regards the water composition. Water hardness of between 8 and 11° gH and a neutral pH are ideal.

FOOD
Although these fish do very well on high quality dry cichlid sticks, they also need live food now and then (including mosquito larvae, small fish and chopped beef heart).

BREEDING
Firemouth cichlids will reproduce easily in the aquarium if conditions are right. In order to speed up the whole process you can gradually increase the temperature in the water to 25°C. The eggs are laid on polished clean stones (slates) and, like the fry, are guarded and cared for by the parent fish. The fry are raised on small live food and fine powdered food (Sera Micron).

SPECIAL REMARKS
These cichlids are very suitable for new aquarists and are one of the most popular cichlid varieties.

Cichlasoma nigrofasciatus

ZEBRA CICHLID

FAMILY
Cichlidae (cichlids)

HABITAT
Central America

SEXUAL DIFFERENCES
Males have longer, more pointed fins and are larger than females, which can be easily recognised by numerous gold-coloured scales on their underside.

LENGTH
Up to about 12 centimetres

ACCOMMODATION
This territorial cichlid belongs in a medium-sized or large aquarium. The aquarium must provide enough refuges for the fish (rocks). Zebra cichlids like to burrow in the bottom, and a material consisting of gravel or sand which is not too coarse and definitely not sharp will

Cichlasoma nigrofasciatus

Cichlasoma nigrofasciatus

therefore be very suitable. Try to prevent the fish from undermining the stones by placing them firmly on the bottom or gluing them down well beforehand.

Plants should not be placed in an aquarium with this species; the fish will not leave the plants or their roots alone. A good motorised filter is essential to keep the water clean. The fish need an enormous amount of oxygen, so add some extra airstones to provide extra oxygen.

SOCIAL CHARACTERISTICS
These fish form a pair which stay mainly within their territory, where they do not tolerate other fish. Most zebra cichlids are particularly aggressive. It is therefore sensible to accommodate them in an aquarium specially designed for this species, without the company of other fish.

TEMPERATURE AND WATER COMPOSITION
23-26°C. The water composition is not very important, as long as the water is clean, pure and rich in oxygen.

FOOD
The zebra cichlid eats cichlid sticks, but it also needs varied live food such as mosquito larvae. Small pieces of beef heart, mussels and snails are also good. The fish also like to eat vegetable food. Occasionally you can give them (blanched) lettuce leaves and watercress, or food tablets for bottom dwellers (Sera Viformo).

BREEDING
In good conditions, breeding these cichlids is quite simple and it is very interesting to observe the typical behaviour of

these fish. The eggs are laid on a stone (slate, earthenware flowerpot) and both parent fish usually provide excellent care and protection for both the eggs and the fry.

VARIANTS
There is an albino variant of the zebra cichlid. This is a pale pinkish fish.

Colisa fasciata

FAMILY
Anabantidae (labyrinth fish)

SUB FAMILY
Trichogasterinae

HABITAT
India and Burma

SEXUAL DIFFERENCES
The difference between the sexes is quite easy to see. The males are much more colourful than the females and also have very elongated fins.

LENGTH
Up to about 12 centimetres

ACCOMMODATION
These fish do very well in peaceful, medium-sized aquaria with plenty of floating plants and peripheral vegetation, subdued lighting and quite a low water level (30 centimetres maximum, but preferably even lower). Dark substrates will bring out the colours much better. The fish like peace and quiet and it is therefore best not to keep them alongside more boisterous fish. They also do not like a current in the water.

SOCIAL CHARACTERISTICS
These fish are usually peaceful towards other aquarium dwellers, but males can sometimes be intolerant of one another. Do not keep them with keen swimmers or, even worse, with aggressive fish. *Barbus tetrazona* (tiger barb) does not belong in an aquarium in which *Colisa fasciatae* are kept, since these fish have a tendency to nibble off their antennae.

TEMPERATURE AND WATER COMPOSITION
24-27°C. The water does not need to be as rich in oxygen since these fish have a "labyrinth", a respiratory organ situated at the back of the head which enables them to absorb oxygen directly from the atmosphere. The fish can adapt to varying water compositions, although it does better in slightly acidic and rather softer water.

FOOD
These labyrinth fish can remain healthy all their lives on varied dry food (Sera Vipan, Sera O-Nip), but they do like some live food such as mosquito larvae, water fleas and fruit flies from time to time.

BREEDING
Breeding Colisa fasciata is similar to breeding *Colisa lalia*, but *C. fasciata* needs more space and it usually builds its bubble nest under a floating plant.

Colisa lalia

DWARF GOURAMI

FAMILY
Anabantidae (labyrinth fish)

SUB FAMILY
Trichogasterinae

HABITAT
South East Asia

SEXUAL DIFFERENCES
The difference between the males and the females can be seen at a glance, since the males have much more striking colouring.

Colisa fasciata

Up to five centimetres

ACCOMMODATION
These attractive little fish do best in smaller aquaria, with plenty of floating plants, dense, feathery-leafed peripheral vegetation, little or no current and a low water level. A dark substrate is also necessary to bring out their colours better.

SOCIAL CHARACTERISTICS
These predominantly peaceful fish are extremely tolerant, both towards their own kind and towards other fish. They are peaceful, if sometimes rather withdrawn, and will actually become shy if kept in an aquarium with very active fish. Aggressive species of fish and tiger barbs have no place in an aquarium with these small fish. The dwarf gourami mainly stays in the middle and top zone.

TEMPERATURE AND WATER COMPOSITION
23-28°C. This fish is not very demanding as regards the water composition.

Colisa lalia, *variant (♂)*

FOOD
Give the dwarf gourami dry food as a basic staple, with some small live food now and then (or Sera San) as a treat. It also likes to eat algae and other vegetable food (dry or fresh).

BREEDING
A mature pair in peak condition can be encouraged to breed in a separate breed-

Colisa lalia, variant *(♂)*

Colisa lalia ♂

ing tank with a very low water level and plenty of floating plants (crystalwort). Gradually increase the temperature to 29°C and ensure that the water is soft (4-8° gH).

The male builds a bubble nest under the surface, usually with the help of fragments of (floating) plants. After entwining, during which the female releases the eggs and they are fertilised by the male, the male picks up the eggs from the bottom and spits them into the bubble nest, where they then hang neatly. The male tends the eggs and will no longer allow the female anywhere near him. You should therefore catch her immediately after spawning to prevent the male from injuring, or even chasing her to death. It is time to remove the male as well when the fish hatch because at this stage he will begin to see them as food himself.

The fry can be raised on fine powdered food (Sera Micron) and tiny live food organisms (for example, slipper animalcules). The small breeding tank should not be aerated. Filtration is unnecessary and may damage the bubble nest. Siphon up dirt and excrement from the bottom now and then to keep the water clean.

VARIANTS
Many different variants of the dwarf gourami are known, such as the mainly red and blue variety. However the original variety is still by far the most popular.

SPECIAL REMARKS
With its tough character and interesting behaviour this fish is very suitable for beginners.

Colisa sota *(syn.* **Colisa chuna***)*

HONEY GOURAMI

FAMILY
Anabantidae (labyrinth fish)

SUB FAMILY
Trichogasterinae

HABITAT
North East India and Assam

SEXUAL DIFFERENCES
During mating and when they feel good, males have a deep copper-coloured body, a bright yellow dorsal fin and a black belly and head, while females tend to be greyish-beige.

LENGTH
Up to 4.5 centimetres

ACCOMMODATION
Colisa sota can very easily be kept in a smaller aquarium in a quiet location. As the fish are very shy, plenty of floating plants (providing shade) and dense peripheral vegetation is necessary. In a sparsely planted and brightly lit aquarium these fish will become anxious and never show their attractive colours. Keep the water level below 25 centimetres. A dark substrate is advisable. The fish prefer still water.

SOCIAL CHARACTERISTICS
The fish prefer to live in the middle and top zone amongst leaves or close to plants. They are best kept in a pair, together with other small, peaceful fish

Colisa sota ♂

such as *Rasbora maculatae. Acanthoph-thalmus kuhlii* (kuhli loach) is a good choice of bottom dweller. It is also good to keep them together with other labyrinth fish.

TEMPERATURE AND WATER COMPOSITION
25-28°C. This fish is not very demanding as regards the water composition.

FOOD
Colisa sota is easy to feed; it eats both small food flakes and live food.

BREEDING
The method for breeding is similar to the other labyrinth fish; the male builds a bubble nest and cares for the eggs.

Colomesus psittacus

FAMILY
Tetraodontidae (puffer fish)

HABITAT
Amazon region

SEXUAL DIFFERENCES
Unknown

LENGTH
In the wild these fish can be quite large, but in the aquarium they are rarely larger than 10 to 15 centimetres.

ACCOMMODATION
Due to its size, this puffer fish belongs in spacious aquaria where there is enough

Colomesus psittacus

vegetation and also plenty of open space for swimming. The substrate, or large parts of it, should consist of washed sand.

SOCIAL CHARACTERISTICS
This is one of the most peaceful puffer fish. While most other members of the family tend to make life difficult for other aquarium dwellers, these fish generally leave them alone. They can be kept either as a pair or in a group. They do not interfere with each other much – and each one tends to keep to itself.

TEMPERATURE AND WATER COMPOSITION
22-26°C. The fish feel most comfortable in soft or medium-hard water with a slightly acidic or neutral pH value.

FOOD
Like all puffer fish, this one also adores snails. it "cracks" the shells with its hard mouth in a fraction of a second. The fish also eats other live food and particularly likes mussels. It sometimes eats dry food "by accident", but that is as far as it goes.

BREEDING
These fish have not yet reproduced in the aquarium.

Colossoma brachyponum *(syn. Piaractus brachypomus)*

FAMILY
Serrasalmidae

SUB FAMILY
Catoprioninae

HABITAT
Amazon region

SEXUAL DIFFERENCES
So far no difference between the sexes has been observed.

LENGTH
These fish can grow to 40 centimetres or longer in the wild, but they usually remain smaller in the aquarium.

ACCOMMODATION
Due to their size and the fact that these are shoaling fish, the aquarium must be

Colossoma brachyponum

extremely spacious and at least two metres long. This variety eats plants very
rapidly, which is why the fish are usually
kept in rocky aquaria. The fish like plenty of current in the water.

SOCIAL CHARACTERISTICS

This fish look rather like piranhas and are
also related to them but unlike their
notorious family members, they leave
other aquarium dwellers in peace. Nevertheless, it is better not to put them with
small fish. They are particularly active
and must be kept together in a small shoal
containing at least five fish, but preferably
with more than that.

TEMPERATURE AND WATER COMPOSITION

23-28°C, 5-18° gH, pH 5-6. Peat filtration.

Corydoras arcuatus

FOOD

These large fish are essentially vegetarians. You can always give them some
greens in the form of cheap, fast-growing
aquatic plants (for example, water thyme),
but blanched lettuce leaves and spinach
are also much appreciated. Most fish also
eat small live food and food flakes.

BREEDING

Little is known so far about the reproduction of these fish.

Corydoras-*soorten*

MAILED CATFISH

FAMILY

Callichthyidae (mailed catfish)

SUB FAMILY

Corydoradinae

HABITAT

Venezuela, Bolivia, Argentina and Brazil,
mainly in flowing water

SEXUAL DIFFERENCES

The difference between the sexes is not
always clear to see. It is true of all
Corydoras varieties that mature males are
rather thinner than females and, in some
varieties, the dorsal fins of the males are
more pointed.

Corydoras sterbai

Corydoras aeneus

Mature fish – depending on the variety – grow to three to seven centimetres long. Most mature *Corydoras* varieties are four to six centimetres long.

ACCOMMODATION
These fish can be kept both in small and large aquaria. One prerequisite is that there must be sufficient plants and that the water level must not be too high; 30 centimetres is usually more than enough. The fish very much appreciate a

current in the water (provided by a powerful filter or airstone), but they also feel at home in still water. They like to burrow in the bottom after food (remnants), so coarse or sharp gravel is not suitable for use as substrate. You can design various places in the aquarium to meet the needs of these fish. A layer of washed sand a few centimetres thick, slightly sheltered by overhanging plants or a piece of petrified wood, will be very suitable for this.

SOCIAL CHARACTERISTICS
All *Corydoras* varieties like nothing better than to commune with other family members. Although they do not form close shoals, they like to be near each other. They form a lively community in the bottom zone of the aquarium and the different varieties get on well together.

These friendly catfish keep to themselves and always leave other aquarium dwellers in peace. Due to their peaceful nature and their typical behaviour, they are suitable bottom dwellers for community aquaria. They are best kept with fish which occupy the middle and top zone.

Beware of keeping these friendly fish together with intolerant or even aggressive

Corydoras *varieties like each other's company*

Corydoras paleatus 'Albino'

fish species, since they will not stand up for themselves. The fish are active by day, in contrast to most other bottom dwellers which only emerge at dusk.

TEMPERATURE AND WATER COMPOSITION

22-26°C. These fish make few demands on the water composition, which makes them very gratifying fish for the new aquarist to keep. However it is best for the welfare of the fish to change part of the aquarium water regularly (about once a week).

FOOD

These fish are true omnivores. They carefully devour all the food which is not eaten quickly enough by the other aquarium dwellers. They also need vegetable food and live or dried food organisms. Food tablets for bottom dwellers are very suitable for this variety of fish (S. Viformo). They also love tubifex.

BREEDING

Breeding is very easy, although for best results a specially adapted breeding tank is more suitable than a community aquarium. All the fish reproduce in more or less the same way, with slight differences: one variety will lay its sticky eggs on plants or aquarium walls, while others dig a hole in which the eggs are deposited. The number of eggs which are laid each time also varies from one variety to another.

The fish must be well fed beforehand, with a varied diet so that they are in good condition. The water in the breeding tank should always be changed little by little. A well suited breeding pair is important if breeding is to be a success. Usually suitable pairs are formed within the shoal, as the fish notice each other because they are always close together.

The ideal conditions to accelerate breeding are a pH of about 6.5 and soft water (4-7° gH) at a temperature of around 26°C. Remove the parent fish after the eggs are laid and raise the fry on fine powdered food (Sera Micron).

VARIANTS

There are innumerable different *Corydoras* varieties, which are not bred variants and all have different markings. C. aeneus is seven centimetres long and is the best known and also the largest. New varieties are being discovered and imported all the time which, at first glance, differ from one another mainly in colour, markings and size. The only genuine bred variant is the "Albino". This small fish is just as robust as the other Corydoras varieties and forms an attractive contrast against a dark bottom.

Corydoras paleatus

Corydoras *varieties like a soft substrate.*

Corydoras schwartzi

Crenicara punctulata
(syn. Aequidens hercules)

RED FINNED CHECKERBOARD CICHLID

FAMILY
Cichlidae (cichlids)

HABITAT
South America, northern part of the Amazon region

SEXUAL DIFFERENCES
The males are generally more brightly coloured than the females, which have more red pigment in their fins.

LENGTH
Up to 12 centimetres

Crenicara punctulata

ACCOMMODATION
This cichlid does not need too big an aquarium. The aquarium can have a moderate amount of vegetation since these fish, unlike many other cichlids, leave plants in peace and are not burrowers. The fish greatly appreciate some shelter in the form of rocks or petrified wood.

SOCIAL CHARACTERISTICS
This cichlid variety is best kept in pairs; that is one pair per aquarium. The males can be rather intolerant of one another. The fish take up a territory and they will leave other fish in peace, as long as they stay out of the area. Do not keep them with shyer, small and less hardy varieties of fish.

TEMPERATURE AND WATER COMPOSITION
22-25°C. Soft and slightly acidic water (pH 6.5) is absolutely necessary in order to keep these fish healthy.

FOOD
These fish are definitely not easy to keep in good condition. They make quite stringent demands in terms of the water composition (this requires some experience and knowledge of chemical water compositions) and they are not easy to feed either. You can try to see whether they will take food flakes or granules (S. Discus), but the fish are much more in need of live food such as mosquito larvae, small fry and tubifex.

BREEDING
So far, little is known about reproduction of this fish in the aquarium, but this species has been studied in the wild. It seems that they, like most cichlid varieties, lay their eggs on stones and that both the brood and the fry are cared for and protected.

SPECIAL REMARKS
The photograph shows an immature fish.

Cynolebias nigripinnis

FAMILY
Cyprinodontidae (egg-laying tooth carps)

SUB FAMILY
Rivulinae

HABITAT
Argentina

SEXUAL DIFFERENCES
The difference between the sexes is quite easy to see. The fins are coloured in the males, while the females have almost colourless fins.

LENGTH
Up to four centimetres

ACCOMMODATION
C. nigripinnis does best in a special aquarium, possibly with some other killifish. A soft, dark substrate, a water level no higher than 30 centimetres, lots of feathery-leafed plants, floating plants and little or no current are all necessary for the well-being of this fish.

SOCIAL CHARACTERISTICS
C. nigripinnis is a very active little fish which can sometimes be rather intolerant of its neighbours in the aquarium.

TEMPERATURE AND WATER COMPOSITION
18-25°C, 3-6° gH, pH 6. The fish do better if parts of the water are regularly changed.

Cynolebias nigripinnis ♂

FOOD
This fish likes food flakes (Sera San). It also needs varied live food such as red mosquito larvae, tubifex, fruit flies and water fleas.

BREEDING
Breeding these small killifish is not easy and is best left to specialists. The eggs are laid in peat dust and have to go through an (artificial) dry season of a few months. To explain this, it is important to know something of the background of these fish. In the wild these fish live in flooded areas. Most of them die in the dry season as the pools in which they live simply dry up. The fertilised eggs remain, however, embedded in and protected against drying by a thick, moist layer of humus. The fish will only hatch from the eggs when heavy rainfall during the rainy season fills the hollows in the jungle with water and, after a short time they will lay eggs themselves before the drought kills them. Nature even makes provision for extreme conditions; it is sometimes known for live fry to hatch from eggs after a few years. This species is not the only killifish to reproduce in this way.

Cyphotilapia frontosa

FAMILY
Cichlidae (cichlids)

HABITAT
Large lakes in Africa

SEXUAL DIFFERENCES
An expert can see small differences in the body shape in mature fish.

LENGTH
In the wild, where the fish live in huge lakes at great depths, these cichlids sometimes grow to 40 centimetres long. In the aquarium they are rarely more than 25 to 30 centimetres long.

ACCOMMODATION
C. frontosa belongs in large, spacious aquaria with plenty of room for swimming and rocks for decoration and refuges. It likes to burrow in the bottom sometimes, but usually leaves plants in peace. Con-

Cyphotilapia frontosa

stantly moving water is preferable to (almost) stagnant water.

SOCIAL CHARACTERISTICS
This variety forms an inseparable pair which takes up residence in a territory. Smaller fish are seen as welcome additions to their diet. In a larger aquarium (over 1.5 metres) with sufficient refuges, these fish can very easily be kept with one or two other (larger) cichlids. The fish will also usually leave a large, solitary catfish in peace.

TEMPERATURE AND WATER COMPOSITION
22-25°C, 9-12°gH, pH 7 8. A powerful motorised filter is necessary to keep the water clear.

FOOD
These fish prefer solid live food such as fry and red mosquito larvae. Pieces of beef heart and mussel also go down well. Some species will also take some dry food (Sera Diskus).

BREEDING
These fish belong to the mouthbrooders. A close-knit pair will reproduce spontaneously under good conditions; you need not lavish any particular care on them. Once the eggs have hatched the female keeps them in its mouth to "brood them". During this period it eats little or nothing, and the fish therefore need to be in top condition before the mating season (spring). The fry use their mother's mouth as a refuge when danger threatens.

Cyprinus carpio 'Koi'

KOI CARP, NISHIKIGOI OR JAPANESE COLOUR[ED] CARP

FAMILY
Cyprinidae (carps and minnows)

SUB FAMILY
Cyprininae

HABITAT
The koi carp has been bred for more than a thousand(!) years in Japan and has developed from the crucian carp. Two wild carp varieties were recently crossbred, resulting in new variants – the mirror carp and leather carp.

SEXUAL DIFFERENCES
The difference between the sexes can actually only be seen when the fish are a

A splendid kohaku koi

Koi carps can grow very big

97

Koikarper met een niet-gestandaardiseerde kleur

LENGTH
Under ideal conditions, in a large lake, these strong and colourful fish can grow to 80 or 90 centimetres or even longer and weigh almost 10 kilograms. In smaller lakes, or large aquaria, they rarely exceed 50 centimetres in length.

ACCOMMODATION
Due to their size and need for sufficient swimming space, only young koi can be kept in (large) aquaria. They must have crystal clear water, rich in oxygen, with a strong current. Under good conditions koi grow very quickly and new, larger, accommodation very soon becomes necessary. The koi like to scour the bottom for food and turn everything upside down in the process; rocks must be glued down firmly! The fish also do not leave plants in peace, even sturdier varieties.

little older. Mature females then have a plumper belly than the males.

Koi carp come in many different colours and patterns.

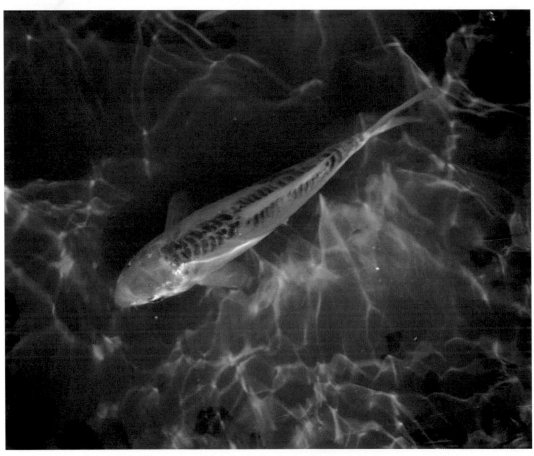

As regards vegetation, only water lilies with well-protected roots (for example in a specially designed basket or a sturdy earthenware flowerpot) can be used. If you keep these fish in a pond, the deepest point should be at least 1.5 metres.

SOCIAL CHARACTERISTICS

Koi carp are very tolerant, both towards their own kind and towards other (much smaller) fish. The fish do not like to be solitary, and prefer to be in a community with other family members. Koi spend practically the whole day actively searching for food. They swim throughout the aquarium and take their food both from both the bottom and from the surface.

TEMPERATURE AND WATER COMPOSITION

4-23°C. Make sure the water does not get too warm in the summer by constantly replacing some of the water with cold, fresh water. The koi is a robust fish which does well in all water compositions, as long as the water is clear and rich in oxygen.

FOOD

The koi is an omnivore. It can be given a special dry food made for koi carp (Sera Koi Plus) as basic staple, supplemented with vegetable food, for example blanched lettuce leaves or soft aquatic plants. It also enjoys all types of live food.

BREEDING

These splendid fish reproduce without any problem in large ponds, given the right conditions. In modern koi farms, the eggs are artificially milked and fertilised. The method used to achieve this is the same as the method used for the goldfish.

VARIANTS

In Japan Koi have been bred and selected for a long time for their slender build, clear colour and precise markings. Nowadays, the fish are also bred in other countries. "Standards" have been established for the diverse range of markings and colours, describing how the distribution of colour, precise shade, shape and scales should look. The recognised colour varieties all have their own (Japanese) name. The "kohaku" (red with white) is the best known and most popular variety. The "shusui" and the

Koi carp

"asagi" are mainly blue-coloured fish with deep orange on their flanks. There is also a gold-coloured fish called "ogon." There are also separate names for the different types of scales which the fish can have and these are added to the names denoting the colours and markings.

Innumerable different combinations are possible. World-wide exhibitions are held, where the most beautiful koi can be seen. Winners of such events are often worth vast sums of money. Fish which come close to the standard are expensive to buy, while koi of an unrecognised colour or marking or with a plump build are relatively cheap. What is more, promising young fish with attractive patterned markings and clear colours do not always grow into equally attractive koi. The colours can intensify under the influence of food and other factors, and they can also fade.

SPECIAL REMARKS

Koi can become very tame if constantly hand fed. They can also live to a ripe old age. In Japan one fish is said to have lived to be older than 200 years, but this is a remarkable exception. A life expectancy of 20 years is more realistic.

Above: Demorgenys pusillus

Below: Enneacanthus obesus

Dermogenys pusillus

FAMILY
Hemirhamphidae (halfbeaks)

HABITAT
Malaysia, Thailand, Vietnam, the Philippines and Indonesia

SEXUAL DIFFERENCES
The males are smaller than the females and can also be recognised by a red spot on the dorsal fin.

LENGTH
Up to about seven centimetres

ACCOMMODATION
This halfbeak lives in the top zone, where it looks for small insects which have fallen into the water. The fish like to swim and therefore, despite their small size, need a large, elongated aquarium. This species can be kept together with other fish, but it is better to keep them in a special aquarium, perhaps with some bottom dwellers. The fish like a current in the water.

Do not forget that halfbeaks are easily frightened and may react by swimming fast at the aquarium wall and possibly fatally injuring themselves in the process. A cover is necessary to prevent them jumping out the aquarium.

SOCIAL CHARACTERISTICS
The males, in particular, are not tolerant of one another, but they rarely have problems with other fish. The best combination is one male with several females.

TEMPERATURE AND WATER COMPOSITION
18-27°C, 9-13° gH, pH 7. Adding some sea salt to the aquarium water now and then will help to keep the fish in good condition.

FOOD
This striking fish mainly eats small insects (fruit flies) from the water surface, but various types of mosquito larvae, water fleas and dry food are also suitable.

BREEDING
The halfbeak is ovoviparous. The young enter the world alive and kicking and can

Dermogenys pusillus

look after themselves immediately. Nevertheless successful breeding of these fish is not simple, as the females produce relatively small batch (10-20 eggs) and the young do not always survive. The parents also eat their own offspring.

SPECIAL REMARKS
D. pusillus is an odd fish which can be kept in the summer months in unheated aquaria and even in garden ponds. These fish are specially bred for fighting, particularly in Thailand, because of their aggressive behaviour. Large sums of money are often gambled on the outcome. The fish do not fight to the death; once one halfbeak has defeated the other it will usually leave it in peace, provided there is enough room.

Diapteron abacinum
(syn. Aphyosemion abacinum)

FAMILY
Cyprinodontidae (egg-laying tooth carps)

HABITAT
West Africa, in shallow waters in the rain-forest

SEXUAL DIFFERENCES
The males are more colourful and larger than the females.

LENGTH
Up to four centimetres

ACCOMMODATION
D. abanicum is usually kept in special aquaria. You can use some petrified wood as decoration, although this is not necessary. Plenty of feathery-leafed plants (for refuge) are vital. Avoid direct sunlight, since the fish prefer rather shaded environment.

SOCIAL CHARACTERISTICS
The males, in particular, can react very aggressively to one another, especially if there are only two or three males in the aquarium. If space allows it, you can usually keep a group of at least six males together with twice as many females without any difficulty. In smaller aquaria it is better to keep only one male with two or three females. These fish can be kept alongside other killifish.

Diapteron abacinum

TEMPERATURE AND WATER COMPOSITION
18-21°C, 7-11° gH, pH 6-6.5

FOOD
D. abanicum is not at all easy to feed, since this fish actually only eats live food. Water fleas (daphnia), brine shrimp (artemia) and tubifex are excellent organisms to give to this killifish as live food, as are black mosquito larvae and fruit flies.

BREEDING
Breeding should be left to fairly advanced aquarists.

Distichodus sexfasciatus

FAMILY
Citharinidae (African characins)

SUB FAMILY
Distichodinae

HABITAT
Republic of Congo

SEXUAL DIFFERENCES
So far no difference between the sexes is known.

LENGTH
In the wild, these fish grow very large, with fish 1 metre long certainly not exceptional. In the aquarium they will not reach anything like this length, but you should count on these fast-growing fish reaching a length of 30 centimetres or more. It all depends on the size of the aquarium in which they are kept.

ACCOMMODATION
These large fish belong in very large aquaria in which the fish have plenty of room to swim, so can only be kept in aquaria at least 1.50 metres in length. They are keen plant eaters, so it does not make much sense putting plants in the aquarium, unless they are cheap plants with tender leaves which the fish can feed on. Decorate the aquarium with rocks, petrified wood and, possibly, plastic aquarium plants.

SOCIAL CHARACTERISTICS
This species is a shoaling fish, so it only feels at a home in a shoal of at least five

Distichodus sexfasciatus

specimens, and preferably more. If they are kept as a solitary fish, they will very quickly develop character defects (aggression).

TEMPERATURE AND WATER COMPOSITION
23-26°C. The fish are not very sensitive to the water composition.

FOOD
These fish are plant eaters. Algae alone are not enough for them. You can feed them on (blanched) lettuce leaves, watercress and spinach, water thyme and special dry foods for plant eaters (Sera Viformo or Sera Flora).

BREEDING
Nothing is known so far about reproduction in the aquarium. This probably has something to do with the fact that the fish never reach their mature size in the aquarium, though this has not been proven.

SPECIAL REMARKS
The fish in the photograph are still im mature and have not yet lost their splendid colours. As they become larger and more mature, the colours disappear and the fish become less attractive to look at. They are also more difficult to keep because of their size and active lifestyle. Think very carefully before buying these fish.

Elassoma evergladei

EVERGLADES PYGMY SUNFISH

FAMILY
Centrarchidae (sunfish)

HABITAT
Southern part of North America (Everglades)

SEXUAL DIFFERENCES
The most obvious difference between the sexes is that the females have almost transparent fins, while those of the males are slightly coloured.

LENGTH
Up to 4.5 centimetres

ACCOMMODATION
These little Americans do best in smaller aquaria. As the fish are rather shy, dense vegetation is required, with plenty of refuges such as petrified wood and stones. A special aquarium, without other fish, is best for studying the behaviour of these fish and perhaps also breeding them.

SOCIAL CHARACTERISTICS
The fish are territorial. Although their appearance is not remarkable at first glance, they soon make up for this by the typical behaviour which they display; they have an unusual way of moving and mainly occupy the bottom zone. They are particularly tolerant of other fish. Unfortunately they are rather shy, and therefore they are rarely seen if their neighbours are active swimmers or less friendly fish.

Elassoma evergladei

These fish can tolerate temperatures of 7-27°C without any problems, but clearly feel at their best in water at temperatures of around 20°C. *E. evergladei* is particularly suited to an unheated aquarium. Allowing the fish to spend the winter in water temperatures of 8-10°C is beneficial to the health of the fish and their willingness to breed. This fish is not very demanding as regards the water composition.

FOOD

These fish will stay in good condition on a basic staple of suitable dry food (Sera Flora), provided their diet is supplemented with water fleas, artemia and tubifex. The fish also need vegetable food (algae).

BREEDING

Once the fish have survived the cold winter period and are in good condition, they will spontaneously start to breed as the temperature rises and lay eggs. These fish are not very enthusiastic about caring for their young, but leave their spawn and fry in peace, so that they generally do not need to be removed.

Enneacanthus obesus

FAMILY
Centrarchidae (sunfish)

HABITAT
Mainly Florida, but also in more northerly American regions.

SEXUAL DIFFERENCES
The difference between the sexes is difficult to establish. The females are often rather plumper during the mating period, because they are carrying eggs.

LENGTH
Up to about 11 centimetres

ACCOMMODATION
This cold-water fish belongs in medium-sized or large aquaria, but can also be kept in outside ponds. The fish are not very demanding in terms of their accommodation, although they do like a current in the water, which you can achieve with a powerful motorised filter.

Enneacanthus obesus

SOCIAL CHARACTERISTICS
The fish like to be with others of their kind, but they can sometimes be aggressive towards other fish. They should not therefore be kept alongside sensitive fish. In terms of temperament, appearance and habits, they strongly resemble the South American cichlids.

TEMPERATURE AND WATER COMPOSITION
This sunfish is a cold-water fish. Beware of overheating; if the water temperature exceeds 23°C, some of the aquarium water should be replaced daily with cold water. Hard water is preferable.

FOOD
Sunfish are gluttons and mainly eat live food such as mosquito larvae, water fleas and small worms. Flies and mosquitoes also go down well, as do small earthworms and frozen food organisms. Not all fish accept dry food. Due to their enormous appetite, it is not always easy to keep these fish through the winter months.

BREEDING
These cichlid-like cold water fish display similar reproductive behaviour to that large fish family. The only difference is that the male usually will not tolerate the female's presence near the nest once her task is over, and you should ideally remove her once the eggs are laid. When the fry hatch, it is best to remove the male as well. The fry can then be raised on small live food.

SPECIAL REMARKS
There are different varieties of sunfish, which are all occasionally sold as pond

fish. They are very well suited to this. Due to their predatory character, they do not belong in a pond with small goldfish or orfes. They are also not suitable company for veiltails. These fish should ideally be kept in a large cold water aquarium specially designed for them.

Epalzeorhynchus bicolor
(syn. Labeo bicolor)

RED FINNED BLACK SHARK

FAMILY
Cyprinidae (carps and minnows)

SUB FAMILY
Garrinae

HABITAT
Thailand, mainly in flowing water

SEXUAL DIFFERENCES
It takes a trained eye to spot the difference between the sexes. When mature, the females are often a little fatter and less intensely coloured than the males.

LENGTH
Up to about 13 centimetres

ACCOMMODATION
The red fin shark belongs in a largish aquarium with subdued lighting. This fish is territorial and likes to hide amongst petrified wood, plants and rocks. As these fish do not burrow in the bottom and also leave plants in peace, they can very easily be kept in aquaria with dense vegetation.

Epalzeorhynchus bicolor

Epalzeorhynchus bicolor

SOCIAL CHARACTERISTICS
Labeo bicolor is a territorial fish. Young fish can be kept together, but older fish are very intolerant. This fish does very well as a solitary specimen in a large aquarium with plenty of vegetation and decorative material. Some will terrorise the other aquarium dwellers, and small and shy fish will very quickly go into hiding.

TEMPERATURE AND WATER COMPOSITION
24-26°C. This fish is not very demanding as regards water composition. Ideally the water should be slightly acidic to neutral (pH 6.5-7) and medium-hard.

FOOD
The red fin shark is an omnivore. It likes dry food, as well as food tablets for bottom dwellers (Sera Viformo). This fish also eats live food and algae and devours food remnants left by other aquarium dwellers.

BREEDING
Unfortunately there have so far been few reports of successful aquarium breeding. However, it is known that the fish display brood care; the males guard and protect both the eggs and the fry from inquisitive or hungry fish. It takes a very long time for young fish to develop the deep velvety-black colour.

Epalzeorhynchus frenatus
(syn. Labeo frenatus*)*

FAMILY
Cyprinidae (carps and minnows)

SUB FAMILY
Garrinae

HABITAT
Thailand, in running water

SEXUAL DIFFERENCES
It is not very easy to distinguish between
the sexes, especially when the fish are still
young. Mature females are rather plumper than the males.

LENGTH
Up to about 13 centimetres

ACCOMMODATION
These fish feel most comfortable in a
largish aquarium with plenty of refuges in
the shape of abundant vegetation, rocks
and petrified wood. They greatly appreciate subdued light. Since these fish do not
burrow in the bottom and leave the plants
in peace, you can easily keep them in
aquaria with dense vegetation.

SOCIAL CHARACTERISTICS
E. frenatus forms a territory in which no
other fish are tolerated. The fry get on
well together, but older fish are very
intolerant or even aggressive towards each
other and often also towards other
aquarium dwellers. The fish are best kept

Epalzeorhynchus frenatus

as solitary specimens. Do not put them
with shy or small varieties of fish, for
these will definitely be chased by
E. frenatus.

TEMPERATURE AND WATER COMPOSITION
24-26°C. This fish is not very demanding
as regards the water composition but, like
the red fin shark, it likes slightly acidic to
neutral, medium-hard water.

FOOD
E. frenatus is an omnivore. As well as dry
food and food tablets for bottom dwellers
these fish also eat algae, (blanched)
lettuce leaves, spinach and live food.

BREEDING
Reproduction is similar to that of the red
fin shark.

SPECIAL REMARKS
This variety strongly resembles the red fin
shark, but is rather less fashionable
because of its paler colours.

Epalzeorhynchus kallopterus

FAMILY
Cyprinidae (carps and minnows)

SUB FAMILY
Garrinae

HABITAT
Thailand and Indonesia

SEXUAL DIFFERENCES
Unknown

LENGTH
Up to about 15 centimetres

ACCOMMODATION
This fish does well in medium-sized or
large aquaria. The fish like to hide; keep
this in mind when setting up the aquarium. Convoluted pieces of petrified wood
will provide an ideal shelter. The fish also
use areas of dense vegetation as refuges.

SOCIAL CHARACTERISTICS
This fish is not very tolerant of its own
kind, so it is best to keep only a single fish
of this variety. Other aquarium dwellers
are usually left in peace. The fish are territorial.

Epalzeorhynchus kallopterus

TEMPERATURE AND WATER COMPOSITION
24-26°C, 4-8° gH, pH 6-7. Change the water regularly.

FOOD
This fish eats both live food and food flakes. Vegetable food forms an important part of the nutritional requirement of this fish and should never be missing from its diet. They also like to eat (blanched) lettuce leaves and special food tablets for bottom dwellers.

BREEDING
Little is known so far about the reproduction of this fish species, but it is assumed to be similar to that of the red fin shark.

Epiplatys dageti

FIREMOUTH PANCHAX

FAMILY
Cyprinodontae (egg-laying tooth carps)

SUB FAMILY
Rivulinae

HABITAT
West Africa

SEXUAL DIFFERENCES
The difference between the sexes is quite easy to spot. The males are usually more colourful and smaller than the females. The male fish are particularly conspicuous because of their fiery red throat area.

LENGTH
Up to 5.5 centimetres

ACCOMMODATION
The firemouth panchax is very suitable for smaller aquaria. Plenty of vegetation and refuges, as well as diffuse lighting (floating plants) and a dark substrate are advisable in order to make this fish feel at home. These fish live in the top zone and can therefore very easily be kept alongside species which mainly occupy the middle and bottom zone of the aquarium.

SOCIAL CHARACTERISTICS
Firemouth panchax are usually calm and peaceful fish, both towards one another and towards other nearby aquarium dwellers. Specimens which develop into intolerant or aggressive fish are definitely exceptions to the rule.

TEMPERATURE AND WATER COMPOSITION
21-25°C, 5-12° gH, pH 6

FOOD
You can give dry food as a basic staple, but the fish also need small live food such as mosquito larvae, artemia (brine shrimps) and small insects (fruit flies) from time to time.

BREEDING
These fish will breed easily if conditions are good. In a breeding tank specially designed for this purpose the temperature should be slightly higher than the fish are accustomed to. The female lays a very large quantity of eggs. In order to ensure that as many as possible are fertilised, it is advisable to put several males alongside

Epiplatys dageti ♂

107

Epiplatys dageti ♂

the female. Keep an eye on the situation, as the males can react aggressively to one another, especially in these circumstances. It is best to remove the parent fish after spawning, as they tend to eat both their own eggs and the fry. Raise the fry on powdered food and extremely small live food (e.g. slipper animalcules).

Erpetoichthys ornatipinnis

FAMILY
Polypteridae (bircher and reedfish)

HABITAT
Republic of Congo

SEXUAL DIFFERENCES
Unknown so far

LENGTH
In the wild, these fish sometimes grow to 45 centimetres long. They are usually smaller in the aquarium.

ACCOMMODATION
This remarkable fish belongs in larger aquaria with plenty of refuges (plants, petrified wood). Fine gravel or washed sand will do fine as a substrate.

SOCIAL CHARACTERISTICS
There are enough natural "frontiers" in larger aquaria with plenty of refuges for several fish to be kept. In all other cases, it is better to keep just one specimen as the fish constantly attack one another. In any case, they feel quite happy as solitary fish. Smaller, less hardy fish do not feel at home in the community; they are seen as a valuable dietary supple-

Erpetoichthys ornatipinnis

Erpetoichthys ornatipinnis

ment. Larger cichlids are a possibility though.

TEMPERATURE AND WATER COMPOSITION
25-28°C. The fish are not very demanding as regards the water composition.

FOOD
Food flakes are scarcely eaten by these fish; they mainly need live food, pieces of meat and fish. Small fish, but also finely chopped pieces of beef heart, earthworms and other solid live food will go down well.

BREEDING
Little is known so far about reproduction.

Eutropiellus buffei *(syn. E. debauwi)*

THREE STRIPED GLASS CATFISH

FAMILY
Schilbeidae (glass catfish)

HABITAT
Nigeria and Republic of Congo, in flowing streams

SEXUAL DIFFERENCES
The difference between the sexes is best seen in the girth of the fish. The males are often more slender than the females.

LENGTH
Up to about 10 centimetres

ACCOMMODATION
This shoaling fish is best suited to quite a spacious aquarium (80-90 centimetres),

with plenty of open space for swimming and a current.
The substrate should be dark in colour; this not only makes the fish feel more at ease, but their colours also stand out better. This fish is not very keen on bright lighting; floating plants such as crystalwort will create naturally subdued light.

SOCIAL CHARACTERISTICS
This very peaceful and quite active shoaling fish must always be kept together with at least five others (and a larger group is even better).

The fish are very tolerant of other aquarium dwellers, but since they are so active they can sometimes turn shyer, slow or sensitive fish upside down with their swimming. These fish, which have their own typical swimming style, prefer to occupy the bottom and middle zone.

TEMPERATURE AND WATER COMPOSITION
23-26°C. The fish are not very demanding as regards the water composition.

FOOD
E. buffei likes both dry food and live food. Tubifex also go down well.

BREEDING
Little is known so far about reproduction.

SPECIAL REMARKS
Three striped glass catfish are undemanding and lively fish which are very suitable for new aquarists.

Eutropiellus buffei

Above: Farlowella acus

Below: Gyrinocheilus aynomieri *"Albino"*

Farlowella acus

FAMILY
Loricariidae (armoured catfish)

SUB FAMILY
Loricaniinae

HABITAT
Amazon region

SEXUAL DIFFERENCES
The females do not have bristles along the head.

LENGTH
Up to 15 centimetres

ACCOMMODATION
This variety will do best in a medium-sized or large aquarium. Always ensure there is plenty of vegetation and decorations (petrified wood) in the aquarium, since these provide excellent refuges for this rather shy fish.

This species is not very keen on running water.

SOCIAL CHARACTERISTICS
The fish get on particularly well with both their own kind and other fish; they like to keep more or less to themselves and have little involvement with other fish in the aquarium. During the day they are usually quiet and keep themselves hidden, becoming active at dusk to go in search of food.

TEMPERATURE AND WATER COMPOSITION
23-26°C. The water quality (clean and clear water is essential) and water composition needs to be very precise for these fish – the water must be very soft (0-4° gH), with a pH of about 6.

FOOD
This striking fish rummages for its food among the plants and on the bottom and polishes off the uneaten remains left by other aquarium dwellers. It also likes tablets specially produced for bottom dwellers.

BREEDING
Unfortunately little is known so far about the reproduction of this striking armoured catfish.

Formosiana tinkhami

Formosiana tinkhami

FAMILY
Balitoridae

SUB FAMILY
Homalopterinae

HABITAT
East Asia, in fast-flowing streams

SEXUAL DIFFERENCES
Unknown

LENGTH
Up to 10 centimetres

ACCOMMODATION
These fish are easily satisfied and can be kept in medium-sized and large aquaria. They feel at home in both flowing and

stagnant water. They appreciate some refuges (overhanging plants are adequate).

SOCIAL CHARACTERISTICS
Although this is not a real shoaling fish, it definitely feels more secure in the company of several others of its kind. It is good-natured both towards others of the same species and other aquarium dwellers, and keeps more or less to itself. *F. tinkhami* prefers to occupy the bottom zone.

TEMPERATURE AND WATER COMPOSITION
18-25°C. The fish prefers soft to medium-hard water with a neutral pH value.

FOOD
This fish eats algae, small live food and food remains from other aquarium dwellers.

Gambusia affinis holbrooki

MOSQUITO FISH

FAMILY
Poeciliidae (livebearing tooth carps)

HABITAT
Southern parts of North America, Mexico

SEXUAL DIFFERENCES
The males are much smaller than the females, they have black spots and also have a gonopodium (see photograph). The females are almost colourless.

LENGTH
The males do not exceed about three to three and a half centimetres. The females can grow to six to seven centimetres long.

ACCOMMODATION
This ovoviparous fish can easily be kept in a small or medium-sized aquarium. It is not very demanding, but it does like dense and feathery-leafed vegetation.

SOCIAL CHARACTERISTICS
These fish are usually friendly towards each another, but do display some aggressive tendencies towards other species of fish. A single male is usually kept together with two or three females because of his active mating behaviour. The fish swim throughout the whole aquarium, but they prefer the top zone.

Gambusia affinis holbrooki ♂

TEMPERATURE AND WATER COMPOSITION
15-30°C. This fish is so robust and tough that it does well in all sorts of extreme water compositions and qualities and also reproduces there. Even the temperature of the water, whether extremely high or low, does not seem to trouble it. Temperatures of around 20°C are best. These fish can even survive for some time in water below ten degrees Celsius and in brackish water.

FOOD
G. affinis is particularly easy to feed. It is a glutton which can live on dry food all its life without any problems (Sera Flora/Sera Premium). It also likes algae. These fish will also greatly appreciate it if you feed them some live red mosquito larvae regularly.

BREEDING
The female is very productive. Like all ovoviparous fish, it gives birth to live young which are immediately able to take care of themselves. However, the parent fish are a major hazard for their own young. The best results will be obtained if a pregnant female, recognisable by her fat belly and dark pregnancy spot just in front of the anal fin, is transferred to a separate tank with plenty of feathery-leafed plants (floating plants such as the mussel plant or a large piece of Java moss will be suitable). Once the fry are born, the mother fish must be removed immediately. The fry can then be reared on fine powdered food (Sera Micron).

Fish of this species do very well in garden ponds and unheated aquaria, as long as temperatures do not fall below 12 degrees Celsius for sustained periods. Breeding is more successful in garden ponds with plenty of vegetation than in small aquaria. Just like *Poecilia reticulata* (*guppy*), this fish is used in various parts of the world to combat the (malaria) mosquito. It therefore appears in the wild in many other places as well as its original habitat.

Gnathonemus petersii

LONG NOSED ELEPHANT FISH

FAMILY
Mormyridae (mormyrid)

HABITAT
Africa, mainly in Cameroon and Nigeria, in stagnant and slow-flowing water.

SEXUAL DIFFERENCES
The males are recognisable by the indentation in the anal fin. The anal fin is straight in the females.

LENGTH
Up to about 18 centimetres

ACCOMMODATION
The elephant fish belongs in larger aquaria. It does not like bright lighting, so floating plants are necessary. The fish will appreciate plenty of refuges in the form of dense vegetation and petrified wood. This variety burrows in the substrate, so you

Gnathonemus petersii

must take care to use a substrate which consists of fine, rounded (and definitely not sharp) gravel or washed sand.

SOCIAL CHARACTERISTICS
These fish prefer to live in the bottom zone. You will not see much of them during the day, since they prefer to hide. They go out in search of food at dusk. Only feed them in the evening, otherwise everything will have been eaten by the other aquarium dwellers before these fish become active. They do best as solitary fish since they are rather intolerant, even aggressive, towards each other. These curious fish will, however, leave other aquarium dwellers alone, as long as they are not too intrusive. The elephant fish is territorial and does not like being interfered with in his territory.

TEMPERATURE AND WATER COMPOSITION
Elephant fish need warmth, and temperatures below 24°C can make them ill. The water composition is not so very important for these fish, though they do not like it when the water is changed. A pH of around 6.5 is ideal.

FOOD
The elephant fish almost exclusively eats food taken from the bottom. It likes and will readily take tubifex and other live food. The fish should also be given some food flakes and small pieces of blanched lettuce.

BREEDING
Unknown

SPECIAL REMARKS
It is not easy to keep an elephant fish in good health. The best results are achieved in an aquarium with a quiet location, "old" aquarium water, a varied diet, and definitely not too many neighbours which will constantly interfere with the fish.

Gobiopterus chuno

GLASS GOBY

FAMILY
Gobiidae (gobies)

HABITAT
South East Asia

SEXUAL DIFFERENCES
None known so far

LENGTH
Up to 2.5 centimetres

ACCOMMODATION
This small transparent fish generally does very well in the smallest aquaria. It greatly appreciates a soft substrate, plenty of refuges and dense vegetation.

SOCIAL CHARACTERISTICS
These peaceful fish get on well both with their own kind and with other species of fish. They keep more or less to themselves and prefer to live on or near the bottom.

TEMPERATURE AND WATER COMPOSITION
24-27°C. The ideal water composition is unfortunately not known, which is probably also the reason why these fish never grow old in the aquarium.

FOOD
The fish mainly eat small live food such as cyclops and daphnia (water fleas).

Gobiopterus chuno

BREEDING
This glass goby has never yet been bred in the aquarium.

SPECIAL REMARKS
Unfortunately this remarkable fish, with its transparent body, is very difficult to keep and, as a result, is seldom imported. Perhaps some advanced aquarists could study this fish, so that in a few years we will know what water composition and food are best suited to these fish.

Gymnocorymbus ternetzi

BLACK TETRA

FAMILY
Characidae (characins)

SUB FAMILY
Tetragonopterinae

HABITAT
Paraguay, Brazil and Bolivia

SEXUAL DIFFERENCES
The males are rather thinner than the females and their dorsal fin is narrower.

LENGTH
Up to six centimetres

ACCOMMODATION
The black tetra is very undemanding. The species can very easily be kept in a community aquarium. The aquarium need not be particularly large, 60 centimetres is enough, although of course the fish will of course also do well in larger aquaria. Plenty of peripheral vegetation and open space for swimming are also advisable, as is a dark bottom, which will bring out their colour better.

SOCIAL CHARACTERISTICS
The black tetra feels happiest in a shoal of at least five fish, but prefers even more of his own kind around him. Solitary fish frequently develop behavioural problems (aggression). These fish can easily be kept with smaller or less hardy varieties of fish, but remember that some fish may well become rather intolerant towards their neighbours as they grow older.

Black tetras mainly occupy the middle

Gymnocorymbus ternetzi

zone in the aquarium and are moderately active.

TEMPERATURE AND WATER COMPOSITION
21-25°C. The black tetra does well in a wide range of water types.

FOOD
These shoaling fish can justifiably be called omnivores. They can live on a (varied) diet of dry food all their lives without any difficulty. They also like vegetable food (Sera Flora) and live food.

BREEDING
Black tetras are free layers and, like other free layers, they eat their own eggs. The parent fish should therefore be removed after spawning.

VARIANTS
There is also a long-finned variety of this fish (see photograph).

SPECIAL REMARKS
Younger fish have pitch-black markings, but they turn grey as they mature. This is not only due to their age, but also to the quality of the food and the water composition.

Gyrinocheilus aynomieri

SIAMESE ALGAE EATER, INDIAN ALGAE EATER

FAMILY
Gyrinocheilidae (algae eaters)

SUB FAMILY
Gyrinocheilinae

HABITAT
Thailand, in fast-flowing streams

SEXUAL DIFFERENCES
The females are somewhat larger and plumper than the males and also have fewer bulges on the mouth.

LENGTH
Fish have been caught in the wild measuring 22 centimetres, but in the aquarium they do not usually exceed about 15 centimetres.

ACCOMMODATION
The Siamese algae eater feels at home in various different types of aquaria. It spends the whole day cleaning algae-covered aquarium walls, plants and decorations and, for this reason, undoubtedly feels more at home in an algae-covered aquarium. The fish also greatly appreciates refuges in the form of convoluted pieces of petrified wood.

SOCIAL CHARACTERISTICS
Young fish will not bother the other occupants and keep more or less to themselves. Older fish can develop the troublesome characteristic of making life difficult for the other aquarium dwellers. The fish are mainly kept as solitary specimens, as they do not always get on well (they are territorial), but a spacious aquarium with plenty of refuges may well offer enough room for two fish. This fish mainly stays at the bottom of the aquarium.

TEMPERATURE AND WATER COMPOSITION
20-27°C. This fish is not very demanding as regards either the temperature or the water quality.

Gyrinocheilus aynomieri

FOOD

G. aynomieri mainly lives on algae. If the aquarium does not contain (any more) algae, feed the fish on special food tablets for bottom dwellers (Sera Viformo) or blanched lettuce leaves and watercress. These fish also eat food remains which fall to the bottom.

BREEDING

It is known that both the male and the female display brood care, but breeding of these fish has so far only occasionally been successful.

VARIANTS

There is one monocolour variety, *G. aymonieri* "Albino".

SPECIAL REMARKS

This is one of the best fish you can buy if you are troubled with too much algae in your aquarium. However the fish only eats algae which is firmly attached to plants, stones and petrified wood, not floating algae or filament algae. Also remember that, as these fish mature, they are difficult to keep in a community aquarium because of their intolerant nature.

Hasemania nana

Hasemania nana

FAMILY
Characidae (characins)

SUB FAMILY
Tetragonopterinae

HABITAT
Brazil

SEXUAL DIFFERENCES
The males are rather more slender in shape than the females, and their colours are also more intense when mature.

LENGTH
Up to five centimetres

ACCOMMODATION
This fish feels very much at home in community aquaria with plenty of (dense) peripheral vegetation and open space for swimming. If the substrate is dark and the light is filtered by floating plants, not only will the colours of these fish stand out better, but the fish clearly feel more comfortable as well. The aquarium does not need to be very big for these fish; an aquarium 60 centimetres wide is sufficient.

SOCIAL CHARACTERISTICS
The silver tipped tetra is a gentle shoaling fish which is very suitable for keeping in a community aquarium. Always keep the fish in a shoal of at least six; silver tipped tetra which are kept alone or in a pair are very shy and will never display their deep copper colour. Keeping them alongside predators or other intolerant species is also not ideal. Silver tipped tetra are moderately active and mainly occupy the middle zone.

TEMPERATURE AND WATER COMPOSITION
20-25°C. These fish are not particularly sensitive to the water composition. They have a slight preference for slightly acidic, soft water.

FOOD
The silver tipped tetra is an omnivore. These fish can easily be kept on a varied diet of dry food, but they also like live food (mosquito larvae and brine shrimps) and algae. Silver tipped tetras hardly ever take food from the bottom.

BREEDING
It is not too difficult to encourage these fish to breed, provided the water composition is right and the two partners "click". To create the right conditions, very soft (3-4° gH) and acidic (pH 5.5) water is required. Only put mating pairs which are in peak condition in the breeding tank. In order to identify from the small shoal of silver tipped tetras which fish are most compatible you should regularly study their behaviour. The breeding tank itself should be filled with plenty of feathery-leafed plants (Java moss, myriophyllum) amongst which the eggs are deposited. Slowly increase the temperature by a few degrees. The parent fish must be removed after spawning because they eat their own eggs. A substrate spawner may offer a temporary solution here.

Helostoma temminckii

FAMILY
Anabantidae (labyrinth fish)

SUB FAMILY
Helostomatidae

HABITAT
Indonesia and Thailand

Helostoma temminckii

nothing to do with mating ritual, since it is virtually only males which display this behaviour towards one another. It is generally assumed that this so-called kissing behaviour is a form of fighting, although it is harmless.
The kissing gourami swims in all zones and is quite active.

TEMPERATURE AND WATER COMPOSITION
24-27°C. This fish is not very demanding as regards either the quality or composition of the water. If there is a shortage of oxygen in the aquarium, its "labyrinth" (an organ at the back of its head) will absorb oxygen directly from the atmosphere. This is characteristic of all labyrinth fish.

SEXUAL DIFFERENCES
There are no discernible differences between the sexes in immature fish. Mature, and therefore larger, females are sometimes recognisable by their rather fatter stomach area.

LENGTH
In the wild these fish can easily reach lengths exceeding 30 centimetres, but they do not usually grow beyond 13-14 centimetres in the aquarium.

ACCOMMODATION
Kissing gouramis are active fish which spend the whole day in search of food. They have small protrusions on their mouths with which they can easily scrape off algae. The kissing gourami can be housed in smaller community aquaria when it is small but you must move it to a more suitable home when it grows larger. Aquaria at least 80 centimetres long are usually large enough for these fish with their cheerful appearance. The water level should never be too high and the fish do not really like a current in the water. Plenty of algae is preferable.

SOCIAL CHARACTERISTICS
The kissing gourami is tolerant towards other aquarium dwellers and can be kept both as a solitary fish and together with several fish. The species is very suitable for the community aquarium. If you have several kissing gouramis in the aquarium, you can observe the typical behaviour for which the fish was given its name. The fish press their sucker-like mouths together and "kiss" until one lets go. Obviously this has

FOOD
The kissing gourami's diet mainly consists of algae and it spends all day carefully cleaning the sides, plants and decorations. If there is no (more) algae to be found in the aquarium, regularly give the fish (blanched) lettuce leaves, watercress, spinach and possibly also special food tablets for plant eaters. Kissing gourami also eat food flakes and live food, but they soon die if they are not given vegetable food.

BREEDING
It is not easy to get these fish to breed. Provide a separate breeding tank each time, with plenty of algae growing in it (in a sunny location). Once they start, kissing gourami are very productive. The eggs float just below the surface. Although the parent fish leave the eggs alone, it is better to remove them after spawning. Rear the fry on small, unicellular organisms such as slipper animalcules, for example. Later they will also eat very fine powdered food (Sera Micron). They eat algae and the small creatures which live in it, so the breeding tank must definitely contain plenty of algae.

VARIANTS
The fish illustrated here is the pink variety, which is very popular among aquarium hobbyists. The variegated (greenish grey) variety is less popular and is more frequently seen in the wild than in the aquarium.

SPECIAL REMARKS
These first-rate algae eaters are a popular edible fish in their country of origin. The fish are specially bred there for this purpose.

118

Hemichromis bimaculatus

RED CICHLID

FAMILY
Cichlidae (cichlids)

HABITAT
Africa, Nile and Congo (Ghana) river areas

SEXUAL DIFFERENCES
Not easy to see: one or more close pairs should come into being after a while if a small group of immature fish are brought together. During the mating season the males have more intense colouring.

LENGTH
Up to about 13 centimetres

ACCOMMODATION
These cichlids do well in medium-sized aquaria with very sturdy plants, plenty of petrified wood and rocks for decoration. The fish like to burrow and dig in the bottom – mainly during the mating season – so beware of loose stones. They very much appreciate clean, clear water rich in oxygen and with a current if possible.

SOCIAL CHARACTERISTICS
This species can very easily be kept in a suitable aquarium together with some other cichlid pairs, even though they are extremely aggressive during the mating season and will tolerate no other fish at all in their territory. Start with a small group of immature fish and take out a pair which separate themselves from the rest. This is almost definitely a suitable mating pair. The red cichlid mainly stays in the bottom zone.

TEMPERATURE AND WATER COMPOSITION
22-26°C. This fish is not very demanding as regards the water composition, as long as the water is rich in oxygen.

FOOD
These fish like to eat live food such as small fish and mosquito larvae, but they also like cichlid sticks.

Natural biotope of Hemichromis bimaculatus

Hemichromis bimaculatus

Hemigrammopetersius caudalis

BREEDING

A well-suited pair will reproduce even in the company of other fish.

Their territory is defended very aggressively, though, so there must be plenty of space for all the fish. The fish lay their eggs on carefully cleaned pieces of petrified wood and stone (slate). Both parents tend the eggs and the fry well.

Hemigrammopetersius caudalis

FAMILY
Alestidae (African characins)

SUB FAMILY
Alestinae

HABITAT
Republic of Congo

SEXUAL DIFFERENCES
The male is characterised by the white stripes on his fins.

LENGTH
Up to about 6.5 centimetres

ACCOMMODATION
This species can be kept very easily in a medium-sized community aquarium with sufficient peripheral vegetation and plenty of space for swimming. A dark substrate and some floating plants will bring out the colours of the fish better.

SOCIAL CHARACTERISTICS
These sometimes rather shy and nervous small fish leave the other aquarium dwellers in peace, but are often chased by more aggressive varieties of fish. They therefore do not belong in an aquarium with predatory species. The fish are at their best and begin to feel more secure in a larger shoal (at least five, but preferably many more fish). They usually occupy the middle zone.

TEMPERATURE AND WATER COMPOSITION
Temperature 22-26°C. These fish make few demands on the water composition.

FOOD
H. caudalis is a real omnivore. A varied diet of different dry foods and some live food now and then keeps these fish in good condition.

BREEDING
Breeding is possible in a separate breeding tank in a sunny location. The fish are free layers and eat their own eggs, so remove the parent fish immediately after spawning. A substrate spawner attached a few centimetres from the bottom will ensure that the fish cannot get to their eggs while mating.

Hemigrammus bleheri

BRILLIANT RUMMY NOSE

FAMILY
Characidae (characins)

SUB FAMILY
Tetragonopterinae

HABITAT
South America (Brazil)

The difference between the sexes is not always easy to see, but the females are usually slightly plumper than the males.

LENGTH
Up to about five centimetres

ACCOMMODATION
The most suitable accommodation for this fish is an elongated aquarium with plenty of free space for swimming. Diffuse lighting, shadowy places (created using floating plants) and a moderate current are desirable.

SOCIAL CHARACTERISTICS
Brilliant rummy noses keep to themselves and are very good-natured towards other fish. The fish feel much more at home in a larger shoal (from seven upwards) than in a smaller shoal. They stay mainly in the middle zone and are active or moderately active.

TEMPERATURE AND WATER COMPOSITION
24-26°C. The water must be soft or very soft (around 2-7° gH) and slightly acidic (pH 6). These fish are very sensitive to waste substances in the water, so try to limit these by feeding moderately (no more than you see the fish eating) and regularly siphoning up dirt from the bottom. Partial changes of water are also necessary to keep these fish healthy.

FOOD
The brilliant rummy nose is an omnivore. The species can survive very well throughout its life on dry food, provided it is varied, but it also likes some small live food now and then.

Hemigrammus bleheri

BREEDING
The brilliant rummy nose breeds within the shoal. If you want to breed these fish, transfer the whole shoal to a separate breeding tank in which you have already created the ideal conditions. The water must be as pure as possible, very soft (1-3° gH) and with a pH of around 6. Peat filtration is necessary. There must also be plenty of feathery-leafed plants among which the fish can lay their eggs, and the aquarium must be in a fairly shady location. Always make sure that the temperature is slowly raised to one or two degrees higher than they are accustomed to. By doing all this, you are imitating the conditions in the wild during the mating season and the fish should breed as a result.

Afterwards they will happily devour the eggs, so you should remove the parent fish after spawning. The fry will hatch after one or two days and can be reared on unicellular organisms (slipper animalcules), microworms and very fine powdered food (Sera Micron). To prevent contamination of the water you must make doubly sure that you do not give them too much to eat.

SPECIAL REMARKS
There are several varieties which look very much like this one and they are frequently confused with one another, especially when the fish are not yet mature. Well-known fish include *Hemigrammus rhodostomus and Petitella georgiae.*

Hemigrammus caudovittatus

BUENOS AIRES TETRA

FAMILY
Characidae (characins)

SUB FAMILY
Tetragonopterinae

HABITAT
Argentina

SEXUAL DIFFERENCES
The females have a fatter stomach area than the males, which are more intensely coloured.

LENGTH
Up to eight centimetres

Hemigrammus caudovittatus

ACCOMMODATION
The Buenos Aires tetra belongs in larger aquaria with plenty of free space to swim, possibly aeration in the water and strong, large-leaved aquatic plants. This species likes to eat plants, so soft and feathery-leafed aquatic plants are only suitable as dietary supplements for this fish and not as decoration. A dark substrate will bring out the colours better.

SOCIAL CHARACTERISTICS
These fish should always be kept in a shoal of about seven. Once mature, the fish will sometimes nibble the attractive long fins of other aquarium dwellers, so remember this when putting together your fish population. Larger and hardier fish are suitable neighbours, because the Buenos Aires tetra likes to "terrorise" other fish as it gets older. You should not therefore keep small, fragile fish in the same aquarium.

TEMPERATURE AND WATER COMPOSITION
17-23°C. The water composition is not particularly important.

FOOD
The Buenos Aires tetra is a real omnivore, but plenty of vegetable food is vital to keep the fish healthy for a long period. Blanched lettuce leaves, watercress, spinach and tablets and food flakes for plant-eating fish are good as well.

BREEDING
It is not difficult to get these fish to reproduce. A separate aquarium is needed with some coarse aquatic plants, and the temperature should be increased slowly. The fish lay their eggs among plants, but they do sometimes tend to eat their eggs. It is therefore better to remove the parent fish after spawning. The fry can be reared on fine powdered food (Sera Micron).

SPECIAL REMARKS
The Buenos Aires tetra can be kept in unheated aquaria and in outside ponds during the summer. This tough and undemanding fish used to be one of the most popular tropical ornamental fish, but in those days not as many different species of fish were imported as now. What is more, technology was not sufficiently developed to offer a suitable living environment to more difficult species.

This fish has now fallen from grace because of the rather intolerant character which it displays towards other fish when older and the fact that they will not leave plants alone.

Hemigrammus erythrononus
(syn. H. gracilis*)*

GLOWLIGHT TETRA

FAMILY
Characidae (characins)

SUB FAMILY
Tetragonopterinae

HABITAT
Guyana and Paraguay, in small shallow streams and flooded areas

SEXUAL DIFFERENCES
The males are thinner than the females and have white-tipped fins.

LENGTH
Up to about 4.5 centimetres

ACCOMMODATION
This fish feels very much at home in aquaria with rather diffuse lighting (floating plants), a dark substrate, plenty of fine-leafed peripheral vegetation and enough open room for swimming in the middle. In such an environment the neon stripes on this fish will light up to spectacular effect. The aquarium need not

be very large; if this variety is not kept with too many other fish, a tank 50 centimetres wide will be large enough. No current is necessary.

SOCIAL CHARACTERISTICS
This shoaling fish must be kept with at least five fish. These fish feel best in a group of twelve or more. Such a large shoal also has much more decorative value. They are very tolerant and good-natured, both towards each other and towards the other fish. Although the small fish like to swim, they are not really boisterous. They mainly occupy the middle zone. These fish should not be kept alongside aggressive or predatory fish.

TEMPERATURE AND WATER COMPOSITION
24-28°C. These small fish can be kept in different water compositions, but preferably in slightly acidic (pH 6.5) and soft water (4-8° gH). Filter through peat now and again.

FOOD
The glowlight tetra is an omnivore; it will readily take both dry food and vegetable food, as well as small live food.

BREEDING
These fish reproduce both as a pair and within the shoal. If you want to get some offspring from your small shoal of glow-light tetras, transfer the whole shoal, or a well-matched breeding pair into a separate breeding tank with plenty of floating plants, feathery leafed plants and very soft water (1-4° gH). Filter over peat. Gradually increase the temperature in the breeding tank but do not let it rise above 29°C.

Hemigrammus erythrozonus

Glowlight tetras are egg eaters, so the shoal should be removed once the eggs are laid. The fry can then be reared on fine powdered food (Sera Micron), micro-worms and unicellular organisms (such as slipper animalcules).

Hemigrammus hyanuary

JANUARY TETRA

FAMILY
Characidae (characins)

SUB FAMILY
Tetragonopterinae

HABITAT
Mainly in the Hyanuary lake in the Amazon region of Brazil

LENGTH
Up to about 4.5 centimetres

ACCOMMODATION
These small fish do well in both smaller and medium-sized community aquaria with plenty of open space for swimming. The fish will fare better if the aquarium is placed in a sunny location.

SOCIAL CHARACTERISTICS
These fish belong in a shoal of at least seven, otherwise they are shy and do not show their colours. They are very peaceful towards other aquarium dwellers. These lively fish are fast swimmers and mainly occupy the middle zone. Do not put them together with predators or intolerant species.

Hemigrammus hyanuary

24-27°C. This variety is not very demanding as regards the water composition, although the fish do prefer soft and rather acidic water.

FOOD

The January tetra is an omnivore. Vegetable food, dry food and small live food are all good for the fish. This species can live solely on a varied diet of different varieties of dry food.

BREEDING

If you want to breed these fish, you should set up a small breeding tank. Morning sunshine in the aquarium is ideal. The pH should be around 6 and the water must be soft (lower than 8° gH). Fit a substrate spawner a few centimetres above the bottom as these free spawning fish are also egg eaters. Rear the fry on fine powdered food.

Hemigrammus pulcher

FAMILY
Characidae (characins)

SUB FAMILY
Tetragonopterinae

HABITAT
Amazon region

SEXUAL DIFFERENCES
Mature females are not difficult to distinguish from males; they clearly have a rounder stomach contour.

LENGTH
Up to about 5.5 centimetres

ACCOMMODATION
These fish feel at home in a medium-sized or smallish aquarium with free space to swim and some peripheral vegetation. A dark substrate and some floating plants are also advisable. A current is acceptable but not necessary.

Hemigrammus pulcher

This is a friendly fish which belongs in a shoal of at least five, but preferably more. It mainly stays in the middle zone, and is placid or moderately active.

TEMPERATURE AND WATER COMPOSITION
22-26°C. This species is not very demanding as regards the water composition. Medium-hard water with a neutral pH is ideal.

FOOD
H. pulcher is an omnivore. This fish can survive very well on a diet of nothing but dry food, as long as it is varied enough (Sera Vipan/Sera O-Nip). The fish does, however, like to eat live food such as tubifex and water fleas from time to time.

BREEDING
Breeding these fish is not easy, partly because they are very sensitive to excess waste substances in the breeding tank and because the partners do not always "click". A male which is ready to mate may also chase a female to death if she is not ready.

The fish are not normally very demanding as regards the aquarium water, but its composition is very important during the mating season. Then they need very soft (2-4 ° gH) and somewhat acidic (pH 6-6.5) water, so peat filtration is a must. Make sure that the tank is shaded and that no direct sunlight can get in. Gradually raise the temperature to around 27-28°C.

If, when the conditions are ideal and the fish are in peak condition, the eggs are a long time coming, you can assume that the pair simply are not interested in each other.

Once the eggs have been laid, remove the parent fish, since they are egg eaters. Rear the fry on microworms, unicellular organisms such as slipper animalcules and fine powdered food (Sera Micron).

Hemigrammus rodwayi

FAMILY
Characidae (characins)

SUB FAMILY
Tetragonopterinae

HABITAT
Guyana

SEXUAL DIFFERENCES
Mature females are recognisable by their plumper stomach.

LENGTH
Up to about five centimetres

ACCOMMODATION
These fish can be kept in both small and medium-sized aquaria alongside friendly species. They are ideal for use in a community aquarium.

Provide feathery-leafed peripheral vegetation. These fish do not need shadowy areas in the aquarium but they will still feel better if the substrate is darker in colour. In this case their colours will stand out better.

SOCIAL CHARACTERISTICS
These small fish are very peaceful and friendly. It is absolutely essential to keep them in a large shoal. Do not put them alongside very boisterous or intolerant neighbours, since there is a chance that they will hide themselves among the plants and never show themselves. They mainly occupy the middle zone and are moderately active.

TEMPERATURE AND WATER COMPOSITION
23-27°C. These fish need soft to medium-hard water.

FOOD
This species likes dry food and small live food.

Breeding these fish takes place in approximately the same way as with other *Hemigrammus* varieties.

VARIANTS
There are two different varieties of *H. rodwayi*: the golden variant and other varieties which are less intensely coloured, but have clear red rings around the eyes. The photograph shows a gold-coloured fish without the red-rimmed eyes.

Hepsetus odoe *'Afrika'*

FAMILY
Hepsetidae

SUB FAMILY
Hepsetinae

HABITAT
Africa (in Senegal and other countries)

SEXUAL DIFFERENCES
Unknown

LENGTH
In the wild, these predators can be up to 80 centimetres long, but in the aquarium they remain much smaller.

ACCOMMODATION
Once it has reached maturity this predatory African fish can actually only be kept in very large aquaria; even a tank two metres long is sometimes too small. The fish must have room to swim and hunt and cannot do this in smaller or

Hepsetus odoe

Hepsetus odoe

narrow aquaria. Decorative materials should not be used in the aquarium because it restricts the space for swimming available for the fish.

SOCIAL CHARACTERISTICS
As the photograph shows, *H. odoe* has small teeth, and it uses them. It is clear that these fish are predators which, once they are older, can no longer be kept with other fish. The fish are seldom any problem to each other. Young fish, until they grow too large, can be kept in the same aquaria as some (robust!) cichlids.

TEMPERATURE AND WATER COMPOSITION
25-28°C. The fish are not demanding as regards the water composition, but the aquarium must be rich in oxygen, well aerated and – above all – kept free of waste substances. Regularly siphon up dirt from the bottom.

FOOD
This large fish eats a lot and only solid live food – pieces of meat and fish and shellfish meat. Small fish, pieces of beef heart, mussel and earthworms are also very good.

BREEDING
This fish has never yet been bred in the aquarium.

SPECIAL REMARKS
Because of its size and the fact that it is a glutton which needs a lot of solid live food, this is not a species of fish which is owned by many people. If it does not get the right type of food, or enough of it, or if there is not enough space in the aquari-

um, it will not live very long. The fish on the picture is still young; when it is larger the contrasting spots will disappear and the fish will turn a uniform gold-silver colour.

Hoplosternum pectorale

FAMILY
Callichthyidae (mailed catfish)

SUB FAMILY
Callichtyinae

HABITAT
South America

SEXUAL DIFFERENCES
The difference between the sexes is not always easy to spot in young fish, but in mature fish the males stand out because of their larger pectoral fins.

LENGTH
Up to about 13 centimetres

ACCOMMODATION
This mailed catfish belongs in a medium-sized or large aquarium in which there are sufficient refuges in the form of petrified wood, rocks and dense vegetation. These fish mainly search for their food at the bottom and, in order to make sure that they do not injure themselves, you can design a special area in the aquarium for this. A thick layer of washed sand is especially suitable for this, preferably situated under some overhanging plants.

SOCIAL CHARACTERISTICS
These fish keep to themselves and usually leave other aquarium dwellers in peace. The males can be rather trouble-some in the mating season. This species can be kept as a solitary fish or in a small group (three or four fish), as long as there is enough room for each, since they form territories into which their own kind are not allowed outside the mating season.

TEMPERATURE AND WATER COMPOSITION
20-26°C. This mailed catfish is not very sensitive to either the pH or the hardness of the water.

FOOD
Since the fish usually lives on the bottom, it eats the remains of the food which the other aquarium dwellers let through. You can also treat these fish by giving them a food tablet for bottom dwellers (Sera Viformo) from time to time.

BREEDING
A breeding pair can be transferred to a separate, somewhat larger breeding tank in which the water level must be very low. The ideal conditions to encourage the fish to reproduce, are soft or very soft water (1-6° gH) and a temperature which is gradually increased to 28°C. The female lays the eggs in a nest of bubbles under large overhanging leaves, where they are looked after by the male.
Catch the female immediately after spawning, since otherwise the male will chase her. It is best to remove the male as well as soon as the fry can swim.

Hoplosternum pectorale

Hoplosternum thoracatum

FAMILY
Callichthydae (mailed catfish)

SUB FAMILY
Callichthynae

HABITAT
South America (Peru, Brazil, Venezuela and Colombia)

SEXUAL DIFFERENCES
The males can only be distinguished from the females during the mating season.

Hoplosternum thoracatum

The males then have a rather pearly coloured belly.

LENGTH
Up to about 18 centimetres

ACCOMMODATION
These fish feel at home in medium-sized or large aquaria (70-100 centimetres wide) with a low water level and refuges such as stones, clusters of plants and petrified wood. They will feel more at ease if the aquarium is not too brightly lit. Due to their burrowing behaviour, although they do spare the plants, a soft bottom (in places) is advisable (see also *Hoplosternum pectorale*).

SOCIAL CHARACTERISTICS
These fish tolerate both their own species and other aquarium dwellers. Only during the mating season are some fish (particularly the males) rather intolerant. You can keep them either as individuals or in a small group.

TEMPERATURE AND WATER COMPOSITION
20-26°C. The water composition is not important.

FOOD
This typical mailed catfish clears up the food which other aquarium dwellers do not finish, but it also like to eat food tablets for bottom dwellers.

BREEDING
Breeding these fish is similar to breeding *Hoplosternum pectorale*.

SPECIAL REMARKS
These are particularly hardy fish, so they are very suitable for beginners.

Hypancistrus zebra

FAMILY
Loricariidae (armoured catfish)

SUB FAMILY
Ancistrinae

HABITAT
Brazil

SEXUAL DIFFERENCES
The sexes can hardly be distinguished from one another at all.

LENGTH
Up to about eight centimetres

ACCOMMODATION
This very spectacularly patterned catfish can very easily be kept in smaller aquaria. There must, however, always be refuges. For these you can for example use petrified wood in convoluted shapes. The fish appreciate dense vegetation.

If you keep several fish alongside one another the aquarium will need to be more spacious (about 80 centimetres wide).

SOCIAL CHARACTERISTICS
These fish have territorial tendencies and therefore cannot get on very well in a small aquarium without refuges.

Hypancistrus zebra

They become more active towards dusk and leave other fish in peace. This variety stays in the bottom zone, usually very close to the refuges.

They are rather shy, so ideally they should not be kept alongside other bottom dwellers; they are easily intimidated by them and will not have a chance at feeding time.

TEMPERATURE AND WATER COMPOSITION
26-29°C. Medium-hard water and neutral acidity are preferable.

FOOD
These fish are omnivores. They mainly stay on the bottom, where they eat food remains. It is also good to give them food tablets for bottom dwellers at dusk every day.

BREEDING
Little is known so far about how these recently discovered fish reproduce, but a number of incidental cases of breeding have already been reported.

Hyphessobrycon bentosi bentosi

ORNATUS

FAMILY
Characidae (characins)

SUB FAMILY
Tetragonopterinae

HABITAT
Brazil and Guyana

SEXUAL DIFFERENCES
The male fish have a crescent-shaped dorsal fin, while the fins of the smaller females are more rounded.

LENGTH
Up to about 4.5 centimetres

ACCOMMODATION
Very suitable for community aquaria with vegetation and moderate dimensions. Although these fish are not keen swimmers, some space for swimming is still advisable. The colours of the fish do not stand out as well against a light substrate (light coloured gravel or sand); so a dark substrate is better.

Hyphessobrycon bentosi bentosi

SOCIAL CHARACTERISTICS
Hyphessobrycon bentosi bentosi is a peaceful and very quiet shoaling fish. It is best to keep them in a shoal of at least seven. Never keep these fish with very boisterous or aggressive varieties of fish, since they will re treat into the vegetation and remain hidden there. They mainly occupy the middle zone.

TEMPERATURE AND WATER COMPOSITION
23-27°C. This small fish is not very demanding as regards the water composition.

FOOD
Hyphessobrycon bentosi bentosi is an omnivore; it will readily take dry food and small live food.

BREEDING
These free layers will seldom reproduce in the community aquarium but if it happens anyway, the eggs will almost definitely be eaten, either by the parent fish or by the other aquarium dwellers.

For breeding, you should therefore transfer the fish to a separate breeding tank with feathery-leafed plants. The water composition is important. During the mating season, the fish need soft (5-9° gH) and slightly acidic water (pH 6.5). Remove the parent fish after spawning. The fry can then be reared on fine powdered food.

SPECIAL REMARKS
Hyphessobrycon bentosi bentosi is very robust, which makes it an ideal fish for beginners. The photograph shows a small fish which is not yet fully mature.

Hyphessobrycon bentosi rosaceus

ROSY TETRA

FAMILY
Characidae (characins)

SUB FAMILY
Tetragonopterinae

HABITAT
Guyana and Paraguay

SEXUAL DIFFERENCES
Like the males of the Hyphessobrycon bentosi bentosi species, males have a long, crescent-shaped dorsal fin.

LENGTH
Up to about 4.5 centimetres

ACCOMMODATION
These fish are an excellent choice if you are looking for shoaling fish to move quietly around your community aquarium. Plenty of vegetation and quiet neighbours are essential, though. This fish will not feel at home in brightly lit aquaria. Too

Hyphessobrycon bentosi rosaceus

strong a current in the water will also not be appreciated. The fish will be very pale in colour in aquaria with a light substrate. A dark substrate and some floating plants (to filter the light) will bring out the colours of the fish much better.

SOCIAL CHARACTERISTICS
These small shoaling fish are very tolerant of one another and also of other fish. Keep them in a small shoal of at least five

Hyphessobrycon bentosi rosaceus

specimens, since solitary fish and smaller shoals will pine away. They are peaceful and very good-natured, so boisterous, large and aggressive fish should not be kept in the same aquarium. They are fairly quiet and prefer to occupy the middle zone.

TEMPERATURE AND WATER COMPOSITION
23-27°C. These little fish are very undemanding as regards the water composition.

FOOD
This species can live on (varied) dry food alone, but will appreciate live food now and then.

BREEDING
Similar to *Hyphessobrycon bentosi bentosi.*

SPECIAL REMARKS
This variety strongly resembles *Hyphessobrycon bentosi bentosi* and is often confused with it. It is a small fish, slightly smaller than *Hyphessobrycon bentosi bentosi*, and a great beginner's fish because of its toughness.

Hyphessobrycon callistus
(syn. Hemigrammus melanopterus)

CALLISTUS TETRA

FAMILY
Characidae (characins)

SUB FAMILY
Tetragonopterinae

HABITAT
South America, mainly in Paraguay

SEXUAL DIFFERENCES
The females have a fuller stomach and more rounded contours. They are also usually slightly paler in colour than the males.

LENGTH
Up to about 4.5 centimetres

ACCOMMODATION
The callistus tetra is a well-known and popular shoaling fish which does very well in smaller or medium-sized community aquaria. In order to meet the needs of these fish, you should ensure that the aquarium is richly planted with feathery-leafed plant vegetation

Hyphessobrycon callistus

and that there is also enough free space for swimming. To enable the colours to show to their best advantage use a dark substrate combined with some floating plants. The callistus tetra will not show its characteristic red colour in a brightly lit aquarium with sparse vegetation and a light bottom.

SOCIAL CHARACTERISTICS
These little fish feel most comfortable when kept in a larger shoal. They are generally very friendly, but older and lonely fish can sometimes develop an intolerant disposition towards other species. They are moderately active and stay mainly in the middle zone.

TEMPERATURE AND WATER COMPOSITION
23-27°C. The water composition is not very important.

FOOD
Callistus tetra is an omnivore; it eats both dry food and live food.

BREEDING
These fish feel at ease in practically any water composition, but if you want to try to get these fish to reproduce, it is definitely necessary to transfer a mature breeding pair in peak condition to a separate breeding tank. The water in the breeding tank should be reasonably soft (4-11° gH) and slightly acidic (pH around 6). Peat filtration is advisable. The callistus tetra is a free layer which eats both its own eggs and the fry after hatching, so remove the parent fish once the eggs have been laid.

Hyphessobrycon erythrostigma
(syn. H. rubrostigma)

BLEEDING HEART TETRA OR TETRA PEREZ

FAMILY
Characidae (characins)

SUB FAMILY
Tetragonopterinae

HABITAT
Peru

SEXUAL DIFFERENCES
The mature males have a much larger, crescent-shaped dorsal fin than the females.

LENGTH
Up to about eight centimetres

ACCOMMODATION
Due to the size that these fish can reach the bleeding heart tetra belongs in a spacious community aquarium which should be at least 80 centimetres long. Provide plenty of peripheral vegetation, open space for swimming, a dark bottom and perhaps some floating plants.

SOCIAL CHARACTERISTICS
This species belongs in a largish shoal. Individuals or smaller shoals (three specimens) will sometimes pine away or become aggressive and will in any case not feel comfortable. This species is definitely good-natured, not only towards each other, but also towards other fish. The fish have a moderate temperament and stay mainly in the middle zone.

Hyphessobrycon erythrostigma ♂

TEMPERATURE AND WATER COMPOSITION
23-27°C, gH 4-10°, pH 6-6.5

FOOD
This fish is an omnivore. It likes to eat dry food and also some small live food.

BREEDING
These fish are not easy to breed. A lot depends on the right water composition (very soft water, 1-3° gH) and a suitable breeding pair. Other details are the same as for other related species.

SPECIAL REMARKS
The bleeding heart tetra looks a lot like both *Hyphessobrycon bentosi bentosi* and *H. bentosi rosaceus*. These fish are also related to each other, but the other species are more easily satisfied with regard to water composition.

Hyphessobrycon flammeus

FLAME TETRA

FAMILY
Characidae (characins)

SUB FAMILY
Tetragonopterinae

HABITAT
Rio de Janeiro area

SEXUAL DIFFERENCES
The females are rather larger than the males and less intensely coloured (particularly on the fins).

Hyphessobrycon flammeus

Hyphessobrycon flammeus

LENGTH
Up to about 4.5 centimetres

ACCOMMODATION
The flame tetra is highly suitable for the community aquarium, which need not be very big. These fish do require plenty of open space for swimming and dense peripheral vegetation. A dark bottom and subdued light will bring out the colours much better.

SOCIAL CHARACTERISTICS
These lively and popular shoaling fish are amongst the most peaceful aquarium fish we know. One requirement is that the fish must be kept in a shoal of at least five. Solitary fish, or fish in too small a shoal, can develop behavioural problems such as aggression towards other fish. Since these fish form huge shoals in the wild, and feel safe and comfortable in them, it is not fair to keep them in an aquarium with just two or three others. Flame tetras have a moderate temperament and swim mainly in the middle zone.

TEMPERATURE AND WATER COMPOSITION
22-25°C. The water composition is of minor importance.

FOOD
The flame tetra will eat almost anything. It likes all sorts of dry food, but also enjoys some small live food occasionally.

BREEDING
It is very easy to encourage these fish to reproduce. A well-suited and mature breeding pair can be transferred to a separate breeding tank with plenty of feathery-leafed plants. Fairly soft water (4-8° gH) and peat filtration are recommended. The fish are free layers and eat their own eggs; it is therefore necessary to remove the parent fish after spawning.

SPECIAL REMARKS
This fish is very suitable for new aquarists since it is easily satisfied and remains healthy in a wide range of water compositions. Pay particular attention to its colour at the time of purchase; many flame tetras have hardly any red pigment at all.

Hyphessobrycon herbertaxelrodi

BLACK NEON TETRA

FAMILY
Characidae (characins)

SUB FAMILY
Tetragonopterinae

HABITAT
Brazil (Rio Taquari)

SEXUAL DIFFERENCES
The females have a fuller stomach and are also rather larger than the males.

LENGTH
Up to about 4.5 centimetres

ACCOMMODATION
This small fish can be easily accommodated in a medium-sized or small community aquarium. They enjoy swimming and must be given the opportunity to do so. Peripheral vegetation is also essential. Since they do not like bright lighting,

Hyphessobrycon herbertaxelrodi

diffuse lighting created by floating plants or long-leafed plants (vallisneria) is advisable. This lighting, together with a dark substrate, will allow the lively pattern of colours on the fish to stand out much better.

SOCIAL CHARACTERISTICS
The black neon is a good-natured fish which allows more aggressive fish to dominate it, so only keep these fish with equally friendly species. It is also necessary to keep the fish in a shoal. A larger shoal, for example with 12 or more specimens, will be much more attractive than a smaller shoal. The fish are quite active and mainly occupy the middle zone.

TEMPERATURE AND WATER COMPOSITION
23-26°C. These little fish do reasonably well in varied water compositions, but soft (4-8° gH) and slightly acidic (pH 6-6.5) water is ideal. Peat filtration is recommended.

FOOD
The black neon enjoys both dry food and small live food.

BREEDING
Breeding these charming small fish is very difficult. Black neons reproduce best of all within the shoal. The future parents have to be in peak condition and, above all, must have been well fed with a varied diet, including small live food. Three or four pairs can be transferred to a breeding tank with feathery-leafed plants. The correct water composition is very important. You will achieve the best results with very soft (0-4°) and acidic (pH 5.5-6) water. The small fish are free layers and eat their own eggs, so remove them after spawning. The fry grow quite slowly and will need microworms and fine powdered food for a long time.

Hyphessobrycon loretoensis

FAMILY
Characidae (characins)

SUB FAMILY
Tetragonopterinae

HABITAT
Western part of the Amazon region

SEXUAL DIFFERENCES
The male differs from the female because of its thinner build.

LENGTH
Up to about four centimetres

ACCOMMODATION
This fish is suitable for smaller or medium-sized community aquaria with plenty of peripheral vegetation and open space for swimming.

SOCIAL CHARACTERISTICS
This lively fish will come into its own in a larger shoal. It is friendly both towards its own kind and other aquarium dwellers. The fish mainly stays in the middle zone.

Hyphessobrycon loretoensis

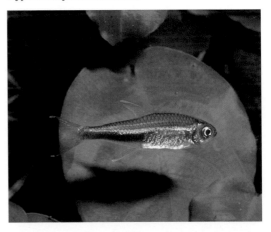

22-26ºC. The species is not very demanding as regards the water composition.

FOOD
This small fish likes to eat dry food (food flakes), but you should also give it some live food now and then, such as tubifex and water fleas.

BREEDING
Little is known so far about reproduction.

Hyphessobrycon pulchripinnis

LEMON TETRA

FAMILY
Charachidae (characins)

SUB FAMILY
Tetragonopterinae

HABITAT
Amazon region

SEXUAL DIFFERENCES
The difference between the sexes is not always easy to establish. The males are generally slightly smaller than the females and the black edging along the anal fin is more intensely coloured.

LENGTH
Up to about five centimetres

ACCOMMODATION
The lemon tetra feels at home in communi-

Hyphessobrycon pulchripinnis

Hyphessobrycon pulchripinnis

ty aquaria with plenty of open, free space to swim, and dense peripheral vegetation. The fish look very dull and colourless in an aquarium with white or light gravel; it is therefore better to put them in aquaria with a dark substrate and some floating plants (crystalwort). Together with soft water (4-8º gH), this will lead to more attractive, deeper colours.

SOCIAL CHARACTERISTICS
The lemon tetra is a peaceful and good-natured fish which prefers to be in a larger shoal. Lemon tetras will gradually pine away if kept individually. Since this species is very friendly and relatively quiet, it is best not to keep them with ill-mannered neighbours. Lemon tetras are very active and occupy the middle zone.

TEMPERATURE AND WATER COMPOSITION
22-26ºC. These fish do well in varied water compositions. Soft, peat filtered water is best for their well-being and colouring.

FOOD
The lemon tetra is easy to feed. It eats both dry food flakes and granules and live food such as water fleas and tubifex.

BREEDING
These fish will sometimes reproduce in a separate breeding tank with feathery-leafed plants, plenty of floating plants and soft water (4-8º gH). The parent fish eat their own eggs and must be removed immediately after spawning. The fry can be reared on fine powdered food (Sera Micron).

Hyphessobrycon werneri

FAMILY
Characidae (characins)

SUB FAMILY
Tetragonopterinae

HABITAT
Brazil

SEXUAL DIFFERENCES
The males can be recognised by their largish, crescent-shaped dorsal fin. They are also often somewhat thinner and more brightly coloured than the females.

LENGTH
Up to 4.5 centimetres

ACCOMMODATION
Like other *Hyphessobrycon* species, this variety can also be kept very easily in a medium-sized community aquarium. The fish appreciate peripheral vegetation, not too much current, rather diffuse lighting with a dark substrate and open space for swimming.

SOCIAL CHARACTERISTICS
This fish is good-natured and leaves other aquarium dwellers alone. It should, however, always be kept in a shoal. It mainly occupies the middle zone.

Hyphessobrycon werneri

TEMPERATURE AND WATER COMPOSITION
23-26°C. The water composition is less important, but soft to medium-hard water would be ideal.

FOOD
This shoaling fish is an omnivore which will gladly eat different sorts of dry food and live food.

BREEDING
Similar to other *Hyphessobrycon* varieties.

Hyphessobrycon werneri

Inpaichthys kerri

FAMILY
Characidae (characins)

SUB FAMILY
Tetragonopterinae

HABITAT
Amazon region

SEXUAL DIFFERENCES
The male can be differentiated from the female by its richer colouring and larger size.

LENGTH
Up to about 4.5 centimetres

ACCOMMODATION
These enthusiastic swimmers will feel very much at home in a community tank which certainly does not have to be very large. A dark bottom and dim lighting will bring out the colours of this fish much better.

SOCIAL CHARACTERISTICS
I. kerri is a friendly and problem-free fish which will cause no trouble to other aquarium dwellers. However this shoaling

Inpaichthys kerri

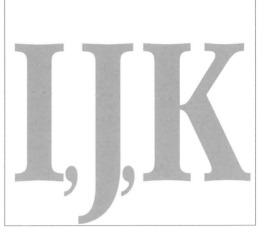

fish will only feel completely in its element with others of its kind. A shoal must always contain at least five fish.

TEMPERATURE AND WATER COMPOSITION
24-28°C. Peat filtration will brighten up the colour of these fish.

FOOD
This small shoaling fish is an omnivore. Both live and dry food will be good for this fish.

BREEDING
Not very easy. A good breeding pair can be transferred to a separate breeding tank with plenty of feathery-leafed plants. Ensure that the aquarium is situated in a shady place and is definitely not brightly lit. To stimulate the fish you can gradually raise the temperature by 2°C. These fish are free layers and happily eat their own eggs, so the parent fish must be removed soon after spawning.
The feathery-leafed vegetation serves as a "hiding place" for the eggs; in a virtually empty aquarium there will not be a single egg left.

Iriatherina werneri

FAMILY
Atheriniidae (silversides)

HABITAT
Australia

Iriatherina werneri ♂

Iriatherina werneri ♀

SEXUAL DIFFERENCES
The difference between the sexes is not only in size – males are larger – but also in the fin ray, which is much longer in the male. The males are also much more colourful than the females during the mating season.

LENGTH
Up to about six centimetres

ACCOMMODATION
These fish do well in medium-sized community aquaria with peaceful neighbours (especially surface and bottom dwellers), provided the water quality is right.

SOCIAL CHARACTERISTICS
These rather active fish are extremely peaceful, both towards each other and in the company of other fish. Since the males have long fin rays, predatory fish, or fish which enjoy nibbling fins, such as the tiger barb, are not a good choice as companions.
These fish mainly swim in the middle zone.

TEMPERATURE AND WATER COMPOSITION
23-27°C. This species prefers hard water (12-20° gH) and a neutral pH.

FOOD
I. werneri eats both dried and live food.

BREEDING
Breeding is absolutely only for specialists.

Julidochromis ornatus

FAMILY
Cichlidae (cichlids)

HABITAT
Along the rocky banks of Lake Tanganyika in Africa.

SEXUAL DIFFERENCES
It is extremely difficult to distinguish the difference between the sexes. Adult females are, however, often larger and fatter than the males.

LENGTH
Up to about 10 centimetres

ACCOMMODATION
This fish does well in smaller aquaria with decorative rocks and stones, to serve as refuges for the fish. They will sometimes "pick" the plants, so it is better to have no plants at all, or to use only very robust plants.
The aquarium should ideally be situated where direct sunlight can shine on it now and then; this encourages algae formation, which the fish enjoy very much.

SOCIAL CHARACTERISTICS
These fish can be very intolerant of other aquarium dwellers. Keeping them as a pair can alleviate this problem. An extremely territorial and somewhat aggressive fish should not be kept in an aquarium with less robust species; take this into account

if you want to buy these fish. If you have a large aquarium, you can keep *J. ornatus* with a few other similar smaller Lake Tanganyika cichlids.

TEMPERATURE AND WATER COMPOSITION
21-24°C, 12-20° gH, pH 8-9.

FOOD
This African cichlid species is certainly not difficult to feed. Cichlid sticks, compressed food tablets (Sera Premium) and algae are a good basic staple, but the fish also enjoy live food such as small fish and mosquito larvae occasionally. You can also give them fine pieces of beef heart.

BREEDING
In the right conditions these fish will breed quite quickly. The eggs and fry are not usually cared for, but they are not eaten either.

Kryptopterus bicirrhis

INDIAN GHOST, OR GLASS CATFISH
FAMILY
Siluridae (true catfish)

SUB FAMILY
Silurinae

HABITAT
Indonesia, Thailand and Malaysia

SEXUAL DIFFERENCES
Unknown.

LENGTH
In very large aquaria and in the wild, the Indian glass catfish can reach 15 centimetres in length, but the fish will generally not be much larger than 10 centimetres in the average aquarium.

ACCOMMODATION
These fish feel at their best in medium-sized or large aquaria with plenty of peripheral vegatation, petrified wood for decoration and a gentle current. They often "stand" as a shoal in an overgrown

Kryptopterus bicirrhis

place in the aquarium, with all their heads facing the same way. Create a shelter of this kind using floating plants or large-leafed plants.

Kryptopterus bicirrhis

SOCIAL CHARACTERISTICS

The Indian glass catfish, with its great decorative value, belongs in a shoal of at least five fish and preferably even more. These fish are mostly peaceful, so you should not put them with rough or more aggressive species. Indian glass catfish are very peaceful fish which usually become rather more active at dusk. They prefer the middle zone.

TEMPERATURE AND WATER COMPOSITION

23-26°C. When it comes to the water composition these fish are easily satisfied.

FOOD

These fish are easy to feed. They eat both small live food and food flakes with no problems. They adore live water fleas.

BREEDING

Not much is known so far about the breeding of this fish.

Ladigesia roloffi

FAMILY
Alestidae (African characins)

SUB FAMILY
Alestinae

HABITAT
Liberia and Sierra Leone

SEXUAL DIFFERENCES
The males are recognisable by their longer fins.

LENGTH
Up to about four centimetres

ACCOMMODATION
These peaceful shoaling fish can be kept in a small to medium-sized aquarium, which must be situated in a quiet spot. This variety is timid, so a dark substrate, plenty of peripheral vegetation and floating plants will help to put them at ease. Above all, this kind of set-up will bring out the colours of the fish.

A cover is necessary because the fish are rather apt to jump out of the water.

SOCIAL CHARACTERISTICS
These fish are easily intimidated and should therefore not be put in the same aquarium with excessively boisterous or aggressive fish. Keep them in a large shoal of at least seven

Ladigesia roloffi

specimens and preferably even more. They prefer to occupy the middle and top zone.

TEMPERATURE AND WATER COMPOSITION
23-26° C. These fish do quite well in various water conditions but they prefer soft and rather acidic water.

FOOD
This variety will readily eat dry food and small live food.

BREEDING
Breeding is not easy. It is important for the breeding tank to be positioned in a very quiet spot where the fish will not be frightened. You can, for example, tape black paper over three sides of the aquarium for this purpose.

You can use some peat as a substrate to put the fish in the right frame of mind and cover two-thirds of the surface with floating plants. The water must be very soft (2-3° gH) and absolutely crystal clear.

Lamprologus *spec. 'Daffodil'*

FAMILY
Cichlidae (cichlids)

HABITAT
Lake Tanganyika in Africa

SEXUAL DIFFERENCES
The males can be identified by their longer fin rays.

Up to about eight centimetres

ACCOMMODATION
These quiet cichlids do well in both smaller and larger aquaria. Shady places, some dense vegetation and refuges are desirable because these peaceful fish tend to withdraw. They do like some current in the water.

SOCIAL CHARACTERISTICS
These interesting and attractive cichlids can be kept with other types of fish in the same community tank almost without difficulty, since they are not too small. The aggression which is often displayed by other cichlids is seldom reported in this variety. These fish are usually kept as pairs, but several specimens in the same aquarium will not cause each other any problems. The fish have a moderate temperament and occupy the lower and middle zone.

TEMPERATURE AND WATER COMPOSITION
22-26°C. The fish like hard water (15-25° gH).

FOOD
These fish are not difficult to feed. They very much like live food, but cichlid sticks are also eaten and can be used as a basic staple.

BREEDING
Breeding these fish is not very difficult. One condition is that they must not be disturbed by other fish. The water com-

position must of course be ideal. Place a flower pot in the aquarium so that a little more than half of it sticks up on a slant above the substrate.
Position this flower pot so that it is in a sheltered, shady place, for example amongst some petrified wood and under overhanging aquatic plants. The eggs will be laid in this pot.

VARIANTS
The "Daffodil" is probably a naturally coloured variant of the well-known Princess of Burundi (*Lamprologus brichardi*), which is much paler.

Lamprologus occelatus

FAMILY
Cichlidae (cichlids)

HABITAT
On the floor of Lake Tanganyika in Africa.

SEXUAL DIFFERENCES
Once they are fully grown, females are a few centimetres smaller than the males.

LENGTH
Up to six centimetres (males).

ACCOMMODATION
This small cichlid variety can easily be kept in a small aquarium. You can use vegetation in the aquarium or not; the fish do not need it and will leave it alone.

Lamprologus *'Daffodil'*

Lamprologus occelatus

They have a typical habit of retreating into empty snail shells. It is therefore a good idea to look for some snail shells (not mollusc shells) which are large enough to serve as homes for these fish. The bottom should ideally consist of well-washed sand, and the fish will partly bury their snail shell.

SOCIAL CHARACTERISTICS
These interesting fish form a territory around the snail shell, into which no other fish are allowed. They mainly stay near the bottom and can therefore be kept together with inhabitants of the middle and top zone. These fish should always be kept in pairs.

TEMPERATURE AND WATER COMPOSITION
22-25°C. Medium-hard to hard water is preferable.

FOOD
This typical cichlid variety mainly eats small shellfish and snails, but also other live food. *Lamprologus occelatus* is not a lover of dry food; it hardly touches it.

BREEDING
The eggs are laid in the snail shell. The female looks after both the spawn and the fry.

Leptobotia mantschurica

FAMILY
Cobitidae (loaches)

SUB FAMILY
Cobitinae

HABITAT
Northern Asia and China.

SEXUAL DIFFERENCES
Unknown.

LENGTH
Up to 20 centimetres

ACCOMMODATION
Due to its size and active lifestyle, this species belongs in a spacious aquarium.

Leptobotia mantschurica

Leptobotia mantschurica

The fish like to search the bottom for food remains and usually only become active at dusk. They can injure themselves on sharp stones; petrified wood or round fossils provide better decoration.

SOCIAL CHARACTERISTICS
This variety is not only good-natured towards its own species, but other aquarium dwellers are also left in peace. The fish are best kept in a small shoal (three to four fish). They prefer to occupy the bottom zone.

TEMPERATURE AND WATER COMPOSITION
The fish can be kept in a unheated aquarium in the living room, but are more active at temperatures above 19°C. They are not very demanding as regards the water composition.

FOOD
These fish will clear up everything that the other aquarium dwellers have not eaten but they also appreciate live food such as tubifex. Do not feed them until around dusk.

BREEDING
Nothing is known so far about the reproductive habits of these fish.

Leuciscus idus

ORFE

FAMILY
Cyprinidae (carps and minnows)

SUB FAMILY
Leuciscinae

HABITAT
Europe

SEXUAL DIFFERENCES
Females are fatter than males.

LENGTH
Up to 70 centimetres. The fish will not grow to this length in small ponds or in the aquarium.

ACCOMMODATION
The orfe is a lively shoaling fish and needs plenty of room for swimming. Largish aquaria with peripheral vegetation is perfectly good accommodation, as are ponds. They do appreciate a current. Only use robust aquatic plants, since they nibble soft-leafed plants.

Leuciscus idus

Orfes are very peaceful shoaling fish and must be kept in a group of at least five specimens, although they prefer more. A solitary orfe will stay alive, but that is about all.

These active fish occupy the middle and top zones. Orfes go well with other cold-water fish but, because of their active nature, they are not ideal company for veiltails.

TEMPERATURE AND WATER COMPOSITION

Orfes are cold-water fish, which means that they must be protected against excessively high temperatures.

If the water temperature remains above 20°C for any length of time, it is advisable to replace part of the aquarium water with cold water every day. The water composition is not very important, but crystal clear water, free of waste materials, will form an ideal environment for these fish.

BREEDING

You will not have much success in the aquarium, but you may be successful in larger ponds. The trouble is that the fish are free layers and quickly eat their eggs, as soon as they are laid.

VARIANTS

The fish shown in the illustration is the golden orfe, but there is also a silver-grey form called the silver orfe. Both varieties are sold by specialist aquarium shops, but the golden orfe is much more popular.

Lucania goodei

Lucania goodei

FAMILY
Cyprinodontidae (egg-laying tooth carps)

SUB FAMILY
Fundulinae

HABITAT
Southern North America

SEXUAL DIFFERENCES
The difference between the sexes is mainly seen in the colouring; the males are more intensely coloured than the females, particularly on the fins.

LENGTH
Up to six centimetres

ACCOMMODATION
This species can be introduced into a medium-sized or small aquarium. These undemanding fish will soon feel at ease as long as there is some petrified wood, feathery-leafed plants and plenty of space for swimming available.

SOCIAL CHARACTERISTICS
These fish are very tolerant of each other, but they can be much less friendly towards other aquarium dwellers.

This species can be kept with other fish, but make sure that they are robust and hardy species. They are very suitable for special aquaria.

TEMPERATURE AND WATER COMPOSITION
These fish feel especially good in unheated aquaria, provided the water temperature remains between 13 and 21°C. Apart from this they make few demands on the water quality.

FOOD
Lucania goodei eats both live and dry food (Sera Flora/Sera Premium).

BREEDING
After a winter period during which the water temperature should be kept quite low, these fish will start breeding under the influence of sunlight and rising temperatures.

There is, however, one difficulty – the females only lay a few eggs each day, and they sometimes carry on doing this for a month. The trouble is due to the greed of the parents, who see the eggs as a welcome addition to their diet. In order to prevent too many eggs being eaten, you must provide plenty of feathery-leafed plants so that the fish cannot find the eggs as quickly.

Give a breeding pair plenty of live food, so that they are not so inclined to devour their own eggs.

You can also float a plastic dish on the surface of the aquarium, and place as many eggs as possible in it each day until spawning is finished.

Natural biotope of Lucania goodei

Macropodus opercularis

PARADISE FISH

FAMILY
Anabandidae (labyrinth fish)

SUB FAMILY
Macropodinae

HABITAT
China, Korea and Vietnam, particularly in still, very shallow water (rice paddies).

SEXUAL DIFFERENCES
The male's fins are longer and more pointed, particularly the outermost fin rays. The males are also noticeably more colourful and larger than the females.

LENGTH
Up to about nine centimetres

ACCOMMODATION
Paradise fish can be kept in both medium-sized and small community tanks, but should not be kept with small or fragile fish. Diffuse lighting (floating plants) and a dark bottom will bring out the colours of the fish much better. These fish do not like a current in the water. Aeration or filtration is not very necessary when setting up a small aquarium specially for a breeding pair. Siphon the excreta from the bottom weekly so that the water is not polluted.

The fish are labyrinth fish, which means that they not only breathe through their gills, but can also take oxygen directly from the atmosphere (above the surface of the water). The water level therefore must not be too high (no more than 30 centimetres).

SOCIAL CHARACTERISTICS
Due to the aggressive nature of the males, it is best to keep only one male in the aquarium. Since males are intolerant towards females outside the mating season, you must definitely make sure that there are enough refuges available for the females.

Females kept together do not cause any problems. Paradise fish are quite peaceful and interesting fish with a thoughtful manner.

Macropodus opercularis ♂

TEMPERATURE AND WATER COMPOSITION
The paradise fish does very well in both unheated and heated aquaria and is almost insensitive to fluctuations in temperature. This is due to its natural biotope: the temperature in the shallow water (rice paddies) where they live can reach 32°C or more during the day in the heat of the sun, but can also cool down rapidly at night. Take care that the temperature does not stay too low for any length of time, and 15°C is the absolute minimum. The paradise fish does well in varied water types and is therefore good for beginners.

FOOD
The paradise fish has a preference for live and frozen food organisms such as red

Macropodus opercularis ♂

mosquito larvae and water fleas, but also eats dry food.

BREEDING
As long as the parents-to-be are in good condition, breeding is definitely not difficult. If you keep them in an unheated (breeding) aquarium without other fish, they will begin to breed when the temperature rises in spring and summer.

The male builds a bubble nest on the surface. When the eggs are laid they fall to the bottom, then they are collected by the male and "spat" into the bubble nest. Remove the female after spawning because she will almost certainly be chased to death by the male once she has made her contribution. The male takes excellent care of the eggs.

Megalamphodus megalopterus

VARIANTS
There are various variants of paradise fish, such as the albino and the darker, almost black, paradise fish. The latter must not be confused with *Macropodus opercularis concolor* (black paradise fish), which is a different species.

SPECIAL REMARKS
The paradise fish was the first aquarium fish after the goldfish and the koi carp to be imported and kept in European aquaria. These fish have been very popular for a long time.

Megalamphodus megalopterus

BLACK PHANTOM TETRA

FAMILY
Characidae (Characins)

SUB FAMILY
Tetragonopterinae

HABITAT
Brazil, Bolivia and Argentina

SEXUAL DIFFERENCES
The males have a larger dorsal fin and much more black pigment on the fins than the females, which have more red pigment.

LENGTH
Up to about 4.5 centimetres

ACCOMMODATION
The black phantom tetra likes to stay amongst and near dense foliage. In small to medium-sized community aquaria they will do fine as long as there is plenty of vegetation and enough open space for swimming. A dark bottom and floating plants will bring out the colours. These fish are fond of moderate current.

SOCIAL CHARACTERISTICS
This fish is friendly both to its own kind and towards other fish. It is best to keep them in a shoal of at least five fish. They are moderately active fish and prefer to occupy the middle zone under over-hanging plants.

23-26° C. This fish imposes hardly any demands on the water composition, but prefers soft water (4-8° gH).

FOOD
M. megalopterus eats both dry flakes and small live food.

BREEDING
The black phantom tetra is not one of the easiest fish to breed. The water must definitely be very soft and also slightly acidic (pH 6-6.5). These fish are free layers. The fry can be reared on unicellular organisms such as slipper animalcules (paramecium).

Megalamphodus sweglesi

RED PHANTOM TETRA

FAMILY
Characidae (characins)

SUB FAMILY
Tetragonopteridae

HABITAT
Colombia, by the banks of large rivers

SEXUAL DIFFERENCES
The females have a fatter stomach.

LENGTH
Up to about four centimetres

Megalamphodus sweglesi ♂

ACCOMMODATION
The red phantom tetra does well in a community tank with other species of fish requiring similar water conditions to itself. Thick, feathery-leafed peripheral vegetation is desirable.

SOCIAL CHARACTERISTICS
This is a very friendly and problem-free fish, which belongs in a shoal with at least five fish. They mainly occupy the middle zone and have a moderate temperament.

TEMPERATURE AND WATER COMPOSITION
22-24°C. These fish can be kept in various water conditions but the ideal is soft water (4-8° gH) and mildly acidic.

FOOD
The red phantom tetra is easy to feed. It readily eats both live and dry food.

BREEDING
The red phantom tetra, just like its relative the black phantom tetra, is not easy to breed. In very soft water (1-2° gH), filtered over peat and with a spawning substrate of Java moss, you may well succeed. The fry can be reared on microscopic food organisms (microworms and unicellular infusoria).

Melanochromis auratus
(syn. Pseudotropheus auratus)

NYASSA CICHLID

FAMILY
Cichlidae (cichlids)

HABITAT
Africa, along the rocky banks of Lake Malawi.

SEXUAL DIFFERENCES
The difference between the sexes can be seen very easily in the yellow so-called "egg spots" on the male's anal fin. Females always have a light background colour, while in the males it is a darker blue or black. Adult males are also several centimetres larger than the females.

LENGTH
Up to 10 centimetres (males).

ACCOMMODATION

This African will do very well in a medium-sized aquarium. You can put plants in the aquarium, since these cichlids do not nibble plants and also do not root around in the bottom. The fish much prefer it if the water is constantly in motion.

SOCIAL CHARACTERISTICS

The male fish, in particular, are very intolerant and can be aggressive. It is wiser to keep only one male in the same aquarium with two or more females.

The fish may still fight with each other, so it is better to buy fish which have been used to each other's company from their youth.

This species forms a territory into which no other fish are allowed so, if you want to keep more species of fish with these, there must be plenty of room in the aquarium and plenty of refuges for the fish.

TEMPERATURE AND WATER COMPOSITION

22-25°C. They do not make any great demands on the water composition outside the mating season.

FOOD

These cichlids eat both cichlid sticks and live food, but they also enjoy a bit of green food (algae) from time to time. You can give this in the form of food tablets (Sera Viformo).

BREEDING

The reproductive habits of these fish are extremely interesting. To get the fish to breed, the water temperature must be raised by one or two degrees. Of course, these fish must have been fed a good and varied diet beforehand so that they are in prime condition. They will readily mate in an aquarium with other fish species, but they may then be aggressive towards the other occupants. The female carries the eggs in her mouth until they hatch, after about two weeks.

VARIANTS

There are no variants of this fish, but their colours are extremely diverse.

Melanotaenia herbertaxelrodi

LAKE TEBERA RAINBOWFISH

FAMILY
Melanotaeniidae (rainbow fish)

HABITAT
New Guinea

SEXUAL DIFFERENCES
It is quite easy to distinguish the different sexes. The males are more intensely coloured than the females and also have a higher back.

LENGTH
Up to about eight centimetres

ACCOMMODATION
These fish like to swim about a lot and therefore need plenty of room. A long aquarium at least 80 centimetres long is essential. Water current is desirable. Peripheral vegetation and decorative material are a possibility, but they must be positioned so as not to hamper the fish as they move about.

SOCIAL CHARACTERISTICS
These active fish are friendly shoaling fish which cause no trouble to other fish, as long as they are not too small. These rainbow fish are very good companions for larger cichlid species. Due to their active and rapid swimming style they can also add variety to a cichlid aquarium with mainly quiet territorial fish.

The fish should always be kept in a shoal of at least five fish. They mainly occupy the middle zone.

Melanotaenia herbertaxelrodi

TEMPERATURE AND WATER COMPOSITION
20-25°C, medium to hard water, pH 7 to 7.5.

FOOD
These fish will eat dry food, but they prefer small live food.

BREEDING
These fish are not difficult to breed. It is important that the breeding tank is large enough (1 metre wide). There must also be plenty of open space for swimming and feathery-leafed aquatic plants available. In the ideal situation, you should put a male with several females in the breeding tank, because the males will chase the females quite vigorously. The eggs are laid on plants. To prevent the parent fish from eating the fry, it is best to remove them immediately after spawning. Like all rainbow fish this variety does not lay all its eggs at once, but the process takes place over a few days. Since the newly-hatched fry are extremely tiny, you must give them extremely small (live) food. This is where slipper animalcules (paramecium) come into their own. It takes a long time for the young to develop attractive colours like their parents.

Melanotaenia lacustris

FAMILY
Melanotaeniidae (rainbow fish)

HABITAT
New Guinea

SEXUAL DIFFERENCES
The males are often more intensely coloured than the females.

LENGTH
10-12 centimetres

ACCOMMODATION
These active fish are at their best in larger and longer aquaria, at least 1 metre long, and with plenty of open space for swimming. A current is desirable, but not essential.

SOCIAL CHARACTERISTICS
These fish are enthusiastic, often even boisterous swimmers and belong in a

shoal with at least five fish. They are peaceful, both towards their own kind and other fish, as long as the neighbours are not too small, in which case they will be seen as food. They are good company for larger cichlids, as long as their needs are the same in terms of water composition.

TEMPERATURE AND WATER COMPOSITION
21-23°C. The fish are not very sensitive to water composition: medium water hardness and pH value are satisfactory.

FOOD
Rainbow fish, the group to which this species belongs, are very easy to feed. They can stay healthy for a lifetime on a varied diet of dry food. They do, however, appreciate some live food now and then. Dry food containing a relatively high proportion of vegetable matter (Sera Flora) is recommended for this species.

BREEDING
In a separate spacious breeding tank, under ideal conditions, a good breeding pair will breed quite quickly. Favourable conditions can be created by getting the water composition right and providing feathery-leafed plants such as myriophyllum and Java moss. The parent fish eat the fry and they should therefore be removed after the eggs are laid. Do not take the fish out of the tank too early, since spawning takes place over a few days.

Young rainbow fish can be reared on fine powdered food from about a week old; during the preceding days even powdered food particles are too large for them. It is therefore absolutely essential to breed fish in an aquarium that has been set up for some time and will therefore usually have microscopically small infusoria available in the water as food.

SPECIAL REMARKS
It is a pity that the attractive colours can take such a long time to appear. The colours of the fish emerge very slowly and are not at their most beautiful until the fish are truly mature.

Melanotaenia macullochi

Melanotaeniidae (rainbow fish)

HABITAT
Australia and New Guinea, in fastflowing, shallow streams and rivers.

SEXUAL DIFFERENCES
The males are rather more colourful than the females and also have larger fins.

LENGTH
Up to about 7.5 centimetres

ACCOMMODATION
This rainbow fish does very well when kept in medium-sized aquaria, as long as you ensure that there is plenty of (feathery-leafed) peripheral vegetation and open space for swimming. The fish appreciate a good current in the water.

SOCIAL CHARACTERISTICS
These fish are easy shoaling fish which not only get on well with their own kind, but also with other species of fish, provided that they are not too small or shy. Cichlids are ideal companions for these colourful fish from "Down Under". These fish are very active and mainly occupy the middle zone.

TEMPERATURE AND WATER COMPOSITION
24-29°C. The fish make few demands on the water composition, but soft acidic water is ideal.

FOOD
These fish eat both small live food and dry food.

BREEDING
Breeding is similar to other rainbow fish.

Melanotaenia praecox

FAMILY
Melanotaeniidae (rainbow fish)

HABITAT
New Guinea

SEXUAL DIFFERENCES
The sexual difference is easy to see in adult fish. The males are always larger than the females and also more colourful.

LENGTH
Up to about six centimetres

SOCIAL CHARACTERISTICS
Despite the fact that these fish like to swim around a lot they will still do well in a medium-sized aquarium because of their small size. They very much like a current in the water, as well as plenty of swimming space and feathery-leafed peripheral vegetation.

SOCIAL CHARACTERISTICS
These fish are extremely peaceful towards other aquarium dwellers. They also get on well with their own kind, but must always

Melanotaenia macullochi

Melanotaenia praecox

Melanotaenia praecox

be kept in a shoal. Due to their rather active habits they are much less suitable companions for timid fish.

TEMPERATURE AND WATER COMPOSITION
22-26°C. This small rainbow fish does well in all kinds of water conditions but rather acidic and soft water is ideal.

FOOD
M. praecox is a real omnivore. It happily eats both dry food and small live food. Every now and then you can give it dry food containing vegetable materials (Sera Flora).

BREEDING
Breeding these fish is very similar to the other rainbow fish mentioned earlier.

Metynis maculatus

FAMILY
Serrasalmidae (American characins)

SUB FAMILY
Myleinae

HABITAT
South America, in fast-flowing rivers in the border regions of Bolivia and Brazil.

SEXUAL DIFFERENCES
The red colour in the adult male's anal fin is much more intense than in the female's.

LENGTH
Up to about 17 centimetres

ACCOMMODATION
Due to their size, lively behaviour and the fact that they are shoaling fish, these fish really do belong in a large aquarium. An aquarium 1.50 metres wide will usually be adequate. These fish are mainly plant eaters, so it makes little sense to put vegetation in the aquarium, or you should plant soft-leafed, cheap and fast-growing varieties which can serve as food. They usually do not like very strong, coarse plants as much, and that also goes for Java moss, so these varieties can be used if you want to provide vegetation in the aquarium.

These fish feel most at home if the water is in constant energetic motion (powerful motorised filter).

SOCIAL CHARACTERISTICS
This species looks like a piranha at first sight, and it is a member of the same family (*Serrasalmus*) but, other than their similarity of build and colour these fish have nothing in common. This species mainly eats vegetable food and is far from aggressive. They should always be kept in a substantial shoal. They mainly occupy the middle zone and are very active. You can keep them with bottom dwellers and maybe one or two pairs of cichlids.

TEMPERATURE AND WATER COMPOSITION
22-26°C. Soft to medium-hard water (4-12° gH) is preferable, at a pH of around 6.5-7.

FOOD
Give these fish dry food for plant eaters (Sera Flora, Sera Premium) and blanched lettuce leaves, spinach and watercress

Metynis maculatus

regularly. They also eat small live food, but only as a supplement.

BREEDING
These fish are quite easy to breed and the fry are also easy to rear. Since they eat their own eggs and other aquarium dwellers will also see them as food, a separate aquarium is an absolute necessity. Obviously, the parents must be removed from the tank after spawning.

Put a substrate spawner a few centimetres from the bottom, to which you can attach large amounts of feathery-leafed plants and Java moss. Peat filtration will encourage the fish to breed.

Select a pair from the shoal which always swim together, and there is a better chance that they will lay eggs. The eggs will be laid amongst the plants. The young can be reared on very fine live food, powdered food (Sera Micron), or a combination of the two.

Microglanis iheringi

FAMILY
Pimelodidae (antennae catfish)

SUB FAMILY
Pimelodinae

HABITAT
Venezuela and Colombia

SEXUAL DIFFERENCES
Unknown

Microglanis iheringi

Microglanis iheringi

LENGTH
Up to about eight centimetres

ACCOMMODATION
This unusual fish can be kept in both smaller and medium-sized aquaria. Since it burrows happily in the bottom looking for food, a soft substrate is ideal.

If necessary you can make a special "burrowing place" for these fish with a layer (a few centimetres thick) of washed sand. Plenty of vegetation and refuges in the form of petrified wood will be more than welcome.

SOCIAL CHARACTERISTICS
The fish look rather surly, but this completely belies their character. They do well when kept in a community aquarium, provided the other inhabitants are equally peaceful. Unlike most antennae catfish, which are very lively swimmers, this species is very placid and slow. These fish are seldom seen during the day, but after dusk they begin to become active and start searching for something to eat.

TEMPERATURE AND WATER COMPOSITION
22-25°C. These fish make few demands on the water composition.

FOOD
M. iheringi is very easily satisfied. Special food tablets for bottom dwellers go down well, as does flaked and small live food.

BREEDING
This species is not yet well established and has not yet been bred.

Moenkhausia pittieri

DIAMOND TETRA

FAMILY
Characidae (characins)

SUB FAMILY
Tetragonopteridae

HABITAT
Venezuela

SEXUAL DIFFERENCES
The male has a larger dorsal fin than the female. He also has a larger anal fin (see illustration).

LENGTH
Up to six centimetres

ACCOMMODATION
The diamond tetra is particularly well suited to the community aquarium, which does not need to be very large. These fish

Moenkhausia pittieri ♂

Koppel Moenkhausia pittieri

like to swim a lot. An aquarium with sufficient open space for swimming and dense peripheral vegetation, giving the fish the opportunity to hide among the plants now and then, is ideal. Against a light background these fish will often appear pale. If the aquarium has a dark bottom and floating plants on the surface as well, these fish will be much more attractive.

TEMPERATURE AND WATER COMPOSITION
Diamond tetras are very peaceful fish. Always keep them in a shoal of at least five, but preferably more of the same species. The fish prefer to spend their time in the middle zone.

FOOD
The diamond tetra eats both dried and small live food with relish and can remain health for its whole life on a varied diet of dry food.

BREEDING
Breeding is not impossible if the conditions are right, that is to say if the water in the breeding tank is very soft (0-5° gH) and there are plenty of shady spots and thick, feathery-leafed plants. Since the parent fish are egg-eaters, it is best to remove them from the aquarium as soon as possible after spawning.

Moenkhausia sanctaefilomenae

RED-EYED TETRA

FAMILY
Characidae (characins)

SUB FAMILY
Tetragonopterinae

HABITAT
South America

SEXUAL DIFFERENCES
The males are usually smaller than the females which, once fully grown, have a fuller stomach.

LENGTH
Up to about seven centimetres

ACCOMMODATION
Red-eyed tetras are perfectly suited for the community aquarium. They can adapt to both aquaria with dense vegetation and moderate vegetation, but floating plants and a dark bottom are desirable in order to bring out the attractive colours of the fish.

SOCIAL CHARACTERISTICS
This species is friendly and leaves other aquarium dwellers alone. Always keep these fish in a shoal, however, since they obviously do not feel comfortable as single fish or in a pair.
These fish are not strong swimmers. They prefer to occupy the middle zone.

TEMPERATURE AND WATER COMPOSITION
21-25°C. These fish make few demands on the water composition.

Moenkhausia sanctaefilomenae

FOOD
The red-eyed tetra is easy to please when it comes to feeding. The fish can remain healthy for a long time on a varied diet of dry food, but they also happily eat live food such as mosquito larvae, water fleas and tubifex from time to time.

BREEDING
This species breeds quite easily in the aquarium, but the parent fish will eat their own eggs, as will the other aquarium dwellers, which are spread all over the place by the females, seeing them as a welcome addition to their diet.
If you want the fry to mature, put the entire shoal in a separate breeding tank with lots of fine-leafed vegetation on the bottom (Java moss). Filter over peat to simulate the conditions which prevail during the mating season – then the fish will be quicker to lay eggs.

Monodactylis argenteus

FINGERFISH, MALAYAN ANGEL FISH

FAMILY
Monodactilae (finger fish)

HABITAT
This species has an enormous range. It is found both in Asia and Africa, along the coast in sea water and in brackish water where freshwater rivers meet the sea.

SEXUAL DIFFERENCES
Unknown.

LENGTH
Up to about 25 centimetres

ACCOMMODATION
Finger fish are not actually freshwater fish, but more brackish or seawater fish. They do not survive for long in fresh water, but in a brackish or seawater aquarium they can grow quite old. This species does not eat any hard-leafed plants, so the edges of the aquarium can be densely planted with coarse plant varieties. The plants must be adapted to the high salt content of the water. The fish enjoy a strong current.

This species is peaceful, lively and sometimes rather shy, but when they are kept in a large shoal, they can overcome their shyness.

TEMPERATURE AND WATER COMPOSITION
24-27°C. Brackish or seawater aquaria.

FOOD
Finger fish are omnivores. They enjoy both live food and food flakes and they can manage vegetable food as well.

BREEDING
Unknown.

Myleus rubripinnis rubripinnis

FAMILY
Serrasalmidae (American characins)

HABITAT
Amazon region

SEXUAL DIFFERENCES
Unknown.

LENGTH
Up to 25 centimetres. They are smaller in an aquarium, depending on the size of the aquarium.

ACCOMMODATION
In view of the size of these fish, the fact that they are shoaling fish and their lively nature, they belong in an aquarium measuring at least 1 metre, but preferably even larger.
They do not like strong light, but do like water which is constantly in motion. This can be provided by with a powerful motorised filter.
These are plant-eating fish, so it is best to decorate the aquarium with stones and petrified wood.

Myleus rubripinnis rubripinnis

LENGTH
In nature these fish can reach 60 centi-metres in length, but in the aquarium they will remain considerably smaller.

ACCOMMODATION
Due to its size, this striking Chinese underwater fish can only be kept in very large aquaria. Aquaria less than a metre wide will quickly become too small. They like to nibble the leaves of soft-leafed plants. They do best with good aeration and also powerful water filtration.

SOCIAL CHARACTERISTICS
This species is peaceful and sometimes rather timid. Keep them in a large shoal (at least seven fish, and preferably even more) then they will be livelier and will feel more secure. A dark substrate will do justice to these beautiful silver fish with their bright red anal fin.
These fish prefer to live in the middle zone.

SOCIAL CHARACTERISTICS
These fish can be kept together with several of their kind, but also as solitary specimens. They are good-natured towards other fish and are mainly found in the bottom and middle zone.

TEMPERATURE AND WATER COMPOSITION
23-26°C. Keep a close eye on the water composition. The pH level should ideally be about six and the hardness of the water must not exceed 14° gH. Filter over peat.

TEMPERATURE AND WATER COMPOSITION
Like most fish which originate from China, this species can tolerate wide variations in temperature. During the summer they can even be kept outdoors in ponds, but bring the fish into warmer surroundings as soon as the temperature remains lower than 16° C for any length of time. The water composition is of second-ary importance.

FOOD
These fish are real plant-eaters, but they will also enjoy small live food. You can give them soft-leafed aquatic plants (water thyme), blanched lettuce, spinach leaves, dry food (Sera Flora) and water fleas to eat.

FOOD
This Chinese fish is an omnivore. These fish eat food flakes, cichlid sticks, live food and (blanched) lettuce, spinach and watercress leaves.

BREEDING
Unknown.

BREEDING
Unknown so far.

Myxocyprinus asiaticus asiaticus

FAMILY
Cyprinidae (carps and minnows)

HABITAT
China

SEXUAL DIFFERENCES
Unknown

Myxocyprinus asiaticus asiaticus

Nannobrycon eques

Nannobrycon eques

FAMILY
Lebiasinidae (killifish)

SUB FAMILY
Pyrrhulininae

HABITAT
Amazon region

SEXUAL DIFFERENCES
As with many fish, the male of this species is more intensely coloured. They are also clearly more slender than the females.

LENGTH
Up to about five centimetres

ACCOMMODATION
This species of fish can be kept very successfully in smaller aquaria. Rich, dense vegetation, petrified wood for decoration, a dark bottom and light filtered through floating plants will provide the ideal aquarium setting for these fish.

SOCIAL HABITAT
These are particularly peaceful fish. They must always be kept in a shoal, since they will otherwise hide among the plants and will not show themselves. The same applies when they are in the company of aggressive or intolerant fish species. They

Left: the natural habitat of Nothobranchius rachovi

are quite placid and have a characteristic way of swimming, with the head higher than the tail. They prefer to occupy the bottom zone.

TEMPERATURE AND WATER COMPOSITION
25-28°C. Soft water (2-10° gH) and a pH of around 6.5. The water must be kept absolutely free from waste materials.

FOOD
These fish make stringent demands on the water composition, but they are a bit easier regarding food. Both dry food (Sera San, Sera Vipan) and small live food (fruit flies and mosquito larvae) go down well.

BREEDING
Breeding these fish is extremely difficult

Nannobrycon eques

161

and should be left to specialists. In order to get the fish to the point where they are prepared to mate they must be fed solely on live food. The water composition and water quality are also extremely specific, and you must bring together a well-matched breeding pair (not a shoal).

The fish eat their own eggs and must therefore be removed from the breeding tank after spawning.

Nannostomus harrisoni

FAMILY
Lebiasinidae (killifish)

SUB FAMILY
Pyrrhulininae

HABITAT
Guyana

SEXUAL DIFFERENCES
The female is rather less intensely coloured, and this is particularly noticeable in the fins.

LENGTH
Up to six centimetres

Nannostomus harrisoni

ACCOMMODATION
A medium-sized aquarium (60-70 centimetres) provides sufficient space for these quiet, rather retiring fish. Plenty of vegetation, floating plants and a dark bottom are desirable.

SOCIAL CHARACTERISTICS
These fish belong in a shoal. They are not strong swimmers and mainly stay amongst or close to vegetation in the top zone.

Too strong a current, boisterous or intolerant neighbours and bright lighting are so threatening to these fish that they will withdraw into the foliage, and are unlikely to be seen any more even during feeding.

TEMPERATURE AND WATER COMPOSITION
25-28°C. Soft water (0-8° gH) and a pH of about 6. The water must be crystal clear.

FOOD
These fish eat dry food and small live food such as fruit flies and larvae.

BREEDING
Breeding is comparable to that of Nannobrycon eques.

Nannostomus trifasciatus

FAMILY
Lebiasinidae (killifish)

SUB FAMILY
Pyrrhulininae

HABITAT
Amazon region, especially Brazil and Guyana

SEXUAL DIFFERENCES
Once they are fully grown, the males are recognisable by their more intense colouring. They are often thinner than the females, too.

LENGTH
Up to six centimetres

ACCOMMODATION
This species is extremely suitable for smaller aquaria. Diffuse lighting, which you can arrange by partly covering the surface with floating plants, plenty of

Nannostomus trifasciatus

The females have slightly shorter fins than the males.

LENGTH
Up to 5.5 centimetres

ACCOMMODATION
This characin does very well in a medium-sized aquarium with sufficient free space for swimming and dense peripheral vegetation.

peripheral vegetation and a dark substrate, will definitely suit these fish best.

SOCIAL CHARACTERISTICS
These fish belong in a shoal and, because of their rather shy and retiring nature, should not be kept with fierce or intolerant fish species. They prefer to stay near or among plants, just below the surface of the water.

SOCIAL CHARACTERISTICS
This is a peaceful shoaling fish which is only at its best in a larger shoal of more than seven fish. These fish should not be kept with fiercer varieties, because these characins with their friendly and placid nature will find that difficult.

TEMPERATURE AND WATER COMPOSITION
25-28°C. The correct water composition is very important for these fish. The water should be very soft and rather acidic.
Just like other pencil fish, they also respond badly to pollution (nitrates) in the water.

TEMPERATURE AND WATER COMPOSITION
24-28°C, preferably rather softer and slightly acidic water (pH of less than 7).

FOOD
These characins, which look very much like the emperor tetra and are in the same family, eat both dry food and live food with relish.

FOOD
N. trifasciatus eats both flakes and live food.

BREEDING
Breeding is not very easy because the few eggs which the fish lay will be just as happily devoured by both parents. It is important that the water should be soft and slightly acidic and that there should be enough feathery-leafed plants to ensure some diffuse lighting. The fry can be reared on fine powdered food and tiny live food organisms.

BREEDING
Breeding these fish should be left to specialists.

Nematobrycon lacortei

Nematobrycon lacortei

FAMILY
Characidae (characins)

SUB FAMILY
Tetragonopterinae

HABITAT
Colombia, in the jungle.

Nematobrycon lacortei

Nematobrycon palmeri

EMPEROR TETRA

FAMILY
Characidae (characins)

SUB FAMILY
Tetragonopterinae

HABITAT
Colombia, in the jungle.

SEXUAL DIFFERENCES
The males are rather larger than the females and can also be identified by the fact that the centre and outermost fin rays on the tail fin are longer. Finally the male's dorsal and anal fins are also longer and the ring around the eyes is more intensely coloured.

LENGTH
Up to about six centimetres.

ACCOMMODATION
The emperor tetra does well in community aquaria, as long as there is plenty of vegetation and the other aquarium dwellers are not too active.
Emperor tetras feel extremely happy in medium-sized aquaria.

SOCIAL CHARACTERISTICS
These fish feel most at home in a shoal of about seven or more fish. You should fish which are not very active as companions for the emperor tetra, for example, hatchet

Nematobrycon palmeri

fish on the surface and Corydoras species as bottom dwellers.

TEMPERATURE AND WATER COMPOSITION
24-27°C. This species is not very demanding as regards the water composition, but they do not feel as comfortable in hard water.

FOOD
The emperor tetra likes to eat both varied dry food and small live food.

BREEDING
Breeding is not easy. The water composition must be extremely precise. Transfer the fish, which will have been fed a varied diet beforehand, into some soft water filtered over peat. The eggs will be laid among feathery-leafed plants.
Since the parent fish eat the eggs, it is wise to remove them as soon as breeding has taken place.

Neolamprologus leleupi

FAMILY
Cichlidae (cichlids)

HABITAT
Africa, Lake Tanganyika

SEXUAL DIFFERENCES
It is to difficult to differentiate between the sexes.

LENGTH
Up to about 10 centimetres

ACCOMMODATION
These Tanganyika cichlids feel most at home in a medium-sized or large aquarium with few plants, but plenty of stones, petrified wood and artificial caves. A fine gravel or sandy bottom is desirable, as well as a good current.

SOCIAL CHARACTERISTICS
These mainly placid fish are, unfortunately, not always friendly towards each other. It is therefore better to keep only one pair. Since this species has rather predatory tendencies, it should normally only be kept in the company of other cichlid species or possibly a larger

Neolamprologus leleupi

Neolamprologus leleupi

(armoured) catfish. They usually stay near the bottom.

TEMPERATURE AND WATER COMPOSITION
23-26°C, medium-hard water, pH 8. The water must be crystal clear and clean. Some aeration is advisable.

FOOD
Unfortunately this fish is not easy to feed. The fish mainly eat live food, and some will even reject dry food. Some specimens take cichlid sticks or frozen food.

BREEDING
These fish will care for their offspring themselves if the conditions are right. You do not need to transfer them to a separate aquarium, since both parent fish will care for both the eggs and the fry and protect them from inquisitive (or hungry) busybodies. The eggs are laid in a hollow.

Neolamprologus signatus

FAMILY
Cichlidae (cichlids)

HABITAT
Africa, Lake Tanganyika

SEXUAL DIFFERENCES
The male is very easy to recognise by the stripes on its flanks. The female is also smaller.

LENGTH
Up to about six centimetres (male).

ACCOMMODATION
This small cichlid can easily be kept in

Neolamprologus signatus

smaller to medium-sized aquaria. The fish need a large snail shell which they can stay near and hide in when danger threatens. The eggs will also be laid here. A substrate of well-washed sand is absolutely vital.

SOCIAL CHARACTERISTICS
This territory-forming species is usually very intolerant and can lash out at both its own kind and other aquarium dwellers. It is best to keep these fish as a pair, together with a pair of other, hardy cichlids. In that case make sure there are sufficient refuges for all fish, so that they will not keep squabbling.

TEMPERATURE AND WATER COMPOSITION
23-26°C. Hard water (10-14° gH), at a pH of 7-8.

FOOD
The fish mainly take live food, such as mosquito larvae and tubifex, but cichlid sticks also go down well.

BREEDING
A well-matched pair does not need to be transferred to another aquarium, but will mate quite well in the cichlid aquarium. The eggs and fry will be cared for by the female.

Nomorhamphus liemi liemi

FAMILY
Hemirhamphidae (halfbeaks)

HABITAT
Celebes

SEXUAL DIFFERENCES
The males are more colourful, especially on the fins, and have a much larger "bulge" on the lower lip, which is typical of these fish, than the females. The males are also much smaller than the females.

LENGTH
Up to about 9 centimetres

ACCOMMODATION
These unusual fish belong in a larger aquarium with plenty of swimming space under the surface. This species likes to swim a lot in the top zone. They also enjoy jumping, so a cover is essential to keep them in the aquarium.

SOCIAL CHARACTERISTICS
Despite the predatory appearance of this fish, it is peaceful and can easily coexist with other fish. It is best to keep these fish in a small group.

TEMPERATURE AND WATER COMPOSITION
23-26°C. The fish are not particularly sensitive to the water composition, but they will feel much more comfortable in soft and slightly acidic water.

FOOD
In the wild this species catches insects and their larvae which fall onto the surface of the water. Feed this fish these types of food organisms to meet their nutritional needs. Dry food is also possible.

BREEDING
The halfbeak is viviparous but, unfortunately, it is not very productive. It is best

Nomorhamphus liemi liemi

to put a cluster of fry in a separate breeding tank (with the same water composition), so that they are not eaten by the parent fish. This is because they are quite large when born and have difficulty hiding.

Nothobranchius patrizii

FAMILY
Cyprinodontidae (egg-laying tooth carps)

SUB FAMILY
Rivulinae

HABITAT
East Africa

SEXUAL DIFFERENCES
It is very easy to see the difference between the sexes – the males are much more colourful than the females, which are virtually colourless.

LENGTH
The males grow to 3.5 or 4 centimetres long. The females remain rather smaller.

ACCOMMODATION
These fish are usually kept in a small special aquarium which is specially set up to meet their specific needs. A significant proportion of the substrate should consist of peat dust. These fish definitely need a variety of refuges, for example in the form of particularly dense vegetation and convoluted pieces of petrified wood.

Nothobranchius patrizii

Direct light coming in from outside is not beneficial to this species, so try to avoid this. The fish also do not appreciate excessively bright aquarium lighting. A thick covering of floating plants will filter the light naturally. They do not like a current.

SOCIAL CHARACTERISTICS
These fish should usually be kept together with a number of other like-minded robust killifish.
The fish normally get on quite well together, but always try to keep more females than males.

TEMPERATURE AND WATER COMPOSITION
20-28°C. Good filtration is essential to keep the water pure but make sure there is not too much movement in the water. Change one-third of the aquarium water each week, since the water will otherwise quickly become polluted. A pH of around 6.5 will be just fine.

FOOD
This species does not eat anything but small live food such as tubifex, small fruit flies, mosquito larvae and artemia. They are gluttons and need to be fed several times a day.

BREEDING
Breeding is similar to other seasonal killifish.

Nothobranchius rachovi

FAMILY
Cypronodontidae (egg-laying tooth carps)

SUB FAMILY
Rivulinae

HABITAT
Africa (mainly Mozambique), in pools which dry out in the dry season.

SEXUAL DIFFERENCES
The difference between the sexes can be seen at a glance – the males are spectacularly coloured, while the females are rather unremarkable in appearance.

LENGTH
Up to five centimetres.

Nothobranchius rachovi

20-21°C and after three to six months pour very soft water at around 18°C on the eggs. Then warm the water to 24°C. In this way you can simulate the natural process whereby the rainy season which fills up the shallow dried up pools in the jungle with a layer of water.

Osteoglossum bicirrhosum

FAMILY
Osteoglossidae

HABITAT
Amazon region, in shallow and stagnant water.

SEXUAL DIFFERENCES
The difference between the sexes cannot be seen properly until the fish are mature. The males have longer fins and are rather thinner than the females.

LENGTH
The fish reach lengths of more than a metre in the wild, but stay smaller in the aquarium.

ACCOMMODATION
N. rachovi is usually kept in a special aquarium. These fish do very well in smaller or medium-sized aquaria, as long as there are plenty of refuges (petrified wood and dense vegetation) and a dark coloured bottom. Like all other killifish, this species does not much like bright lighting and likes to live in quite still water.

SOCIAL CHARACTERISTICS
You can accommodate these fish in a substantial group with several males and twice as many females, or a single male and two or three females. If there are just two or three males in the aquarium, they will always fight. Because of their lifestyle and fact that the species makes high demands on the water composition, they are not suitable for a community aquarium.

TEMPERATURE AND WATER COMPOSITION
20-23°C, 4-12° gH, pH 6.5-7.

FOOD
The fish will eat dry food (Sera San) well, but they also need live food such as mosquito larvae, fruit flies and artemia (brine shrimps).

BREEDING
Breeding is similar to that of other seasonal killifish, but the difference with these fish is that they do not lay their eggs in a spawning substrate or Java moss, but simply on the bottom which, for breeding, should consist of peat dust. The eggs must undergo an artificial dry period of about six months if they are to hatch.

Put the eggs away in a plastic bag with moist peat dust at a temperature of

ACCOMMODATION
Due to the size of these fish, an aquarium about two metres long will very soon be needed. The fish are mainly to be found in the top zone, directly below the surface, so there must be sufficient swimming space there. It doesn't make much difference to them if the water is constantly in motion or if it is still.

A covering is essential because the fish

Osteoglossum bicirrhosum

have a tendency to leap out above the surface of the water, particularly if they see insects.

SOCIAL CHARACTERISTICS
This unusual fish is far from friendly. It can be aggressive, both towards its own kind and towards other aquarium dwellers. It should therefore be kept alone or with a few robust cichlids which occupy the bottom zone.

TEMPERATURE AND WATER COMPOSITION
25-29°C. These fish like the water to be slightly acidic (pH 6-6.5) and not too hard.

FOOD
In the wild this species mainly eats other fish and insects. They also need a similar diet in an aquarium, but they will also take cichlid sticks and freeze-dry food as well.

BREEDING
This fish incubates its eggs in its mouth (mouth brooder), where they are safe from any egg-eaters. It can take up to two months before the fry emerge from the mouth. By that time they are extremely large. It is obviously not possible to breed these fish in the aquarium due to lack of space.

Otocinclus affinis

FAMILY
Loricariidae (armoured catfish)

SUB FAMILY
Hypoptopomatinae

HABITAT
South-east Brazil

SEXUAL DIFFERENCES
Adult females are rather fatter and larger than adult males.

LENGTH
Up to about five centimetres

ACCOMMODATION
This species can be accommodated very comfortably in a small aquarium, but there must be enough refuges in the form of dense vegetation, petrified wood and stones. These fish like a current in the water, since they are accustomed to this in their natural habitat. They also like a rich supply of algae in the aquarium (in a partly sunny position).

SOCIAL CHARACTERISTICS
These fish are peaceful, both towards their own kind and with other fish. They mainly occupy the bottom zone and become active towards dusk, when they become quite active, grazing (algae) on the plants, stones and petrified wood. They like to interact with a few others of their kind.

TEMPERATURE AND WATER COMPOSITION
21-25°C. These fish do not make very high demands on the water composition, but the water must be crystal clear and as pure as possible.

FOOD
These fish only eat vegetable food. Once all the algae has been eaten, you can feed these fish with vegetable food tablets (Sera Viformo), but it is better to ensure that there is always a continuous supply of algae for the fish.

BREEDING
In good conditions, these fish will sometimes lay their eggs on the plants. The parent fish leave the eggs alone, but other aquarium dwellers will see them as a tasty snack. It is better to put the fish in a separate aquarium if you want them to breed.

Otocinclus affinis

Pachypanchax playfairy

PLAYFAIR'S PANCHAX

FAMILY
Cyprinodontidae (egg-laying tooth carps)

SUB FAMILY
Rivulinae

HABITAT
Madagascar, Zanzibar and the Seychelles

SEXUAL DIFFERENCES
The males are more intensely coloured than the females, which also have a dark spot on their dorsal fin.

LENGTH
Up to nine centimetres, depending on how much space is available.

ACCOMMODATION
This is one of the few killifish which will also do well in a community aquarium. They do like a dark substrate though, and plenty of refuges in the form of dense vegetation and petrified wood. A cover is essential; these fish quite often leap out above the surface, particularly if they have an insect in their sights. They prefer to occupy the top zone, usually just under the surface.

SOCIAL CHARACTERISTICS
The panchax does well in pairs. These fish can be kept with other fish without any problems.

TEMPERATURE AND WATER COMPOSITION
23-25°. The fish do not make any great demands on the water composition, but they prefer medium-hard and neutral water.

FOOD
The diet for these fish consists of live food such as insects (flying ants, fruit flies) and insect larvae (mosquito larvae). They will also happily eat dry food and dried and frozen food organisms.

BREEDING
These fish mate as a pair. The eggs are laid on feathery-leafed plants. One inconvenience is that they do not lay all

Pterophyllum scalare *(spotted variant)*

Pachypanchax playfairy

their eggs at once, but take several days over it and eat the eggs as they go. It is therefore necessary regularly to scoop out the eggs which have already been laid and put them in a separate aquarium, or shallow dish, with water at the same temperature (floating on the surface of the breeding tank). The fry eat tiny live food organisms.

Panaque nigrolineatus

GOLD NUGGET PLEC

FAMILY
Loricariidae (armoured catfish)

SUB FAMILY
Ancistrinae

Panaque nigrolineatus

Panaque nigrolineatus

This species is extremely friendly, both with its own kind and towards other fish. Despite its size, *P. nigrolineatus* can easily be kept with other smaller fish. This fish hides during the day, but after dusk and during the night it becomes active and goes looking for food. These fish prefer to occupy the bottom zone and scrape algae off the windows, plants, stones and petrified wood.

TEMPERATURE AND WATER COMPOSITION
22-26°C. The water composition is not important, but it is vital for the water to be clear and always in motion.

FOOD
This catfish only eats vegetable food. If there is not enough algae (left) in the aquarium, you must give this fish supplements of flaked plant food, food tablets (Sera Flora/Sera Viformo) and blanched green food.

BREEDING
Unknown.

SPECIAL REMARKS
Because of its feeding preferences, this fish is a perfect choice if your aquarium is covered with a lot of algae.

Panaque suttoni

FAMILY
Loricariidae (armoured catfish)

SUB FAMILY
Ancistrinae

HABITAT
Columbia

SEXUAL DIFFERENCES
The difference between the sexes is not yet known.

LENGTH
These fish can reach more than 20 centimetres in length in large aquaria with sufficient current, but they grow much larger in the wild.

ACCOMMODATION
This lively and active catfish belongs in a spacious aquarium with a powerful motorised filter to keep the water constantly in motion. Just like other catfish, they need refuges in the form of rocks and petrified wood. They much prefer an aquarium with algae to one which has just been set up.

HABITAT
South America (Amazon)

SEXUAL DIFFERENCES
Unknown

LENGTH
Up to 20 centimetres, but they usually remain rather smaller in the aquarium.

ACCOMMODATION
Due to its size and active lifestyle, *P. suttoni* is best kept in a largish aquarium. You must make sure that there are enough

Panaque suttoni

Panaque suttoni

refuges (for example rocks, petrified wood, thick, coarse-leafed plants, etc.). It is important to filter the water strongly, so that there is a strong current.

SOCIAL CHARACTERISTICS
These fish are very peaceful in every respect, both with each other and with the other aquarium dwellers. They keep to themselves. They hide during the day, and they usually do not become active until evening falls.

TEMPERATURE AND WATER COMPOSITION
21-25°C. These fish are not at all demanding as regards the water composition. The water does need to be very pure and clear, with a strong current.

FOOD
In the first instance this species eats algae and dried vegetable food (Sera Flora/Sera Premium), but this fish can usually also manage the food which the other inhabitants of the aquarium have not eaten and has fallen to the bottom.

BREEDING
So far there has been no successful breeding of these fish.

Pangasius pangasius

FAMILY
Pangasiidae (catfish)

HABITAT
The range of this fish species is large and covers almost the whole of Asia.

SEXUAL DIFFERENCES
Unknown.

LENGTH
In their natural habitat these unusual fish grow to more than a metre long, but they do not achieve this size in an aquarium due to the restricted space.

ACCOMMODATION
Because of their size and particularly active lifestyle, these fish only belong in largish aquaria, i.e. aquaria which are at least two metres long. They need a lot of swimming space.

SOCIAL CHARACTERISTICS
These fish are extremely lively: they swim vigorously through the aquarium all day long, eating whatever they encounter. They mainly occupy the middle and bottom zone.

TEMPERATURE AND WATER COMPOSITION
22-27°C. The water composition is not very important, but strong filtration is

Pangasius pangasius

Pangasius pangasius

vital. The water must always be in motion, just like the fish themselves.

FOOD
Above all this fish wants to eat a lot. Dry food (blanched) green food and live food will be taken readily and enjoyed.

BREEDING
Nothing is known so far about the breeding habits of this species.

SPECIAL REMARKS
Due to the large size of this fish (it also grows fast) and its enthusiastic swimming, this species is not really suitable for the average aquarium enthusiast. It quickly becomes a difficult and expensive affair keeping *P. pangasius* (and perhaps more than one specimen) in an appropriate space which also has to be heated and filtered.

Pantodon buchholzi

BUTTERFLY FISH

FAMILY
Pantodontidae (butterfly fish)

HABITAT
West Africa, in slow-flowing and calm, stagnant waters among dense vegetation.

SEXUAL DIFFERENCES
The difference between the sexes can be seen from the various types of tail fins; the foremost rays of the anal fins are extremely elongated in the male, while the females are rounded. The illustrations show male specimens.

LENGTH
Up to about 14 centimetres.

ACCOMMODATION
The butterfly fish belongs in a medium-sized or large aquarium, but these fish are also often kept in a paludarium. Butterfly fish usually occupy the top zone, just under the surface, and that is where they need space. No current is necessary the fish does not actually like it. Dense vegetation, particularly overhanging leaves, and some floating plants will quickly make these fish feel at home.

Like most fish which take their food from the surface of the water, the butterfly fish is somewhat prone to leaping out of the water, especially if it senses a tasty insect nearby. Their ability to jump is tremendous; they have been seen to leap

Pantodon buchholzi ♂

Pantodon buchholzi ♂

174

more than two metres in the wild. A cover is therefore absolutely essential.

SOCIAL CHARACTERISTICS
This striking fish species is, unfortunately, not the most sociable. Smaller fish, and fish which cannot get out of the way quickly (for example long-finned types), will be chased and bitten. These fish can be kept with other species, but they must be robust and hardy varieties which occupy the bottom and middle zone. These fish also do not always get on with each other, but they do very well as solitary specimens.

TEMPERATURE AND WATER COMPOSITION
24-28°C. These fish are not very demanding as regards the water composition, but they do prefer the water to be not too hard and neutral or slightly acidic (pH 6.5-7).

FOOD
The butterfly fish eats mainly live food, insects and their larvae in particular. You can give them specially bred fruit flies to eat, or mosquitoes and flies, as long as they are not too big. Dry food will be well received, but it will not do as a basic staple for this species.

BREEDING
These fish are not easy to breed. Under ideal conditions (that is to say, a well-matched pair in a separate breeding tank, the right water composition and a slightly higher temperature than the fish are used to) you may be lucky.

The eggs float on the surface and the fish hardly look at them, but for safety it is better to remove the parent fish or scoop up the eggs and transfer them into a separate aquarium. In the latter case, always use water from the breeding tank so that the water temperature stays the same.

Papiliochromus altispinosus

FAMILY
Cichlidae (cichlids)

Papiliochromis altispinosus

Northern part of South America

SEXUAL DIFFERENCES
The two sexes look very similar and can only be distinguished by an expert; provided that the fish are fully-grown. Mature females have a rather fuller stomach.

LENGTH
Up to about eight centimetres.

ACCOMMODATION
These small cichlids should be kept in a medium-sized or large aquarium. This is one of the few cichlid varieties which do not root around in the soil at the bottom of the tank. They do appreciate some refuges though. Dense vegetation, petrified wood and stones will be perfectly adequate, but the fish will be even happier with a good-sized, half-buried flowerpot (laid on its side).

SOCIAL CHARACTERISTICS
These fish are relatively good-natured, but smaller fish will be seen as food. They do very well with other hardy cichlid species. It is best to keep these fish in pairs. It is very difficult to tell whether two fish really are a pair, so you must observe the fish in the shop for some time. Within a larger group, pairs of fish usually form naturally and swim together.

TEMPERATURE AND WATER COMPOSITION
23-26°C. These fish prefer medium-hard water with a pH of about 6.5 or 7.

FOOD
These cichlids like dry food (cichlid sticks) and also live and frozen food organisms.

Paracheirodon axelrodi

BREEDING
A pair will breed in a community aquarium, given the right conditions, provided they are not constantly disturbed by the other aquarium dwellers. Both the eggs and the fry will be protected and cared for.

Paracheirodon axelrodi

CARDINAL TETRA

FAMILY
Characidae (characins)

SUB FAMILY
Tetragonopterinae

HABITAT
Around the edge of the Amazon region, mainly in the Rio Negro and Orinoco rivers.

SEXUAL DIFFERENCES
The males are thinner than the females, whose stomach is fuller and also rather "paler".

LENGTH
Up to about five centimetres.

ACCOMMODATION
Cardinal tetra can be kept in a smallish aquarium but, because these fish are enthusiastic and vigorous swimmers, a medium-sized aquarium is a better choice. They can be kept with a range of fish species and their friendly nature makes them well suited for the community aquarium.
Very brightly lit aquaria are not very suitable for this species.

Paracheirodon axelrodi

A dark substrate, sufficient peripheral vegetation and floating plants will make these fish feel at home and present them at their best. They do enjoy a current in the water, but this is not essential.

SOCIAL CHARACTERISTICS
These fish are particularly peaceful, both towards each other and with other aquarium dwellers.Cardinal tetras form shoals of thousands of fish in the wild. Obviously we cannot achieve this in the aquarium, but you should remember that a substantial shoal, from around twenty fish, is not only better for the fish themselves, but is also a spectacular sight. The cardinal tetra is an active little fish which prefers to inhabit the middle zone.

TEMPERATURE AND WATER COMPOSITION
24-28°C. The ideal values are soft or very soft (2-8° gH) and slightly acidic (pH 6) water but the fish will sometimes do well for a long time in water which differs from this. If you want to enjoy your shoal of cardinal tetras for a longer period, you must meet their needs concerning water quality.

FOOD
The cardinal tetra is not difficult to feed. It very much likes dry food and small live food such as tubifex and water fleas.

BREEDING
It is very difficult to persuade cardinal tetras to mate. What is more the fry are very sensitive and prone to disease.
Always use a separate breeding tank which has been disinfected beforehand. Also disinfect all other materials that you use. Aeration is not necessary in the first instance. The breeding tank should never be in a well-lit position; both the parent fish and the fry will do much better if the lighting is dim.
Cardinal tetras are egg-eaters, so a substrate spawner fixed a few centimetres above the bottom is absolutely necessary. These fish are free layers and prefer to lay their eggs over Java moss. The fry can be fed during the first week on microscopic live organisms and fine powdered food will do after that.

Paracheirodon innesi

NEON TETRA

FAMILY
Characidae (characins)

SUB FAMILY
Tetragonopterinae

HABITAT
The upper reaches of the Amazon region, in small jungle streams.

SEXUAL DIFFERENCES
The males are slimmer than the females, which can be recognised by their fatter stomachs.

LENGTH
Up to four centimetres.

ACCOMMODATION
The neon tetra will do excellently in a smaller community aquarium, which does not

Neon tetras are shoaling fish

Paracheirodon innesi

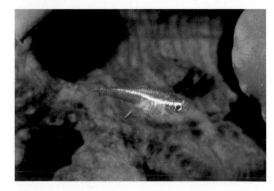

need to be very large. Peripheral vegetation and some floating plants are preferable, as is a dark substrate. Darker coloured gravel will do very well. These lively and popular fish enjoy a current in the aquarium.

SOCIAL CHARACTERISTICS
Neon tetras are shoaling fish and therefore belong in a largish shoal. This will make these fish feel safe and comfortable. Above all, such a large shoal is a much more attractive sight. They leave other fish alone but, conversely, these fish should never be kept with predatory fish. Neon tetras mainly stay the middle zone and are quite active.

TEMPERATURE AND WATER COMPOSITION
21-24°C. These fish do well in various different water compositions, but they definitely prefer soft to medium-hard water and a pH value of around 6 to 6.5.

FOOD
These fish are easy to feed. They eat both dry and small live food.

BREEDING
As regards breeding, the neon tetra is comparable to the cardinal tetra (*Paracheirodon axelrodi*), but the neons are actually easier.

VARIANTS
A long-finned neon tetra has now been bred, albeit only on a very small scale.

Paracheirodon innesi *(variant)*

There is also a less colourful variety in which the blue pigment is concentrated mainly on the head. Neither of these variants are very popular.

SPECIAL REMARKS
Like the cardinal tetra, the neon tetra is one of the most popular fish. Beginners often get them mixed up. The neon tetra not only stays smaller than the cardinal, but it always has a white stomach, while the cardinal has a red stomach. If you are starting out as an aquarist and cannot choose between the two varieties, it is best to choose a shoal of neon tetras.
This species is easier to satisfy and also tougher.

Paracyprichromis brieni

FAMILY
Cichlidae (cichlids)

HABITAT
Africa, Lake Tanganyika

SEXUAL DIFFERENCES
The males are rather larger and more colourful than the females.

LENGTH
Up to about 10 centimetres.

ACCOMMODATION
These lively cichlids need space and an aquarium at least 1 metre wide is therefore essential. Decorate the aquarium with petrified wood, stones and plenty of peripheral vegetation.

SOCIAL CHARACTERISTICS
These fish can be kept in pairs but since they like to form larger groups in the wild, you can also keep them in an aquarium with several of the same species. These fish are reasonably good-natured, both towards their own kind and towards other aquarium dwellers, but small fish are seen as food.

TEMPERATURE AND WATER COMPOSITION
23-27°C. The water composition is not very important, but a neutral pH value and medium to moderately hard water is preferable.

Paracyprichromis brieni

Peckoltia vittata

FAMILY
Loricariidae (armoured catfish)

SUB FAMILY
Ancistrinae

HABITAT
Amazon region.

SEXUAL DIFFERENCES
Unknown.

LENGTH
Up to about 15 centimetres.

FOOD
This species eats both dried and live food.

BREEDING
Paracyprichromis brieni is a mouth brooder. This is not a very productive species.

ACCOMMODATION
This armoured catfish does best in a medium-sized aquarium in which there are plenty of algae available. Sufficient refuges, mainly in the form of convoluted pieces of petrified wood and suitable plants, are absolutely essential for these

Peckoltia vittata

fish. They also need a strong current in the water.

This species is usually very peaceful, both in respect to other fish and with their own kind. They keep to themselves.

They usually "sleep" during the day in a sheltered place and you will not very often see them swimming, but when evening falls they become active and go out looking for food.

TEMPERATURE AND WATER COMPOSITION
23-25°C. This fish does well regardless of the water composition, but it does need absolutely crystal clear and pure water. A powerful motorised filter will come in handy here.

FOOD
This species only eats vegetable food, with the emphasis on algae. If there is not enough algae available in the aquarium (any more) it will definitely be necessary to feed this fish on vegetable food tablets and/or blanched lettuce leaves. Food should not be given until dusk, otherwise the other aquarium dwellers will have eaten it before this fish goes out looking for food.

BREEDING
So far, not much is known about how these fish reproduce.

Pelvicachromis humilis

FAMILY
Cichlidae (cichlids)

HABITAT
West Africa

SEXUAL DIFFERENCES
The fin ends in the males are pointed, while those of the female are more rounded. The males are also larger.

LENGTH
Up to 12 centimetres (male)

ACCOMMODATION
These fish like to stay near and in their refuge. This might be a convoluted piece of petrified wood or a rock formation sheltering the fish from above. The substrate should not be too coarse or sharp since otherwise these fish, which enjoy rooting around in the bottom, could be injured.

Pelvicachromis humilis particularly appreciates a shady aquarium; you can create shady spots using overhanging plants and floating plants. The aquarium water must be continuously in motion.

SOCIAL CHARACTERISTICS
These fish form inseparable pairs which withdraw into a territory. You definitely should not keep them with small or slow species. However it is quite possible to keep them together with larger and faster swimming fish, other cichlids or larger catfish.

TEMPERATURE AND WATER COMPOSITION
23-26°C, 4-10° gH, pH 6 – 7.

FOOD
P. humilis is not difficult to feed. Cichlid sticks and dried and frozen food organisms will be eaten readily. Also give the fish some live food.

Pelvicachromis humilis

Pelvicachromis humilis ♀

If you want some offspring from your pair of *P. humilis*, you must make the water softer (Up to about 2° gH). The pH level should be about 6. In this way you will be coming close to the water values which prevail during the mating season. The fish respond to this by laying their eggs in the hollow.

Both parent fish tend and protect not only the eggs but also the fry.

Pelvicachromis pulcher

PURPLE CICHLID

FAMILY
Cichlidae (cichlids)

HABITAT
West Africa (Cameroon and Nigeria)

SEXUAL DIFFERENCES
It is easy to see the difference between the sexes, certainly when the fish are mature. The females are smaller and somewhat fatter than the males. The females also have a red-coloured belly and rounded fins, while the fins on the male are pointed.

LENGTH
Up to 10 centimetres (male).

ACCOMMODATION
The purple cichlid has been known and loved for a long time and can be kept either in small or medium-sized aquaria. It is very important for this species to have

Pelvicachromis pulcher ♀

Pelvicachromis pulcher ♂

cave-like refuges. These can be in the form of stones or petrified wood, but you will see that if you bury an inverted flower-pot (with the hole enlarged and the sharp edges filed smooth) a few centimetres into the gravel, that these fish will have taken possession in no time at all. They will certainly do so if the pot is situated in a sheltered position amongst or under some plants.

Since these fish like digging in the bottom, a thick layer of small, rounded gravel is desirable. A current is acceptable, but the fish will tend to look for calmer spots.

SOCIAL CHARACTERISTICS
Purple cichlids fit in very well in a community aquarium, as long as there is absolutely no overcrowding because the fish are territorial. Other fish which stray into the territory will be chased away, but otherwise the purple cichlid will leave them alone and will seldom attack them. They are always kept as a pair and the two

Pelvicachromis pulcher

Pelvicachromis pulcher *with fry*

stay very close together. They look for food among the plants and in other sheltered places near the bottom.

TEMPERATURE AND WATER COMPOSITION
22-25°C. They make few demands on the water composition. In the wild these fish even live in coastal areas in brackish water.

FOOD
The purple cichlid eats everything except plants and algae. They are perfectly capable of living on a varied diet of dry food, but live food and frozen food organisms will be much appreciated from time to time.

BREEDING
Many aquarists agree that purple cichlids are easy to breed. Often you do not need any modifications in the water composition and you do not usually have to create any special circumstances to put the fish in the mood to breed. If you do want to accelerate the process, it helps if the water is slightly on the acidic side, at around 6 or 6.5 pH. The eggs will be laid in the flowerpot and tended and cared for by both parents. The numerous fry will also be looked after and protected.

During this period the purple cichlids are obviously much less tolerant of the other aquarium dwellers, which is of course quite reasonable. Their young will do well on fine powdered food (Sera Micron) and the smallest live food such as newly-hatched brine shrimps (artemia), which you can easily breed. The eggs of these food organisms can be bought in all specialist aquarium centres. You can leave the fry with the parent fish for some time. By watching the behaviour of the parent fish you will see for yourself when they have had enough.

SPECIAL REMARKS
Because of its interesting behaviour and toughness, the purple cichlid is a very suitable fish for beginners.

Pelvicachromis roloffi

FAMILY
Cichlidae (cichlids)

HABITAT
West Africa

SEXUAL DIFFERENCES
The difference between the sexes is easy to see. The females are smaller and fatter than the males and have a pinkish-purple coloured stomach. The males have longer and more pointed fins.

LENGTH
Up to about eight centimetres (male)

ACCOMMODATION
This cichlid, a relative of the purple cichlid, needs plenty of refuges. These might be convoluted pieces of petrified wood, some stones or a half-buried flowerpot. These fish do not much like bright lighting; plant lots of vegetation in

Pelvicachromis roloffi ♀

Pelvicachromis roloffi ♂

the aquarium and allow plants to float on the surface to create shadowy places.

This species does dig around on the bottom now and then. To prevent injury to this fish, the substrate should consist of well washed coarse sand or fine gravel.

SOCIAL CHARACTERISTICS
This species is territorial. A pair stays close together and is always to be found close to its refuge. The fish are usually quiet, peaceful and cautious and will do well in a community aquarium, as long as there is enough space available for all the inhabitants. This species mainly occupies the bottom zone.

TEMPERATURE AND WATER COMPOSITION
24-26°C. In their natural habitat these fish live in shallow waters in the jungle. Partly due to the many leaves and roots in the water it is very acidic and very soft (pH 6, 2-3° gH). The fish also prefer somewhat softer water in an aquarium, but they are very adaptable and can also be kept in harder and less acidic water.

FOOD
These small cichlids are not very difficult to feed. Dry food will go down well and they will also eat vegetable food occasionally. However they do like some small live food such as mosquito larvae, tubifex and water fleas on a regular basis.

BREEDING
For breeding these fish are quite similar to the purple cichlids, but the main difference lies in the water composition. *P. Roloffi* is more inclined to reproduce in very soft water.

Pelviciachromis suboccelatus

FAMILY
Cichlidae (cichlids)

HABITAT
West Africa, in coastal regions.

SEXUAL DIFFERENCES
Both sexes are very easy to recognise. The male fish are much larger than the females and have tapering fins. The females are also conspicuous because of their more intense colouring.

LENGTH
Up to 10 centimetres (male).

ACCOMMODATION
These cichlids will do best when housed in a medium-sized aquarium. The fish prefer to occupy the bottom zone and rarely venture far from their territory. It is definitely necessary to provide plenty of

Pelvicachromis suboccelatus ♀

Pelvicachromis suboccelatus ♂

refuges, such as larger convoluted pieces of petrified wood, rocks or possibly an upside down flowerpot (obviously with an enlarged opening and any sharp edges removed).

These fish like to burrow in the bottom. A fine and definitely not sharp gravel bottom will allow them to do this.

SOCIAL CHARACTERISTICS

These cichlids are kept in pairs. They form a territory and will not allow any other fish into it, but they are not really aggressive and that is why they can also be kept in a community aquarium.

If the other fish in the aquarium are too small their lives may not be quite safe with these fish, so it is best to keep them alongside robust species. Make sure that there is enough space for them to form territories because overcrowding will oblige them to constantly attack the other fish.

TEMPERATURE AND WATER COMPOSITION

22-25°C. They are not very demanding as regards the water composition, but if these fish obviously do not feel at ease when there is sufficient food and plenty of refuges, add a few tablespoons of (iodine free) salt to the water.

FOOD

These fish eat both dried and live food as well as frozen food organisms.

BREEDING

When it comes to breeding these cichlids are similar to the purple cichlid.

Pelvicachromis taeniatius

FAMILY
Cichlidae (cichlids)

HABITAT
West Africa, in coastal regions

SEXUAL DIFFERENCES

The males and females are easy to distinguish; the males are larger and have larger and more pointed fins, while the females are smaller and fatter and have pinkish-purple colouring on their bellies.

LENGTH
Up to 10 centimetres (♂)

ACCOMMODATION

These cichlids are not very fond of bright light and you should therefore provide some floating plants on the surface and plant the aquarium with abundant large, coarse-leafed plant species. This makes it possible to create areas of shadow. Like all members of this cichlid family, *P. taeniatius* needs refuges in the form of an upturned or half-buried flowerpot, stones or convoluted pieces of petrified wood. This species likes to dig. A soft bottom consisting of sand, small rounded gravel or a combination of these is very suitable, since it will ensure that the fish cannot hurt themselves.

SOCIAL CHARACTERISTICS

These fish live in pairs and mainly stay around their territory near a refuge (close to the bottom). Other fish will usually be left alone, as long as they do not come inside their territory. There must

Pelvicachromis taeniatus ♂

Pelvicachromis taeniatus ♀

therefore be enough space in the aquarium for all the inhabitants. You can keep this species in a largish community aquarium.

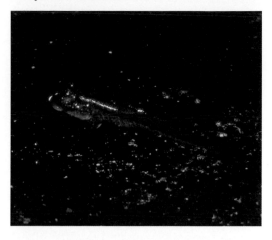

TEMPERATURE AND WATER COMPOSITION
23-25°C. P. taeniatus is highly adaptable, but will do much better, and will also breed more quickly, in slightly acidic and soft to medium-hard water.

FOOD
Both live food (mosquito larvae, tubifex, brine shrimps and water fleas) and frozen food organisms go down very well, but these fish can also easily survive on dry food. Every now and then give them a food tablet containing plenty of vegetable food, since P. taeniatus does need this occasionally.

BREEDING
As regards breeding this fish is similar to Pelvicachromis pulcher (purple cichlid) but breeding is generally less successful.

Periopthalmus barbarus

BLOTCHED MUDSKIPPER

FAMILY
Gobiidae (gobies)

HABITAT
The mudskipper is found in various parts of the world. It lives near sandy banks in brackish water in coastal areas of Africa and Australia, as well as South East Asia.

SEXUAL DIFFERENCES
Unknown

LENGTH
From 10 to 14 centimetres

ACCOMMODATION
The mud skipper lives partly in and partly out of the water. The aquarium must therefore be specially designed for these fish. The bottom consists of sand. The tank can be decorated with petrified wood and stones and marsh plants such as spathiphyllum and *Acorus gramineus*. The area underwater must gradually slope up to the bank area.

Mudskippers are very sensitive to cold

and drying out; a properly sealed cover is essential to prevent heat loss.

SOCIAL CHARACTERISTICS
These unusual creatures form a territory into which they will not tolerate any of their own kind. The largest part of the day is spent "sunning", which involves the fish lying in a shallow area of water. If you want to keep more of the same fish, you will need a spacious aquarium (at least 80 centimetres wide).

TEMPERATURE AND WATER COMPOSITION
26-30°C. Mudskippers are brackish water fish, which means that the water composition must be halfway between seawater and fresh water.

FOOD
Mudskippers eat both dry food and tubifex.

BREEDING
So far there have been no reports of successful breeding.

Petitella georgiae

CONGO TETRA

FAMILY
Alestidae (African characins)

SUB FAMILY
Alestinae

Congo River and surrounding area (Africa)

SEXUAL DIFFERENCES
The difference between the sexes is clearly visible. The males are larger and have longer fins than the females.

LENGTH
Up to about 11 centimetres.

ACCOMMODATION
This large and fast swimming shoaling fish is best kept in a rather large, elongated aquarium. There will not be enough space in small aquaria for this fish to swim around. It appreciates peripheral vegetation. A dark substrate and floating plants will bring out its colours to best effect.

SOCIAL CHARACTERISTICS
The Congo tetra is a very good-natured shoaling fish which leaves other aquarium dwellers in peace.
Always keep these fish in a shoal of at least seven fish and do not put them with aggressive species. They mainly occupy the middle or top zone.

TEMPERATURE AND WATER COMPOSITION
24-26°C, pH 6 or 6.5. These fish feel more comfortable in soft water than in hard or medium-hard water. Filter over peat.

FOOD
The Congo tetra eats almost everything it encounters. Various types of dry food, mosquito larvae, small insects, water fleas and also vegetable food (blanched lettuce leaves) will all go down well.

BREEDING
Breeding these fish is definitely not easy. It all depends on the correct water composition (3.5° gH, pH 6), plenty of peace and quiet, diffuse lighting and a compatible pair in peak breeding condition.
The fish are free layers and eat their own eggs.

SPECIAL REMARKS
The disadvantage of keeping this well-known African, other than that it is difficult to keep it healthy, is that it sometimes has a tendency to nibble soft-leafed plants. To prevent this use harder plant varieties in the aquarium and give the fish regular vegetable food.

Phenacogrammus interruptus

FAMILY
Pimelodidae

SUB FAMILY
Pimelodinae

HABITAT
South America

SEXUAL DIFFERENCES
None yet known.

LENGTH
Up to 15 centimetres.

ACCOMMODATION
These catfish will do best in a rather spacious aquarium (at least 80 centimetres). They need plenty of refuges, some shady areas and a dark substrate,

Petitella georgiae

Phenacogrammus interruptus ♂

and prefer a current in the water. You will rarely catch sight of them in an aquarium which is too strongly lit. This species likes the twilight hours.

SOCIAL CHARACTERISTICS
This catfish is a good-natured aquarium inhabitant which does very well in community aquaria. They prefer to occupy the bottom zone, staying near the refuges. They can be kept either as solitary fish and in small groups, but they do not form a real shoal. They usually hide during the day and you will not often catch sight of them, but they come out of their refuges at dusk and begin to search for food.

They are also active at night, even if it is dark; they find their way around by using their antennae.

TEMPERATURE AND WATER COMPOSITION
22-26°C. The water composition is not very important, but keep the water pure and clear and strongly filtered. Regularly changing part of the aquarium water is also desirable.

FOOD
This fish actually eats everything. First of all it will track down and clean up food which the other aquarium dwellers have not eaten. It also needs food tablets for bottom dwellers (Sera Viformo). Small live food or frozen food organisms (tubifex) will also be taken happily by these eye-catching fish. You should certainly not feed these fish before dusk.

BREEDING
Nothing is known so far about the breeding habits of these fish.

Phenacogrammus interruptus ♀

Pimelodus pictus

FAMILY
Pimelodidae

SUB FAMILY
Pimelodinae

HABITAT
South America

SEXUAL DIFFERENCES
None yet known.

LENGTH
Up to 15 centimetres.

ACCOMMODATION
These catfish will do best in a rather spacious aquarium (at least 80 centimetres). They need plenty of refuges, some shady areas and a dark substrate, and prefer a current in the water.

You will rarely catch sight of them in an aquarium which is too strongly lit. This species likes the twilight hours.

SOCIAL CHARACTERISTICS
This catfish is a good-natured aquarium inhabitant which does very well in community aquaria. They prefer to occupy the bottom zone, staying near the refuges. They can be kept either as solitary fish and in small groups, but they do not form a real shoal. They usually hide during the day and you will not often catch sight of them, but they come out of their refuges at dusk and begin to search for food.

They are also active at night, even if it is dark; they find their way around by using their antennae.

TEMPERATURE AND WATER COMPOSITION
22-26°C. The water composition is not very important, but keep the water pure and clear and strongly filtered. Regularly changing part of the aquarium water is also desirable.

FOOD
This fish actually eats everything. First of all it will track down and clean up food which the other aquarium dwellers have not eaten. It also needs food tablets for bottom dwellers (Sera Viformo). Small live food or frozen food organisms (tubi-

fex) will also be taken happily by these eye-catching fish. You should certainly not feed these fish before dusk.

BREEDING
Nothing is known so far about the breeding habits of these fish.

Poecilia melanogaster
(syn. Limia melanogaster*)*

FAMILY
Poeciliidae (egg-laying tooth carps)

SUB FAMILY
Poeciliinae

HABITAT
(Fresh water) streams and small lakes in Haiti and Jamaica.

SEXUAL DIFFERENCES
The males are recognisable by the gonopodium, an anal fin transformed into a sexual organ. They also have more yellow pigment in their tail fin than the females.

LENGTH
Up to about six centimetres.

ACCOMMODATION
This species does outstandingly well in smaller community aquaria in which there is not only sufficient swimming space (primarily in the top zone) but also feathery-leafed, dense vegetation. The fish like to graze on algae, so they will prefer an older aquarium in which algae has already formed.

SOCIAL CHARACTERISTICS
Since the males actively chase the females and continuously try to mate with them, it is better to keep more females than males. Males are tolerant of each other and will also leave other fish in peace.

TEMPERATURE AND WATER COMPOSITION
22-26°C. These fish are easy to satisfy as regards the water composition, but hard water is definitely preferred to soft water.

Poecilia melanogaster ♂

LENGTH
Up to about 6.5 cm

ACCOMMODATION
These viviparous fish can easily be kept in a smallish aquarium. Free space for swimming, particularly in the top zone, and dense, feathery-leaved peripheral vegetation are both desirable.

SOCIAL CHARACTERISTICS
These fish are problem-free in company with their own kind and other aquarium dwellers. They are very lively, however, and timid fish cannot always cope with this. Since the males are fanatical about chasing the females, it is best to keep more females than males.

FOOD
Both small insects and their larvae will go down well. Dry food will do very well as a basic staple, as long as it contains vegetable foodstuffs (Sera Flora/Sera Premium).

TEMPERATURE AND WATER COMPOSITION
22-26°C. This fish is not very demanding as regards the water composition. If they do not do very well you can add a few tablespoons of (iodine free) cooking salt to the water in the aquarium.

FOOD
These fish eat algae, live food and flaked food (Sera Flora)

BREEDING
The females regularly conceive and bear live young which can look after themselves immediately after birth. The strongest fry will survive in an aquarium with dense vegetation, plenty of floating plants and Java moss, but if you want to keep more young, you can put a heavily pregnant female, recognisable by the black pregnancy spot on her anal fin and her fat stomach, into a separate aquarium with dense vegetation. The fry eat mainly algae, so they will have more food at their disposal if the aquarium is situated in a sunny spot.

BREEDING
This species is viviparous and under the right conditions the female will regularly bear young which are able to look after themselves immediately after birth. The fry can be reared on fine powdered food (Sera Micron). They also like to eat algae.

Poecilia perugiae

FAMILY
Poeciliidae (egg-laying tooth carps)

SUB FAMILY
Poecilinae

HABITAT
Haiti

SEXUAL DIFFERENCES
The males are recognisable by their anal fin which has been transformed into a sexual organ, the gonopodium.

Poecilia perugiae ♂

Poecilia perugiae ♀

Poecilia reticulata
(syn. Lebistes reticulatus)

GUPPY

FAMILY
Poeciliidae (egg-laying tooth carps)

HABITAT
The original sources of this particularly well-known fish are Central and South America (Brazil and Barbados). Since these fish are released in large numbers all the year round to combat malaria mosquitoes, we now encounter them in many different areas all over the world.

It has been found that they can cope - and breed in – the most diverse water conditions in the wild. They are particularly adaptable, as is demonstrated by the fact that guppies are found not only in fresh and brackish water, but also in pure sea water.

SEXUAL DIFFERENCES
The males are distinguishable by their anal fin which has been transformed into a reproductive organ, called a "gonopodium" in ovoviparous fish. The males are also significantly smaller and slimmer than the females. They are often also much more colourful, especially on the body.

LENGTH
Up to about six centimetres (♂).

ACCOMMODATION
Guppies are not very demanding and can very easily be kept in smaller aquaria. Plenty of fine-leafed vegetation is desirable. These fish can look very pale against a white or light-coloured substrate. A darker gravel bottom is therefore more suitable.

SOCIAL CHARACTERISTICS
These lively fish are extremely tolerant, not only towards each other, but also towards other fish, which makes them eminently suitable for the community aquarium. Since guppy males almost never stop attempting to mate with the females, it is better to keep more females than males.
The male variants often have very long fins, as a result of which they make an easy target for less friendly fish species. Do not keep them together with intolerant or predatory fish. Guppies are strong swimmers which visit all the zones, but prefer to occupy the very highest zone.

TEMPERATURE AND WATER COMPOSITION
17-27°C. These fish do well in very diverse water conditions, but a pH close to

Poecilia reticulata ♀

Poecilia reticulata ♂

Poecilia reticulata ♀

Poecilia reticulata ♂

neutral and water which is not too hard (less than 25° gH) is ideal. A small amount of added sea salt will be appreciated. You can also use cooking salt, as long as it is iodine free.

FOOD
Guppies are omnivores and do very well on dry food to which extra vegetable material has been added (Sera Flora/Sera Premium). They have been nicknamed mosquito fish because they can consume a large number of (red) mosquito larvae in a short time. These must certainly not be omitted from their diet. Water fleas and artemia (brine shrimps) are also taken with pleasure.

BREEDING
Guppies are very fertile fish, which has led to their sometimes being nicknamed "million fish". From a single mating session the female guppy can produce several clusters of 10-70 fry each at intervals. The fry can look after themselves immediately after birth, but they are often seen by their parents or other residents of the aquarium as a tasty snack. In community aquaria with sufficient refuges in the form of Java moss, feathery-leafed vegetation and floating plans, the strongest fry will survive without any special care.

They will grow very nicely on a diet of fine powdered food and recently hatched artemia.

If you want to keep more of the fry alive you can transfer the pregnant female, who can be recognised by her fat stomach and black pregnancy spot, to a separate tank with plenty of vegetation.

VARIANTS
A huge number of different types of guppies have been bred, and they differ not only in colouring but also in the shape of the tail. The most familiar of these will be the flag tail or triangle tail, but there are also undersword, oversword, double sword, spade tailed, round tailed and spear tailed guppies.

The best known guppy variants are the red, black and variegated, but the "snakeskin" and a yellow and black variety are also extremely fashionable. We mainly find the tough, short-tailed original guppies in the wild, but even these fish are not all uniform in colour. The females are not usually the best when it comes to rich colouring, but longer-finned females and females with better colouring have also been bred over the years.

Poecilia reticulata, *wildvang*

Poecilia reticulata *(double sword)* (♂)

Poecilia reticulata *(snakeskin)* (♂)

Because of their great adaptability, guppies are often underestimated. The wild-caught guppies, which are occasionally imported, are much stronger than the specially bred variants.

Poecilia sphenops

BLACK MOLLY

FAMILY
Poeciliidae (egg-laying tooth carps)

HABITAT
The black molly is not found in the wild. The original form came from Mexico.

SEXUAL DIFFERENCES
Males can be distinguished from the females by the anal fin, which has been transformed into a sexual organ (gonopodium).

LENGTH
Up to about six centimetres.

ACCOMMODATION
These lively fish can easily be kept in smaller aquaria, but they do need dense peripheral vegetation and plenty of space for swimming. A coating of algae is more than desirable.

SOCIAL CHARACTERISTICS

Black mollies are very peaceful both towards each other and towards other fish, which makes them extremely suitable for a community aquarium. They are eye-catching, active and much-loved aquarium dwellers.

Unfortunately they are somewhat susceptible to diseases such as white spot and fungus. These unpleasant conditions can arise as a result of stress (overcrowding or transportation) and excessively low water temperatures. In spite of this they are strong and usually respond well to medication.

TEMPERATURE AND WATER COMPOSITION

26-28°C. These fish make few demands on the water composition, but a regular addition of a few heaped tablespoons of sea salt (or cooking salt without iodine) is necessary to keep them in good health.

FOOD

The black molly is principally an algae eater. This species can remain healthy all its life if kept on dry food with a large quantity of vegetable food in it (Sera Premium/Sera Flora). They will graze algae from the stones and plants.

A suitable living environment for a black molly is an aquarium which has been use for some time and is situated where direct sunlight can shine on it now and then. Algae will already have formed in an aquarium of this kind. Small live food is also readily taken.

BREEDING

Black mollies are ovoviparous fish, which means that they produce live young which can look after themselves when born.

Poecilia sphenops *(lyre-tailed variant)* (♀)

In a less crowded aquarium with sufficient refuges and algae growth, the strongest fry will survive without any special care. They can be fed on fine powdered food.

VARIANTS

The black molly as we know it, is a variant form which is not found in the wild. The wild-caught *Poecilia sphenops* is almost transparent, with only a few black flecks and a blue, metallic lustre on the body. The black molly is therefore the result of breeding, presumably as a result of crossing the flecked *P. Sphenops* with sailfin mollies. These varieties will cross-breed quite readily if they are kept in the same aquarium. It is therefore better not to do this.

Lyre-tailed varieties, sailfin varieties and spotted mollies are also known.

Poecilia sphenops *(spotted variant)*

Poecilia sphenops *above* (♂), *below* (♀)

Poecilia velifera

Poecilia velifera *(golden variant)* (♂)

FAMILY
Poeciliidae (egg-laying tooth carps)

HABITAT
Mexico, particularly in brackish water on the Yucatan peninsula.

SEXUAL DIFFERENCES
Apart from its reproductive organ (gonopodium) the mature male can also be distinguished by its enormous dorsal fin.

LENGTH
Up to about 18 centimetres, but these fish usually stay smaller due to lack of space.

ACCOMMODATION
Giant sailfin mollies are strong swimmers and therefore belong in larger aquaria with sufficient swimming space. A width of 80 centimetres is the minimum. The fish like a current in the water. Since they

like eating algae, a recently set up aquarium is not (initially) suitable for them. A much better home will be an aquarium which has been in use for longer and contains plenty of algae.

SOCIAL CHARACTERISTICS
Giant sailfin mollies are active and boisterous swimmers. They do not therefore belong in an aquarium with shy or sensitive fish. They are extremely peaceful with respect to other aquarium dwellers

Poecilia velifera *(original form)*

and do very well in a community aquarium with other friendly species.

Giant sailfin mollies can be kept either as a pair or in a group. Dominant males will sometimes make life difficult for weaker males of the same species. Intervene early on if you notice this happening.

TEMPERATURE AND WATER COMPOSITION
25-28°C. They prefer quite hard water. Add a tablespoonful of sea salt or iodine-free cooking salt to every 10 litres of water.

FOOD
Giant sailfin mollies are omnivores and eat a lot, with a predilection for algae and other vegetable food. These fish will greedily consume dry food, but always give them dry food which mostly consists of vegetable material (Sera Flora/Sera Premium). They will also happily eat live food.

BREEDING
These ovoviparous fish can give birth to large clusters (up to 70 fish). The fry can take care of themselves immediately after birth, but rearing these small fish until they are large adult specimens is extremely difficult. The best breeders put the fry in a very spacious aquarium with strong aeration and sufficient current in the water. Make sure the aquarium is in sunlight now and then, so that plenty of algae can grow, and add some salt to the water regularly.

It can sometimes take as much as two years until the male's characteristic high sailfin is fully developed and it will not develop at all in smaller aquaria, or if the fish are not bred under ideal conditions.

VARIANTS
Giant sailfin mollies can be obtained in various colours. The "natural colour" is easily the most recognisable and frequently seen colour. The gold coloured giant sailfin molly, with or without red eyes, and the silvery-white and spotted varieties are also very fashionable.
Poecilia latipinna is a separate species which is often confused with the giant sailfin molly and will cross-breed with it (as it also will with the black molly). Always keep these varieties separate from each other.

SPECIAL REMARKS
Despite the great popularity of these fish, they are not easy to keep in good condition. Too low a water temperature, which causes the fish to lose weight and "oscillate", is the most common complaint, but too little added salt or a diet containing insufficient algae will also cause your fish to become sick.

Potamotrygon motoro

OCELLATED FRESHWATER STINGRAY

FAMILY
Potamotrygonidae (freshwater rays)

HABITAT
South America

SEXUAL DIFFERENCES
Unknown

LENGTH
Up to about 60 centimetres.

ACCOMMODATION
These are a very special fish species which need space and therefore belong in a very large, roomy aquarium. Plants will restrict their freedom of movement, so it is better to remove them, but floating plants can obviously remain. The fish need well-washed sand as a substrate, and like to dig around in it.

SOCIAL CHARACTERISTICS
These fish are not often combined with other fish because they see them as a welcome supplement to their diet. Imma-

Potamotrygon motoro

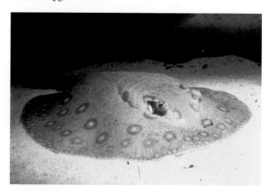

ture fish will go well with large surface dwellers or a few others of their kind, but older fish live practically alone. It is therefore best to keep only one specimen in the aquarium. These rays are quite active and lively and move around the aquarium in a remarkable way.

TEMPERATURE AND WATER COMPOSITION
23-26°C. These fish do not make great demands on the water composition, although rather soft, slightly acidic water is ideal. Make sure the water is free of waste matter. The fish like some movement in the water (strong filtration).

FEED
Young fish eat small live food such as artemia, mosquito larvae and small snails. Larger rays need more solid food, and like fish, large snails, earthworms, shrimps, pieces of meat and fish, mussel flesh and crab. Dry food will sometimes be accepted by both adults and fry.

BREEDING
These unusual fish have not yet been bred in the aquarium, but in the wild it has been observed that the fish give birth to live young.

SPECIAL REMARKS
Take care with this freshwater ray. It may sting if it gets the idea that it is being threatened.

Pristella maxillarus (syn. Pristella riddlei)

PRISTELLA

FAMILY
Characidae (characins)

SUB FAMILY
Tetragonopteridae

HABITAT
Brazil, Surinam, Trinidad, Venezuela and Guyana, in both running and stagnant water.

SEXUAL DIFFERENCES
The females are larger and have a fuller stomach.

Up to about 5.5 centimetres.

ACCOMMODATION
The pristella is rightly described as a fish for beginners because it is particularly undemanding. This species will feels at home in all kinds of community aquaria, provided that there is enough peripheral vegetation. A dark substrate and slightly dimmed light will optically help to improve their colour.

SOCIAL CHARACTERISTICS
This species must be in a shoal of at least seven or preferably even more fish. Solitary pristellas, or those in smaller groups, remain pale and never show their red tail fin and yellow dorsal fin with black and white spots.

These fish are extremely good-natured and therefore cannot be kept in the same aquarium with predatory fish. They are quite active and usually swim in the middle zone.

TEMPERATURE AND WATER COMPOSITION
22-26°C. The water composition is almost irrelevant, but if you want to take the best possible care of these fish, soft and slightly acidic water (filtered over peat) is ideal.

FOOD
Pristellas like various types of dry food, and also enjoy small live food.

BREEDING
If you want to breed these fish you must select a well-matched breeding pair and put them in a separate breeding tank. Of course, you must already have given the fish a good and varied diet so that they are in peak condition. Gradually increase the temperature in the aquarium by no more than 2°C and ensure that the water composition is optimum.

If nothing has happened within a few days, it is very probable that the breeding pair are incompatible and you can try again later with another pair. The fish are free layers and eat their own eggs.

Procatopus similis

FAMILY
Cyprinodontidae (egg-laying tooth carps)

HABITAT
Coastal regions of West Africa.

SEXUAL DIFFERENCES
The males are much more brightly coloured and larger than the females.

LENGTH
Up to about four centimetres.

ACCOMMODATION
The species can be kept in a small special aquarium together with a number of other peaceful killifish. A dark substrate, possibly consisting partly of peat dust, a thick covering of floating plants and luxuriant peripheral vegetation will benefit these fish, which also appreciate a current in the water. They are not real shoaling fish, but they do enjoy having others of their own kind for company.

SOCIAL CHARACTERISTICS
These fish are normally very peace-loving

Pristella maxillarus

Procatopus similis

and the males are very tolerant of each other. These fish can therefore very easily be kept in a community aquarium with other fish which make the same demands in terms of their environment.

TEMPERATURE AND WATER COMPOSITION
25-27°C, 8-12° gH, pH 6.5 to 7. Add some sea salt to the water now and then.

FOOD
These killifish mainly eat live food such as artemia, mosquito larvae and tubifex. They will also take dry food.

BREEDING
Breeding these fish is not easy and is best left to specialists.

Pseudancistrus leopardus

FAMILY
Loricariidae (armoured catfish)

SUB FAMILY
Ancistrinae

Pseudancistrus leopardus

Pseudancistrus leopardus

HABITAT
Brazil, in streams with fast running water.

SEXUAL DIFFERENCES
It is virtually impossible to distinguish the sexes outside the mating season. During the mating season, the male has bulges on his pectoral fins.

LENGTH
20 to 35 centimetres, depending on the size of the aquarium.

ACCOMMODATION
Since these catfish can grow quite large,

you should keep them in a good sized aquarium. A metre wide is, nevertheless, the minimum. These catfish very much like to burrow, so they are ideal neighbours for a cichlid aquarium set up with stones and petrified wood to accommodate more "enterprising" fish species. They very much appreciate a current in the aquarium and you can provide this with the help of a powerful motorised filter. You should also remember to provide refuges and to make sure the lighting is not too bright.

SOCIAL CHARACTERISTICS
You can keep several fish together without any problems. These fish tend to keep to themselves and leave other aquarium dwellers alone. They prefer to occupy the bottom zone. During the day you will hardly see them at all, but towards evening they become active and go around looking for food.

TEMPERATURE AND WATER COMPOSITION
25-27°C. The water composition is not very important, but the water must be crystal clear. These fish are extremely sensitive to pollution in the water, so you should change one-quarter of the aquarium water at least fortnightly.

FOOD
P. leopardus clears up everything that the other aquarium dwellers leave behind, but they mainly need algae and other vegetable food. You can give them blanched lettuce leaves and spinach and they will also take food tablets with a high vegetable content (Sera Viformo, Sera Premium).
Feed these fish after dusk; they will probably not be interested earlier.

BREEDING
Unknown.

Pseudocrenilabrus nicholsi

FAMILY
Cichlidae (cichlids)

HABITAT
Africa

SEXUAL DIFFERENCES
The males are much more colourful than the females.

LENGTH
Up to about eight centimetres.

ACCOMMODATION
These small cichlids can be kept in an average sized aquarium. The fish like to root around in the substrate so take care that the gravel is fine and is definitely not sharp. Small stones must be secure on the base of the aquarium so that the fish cannot undermine them during their "excavation work". For the same reason it is wise to use only very strong plants and also to protect their roots.
The fish like to be able to retreat into a "cave"; you can create this type of place using stone formations or convoluted pieces of petrified wood. An earthenware flowerpot (with the hole enlarged), up-turned or lying on its side half-buried in the gravel, will often be exploited.

Pseudocrenilabrus nicholsi *with fry in its beak*

Pseudocrenilabrus nicholsi

Pseudocrenilabrus nicholsi *with fry*

SOCIAL CHARACTERISTICS
P. nicholsi is, unfortunately, not the most friendly of cichlids. The fish form a pair which take possession of a territory and defend the borders vigorously. It is therefore best to keep a single breeding pair in a small or medium-sized aquarium. If you have a more spacious tank with plenty of refuges, then other cichlids and, possibly, a catfish, can live there as well.

TEMPERATURE AND WATER COMPOSITION
23-25°C. These fish do not make any great demands on the water composition, but a powerful filter is essential to keep the aquarium water pure and constantly in motion.

FOOD
The species almost exclusively eats various kinds of live food such as water fleas, mosquito larvae and artemia.

BREEDING
It is not very difficult to breed these fish. They do not need to be put in a separate breeding tank. The female takes the fertilised eggs in her mouth and they stay there until they hatch out. Since she does not eat throughout this period, she must be fed well beforehand on a variety of live food. When the time comes, the fry swim out, but when danger threatens and at night, they still return to their mothers mouth for protection.

Pseudomugil furcatus
(syn. Popondetta furcata*)*

FAMILY
Pseudomugilidae (rainbow fish)

SUB FAMILY
Pseudomugilinae

HABITAT
New Guinea

SEXUAL DIFFERENCES
The males can be distinguished by their clearer colours and the striking fin shape.

LENGTH
Up to about five centimetres.

ACCOMMODATION
These shoaling fish can be kept in an average sized aquarium. They prefer plenty of feathery-leafed plants. Floating plants and a dark substrate will not only bring out their colours to best effect, but they will also feel much more comfortable as well.

SOCIAL CHARACTERISTICS
This is a very elegant and peaceful fish which must be kept in a shoal of at least five fish and preferably even more. They leave other aquarium dwellers in peace. These fish occupy the middle zone and keep moving all the time.

TEMPERATURE AND WATER COMPOSITION
24-26°, medium-hard water, pH 7 or 8.

Pseudomugil furcatus

FOOD
The fish eat both small live food and good quality dry food.

BREEDING
These fish usually mate within the shoal and lay their eggs among feathery-leafed plants.

Pseudomugil gertrudae

FAMILY
Pseudomugilidae

SUB FAMILY
Pseudomugilinae

HABITAT
Australia and New Guinea

SEXUAL DIFFERENCES
The males are much more colourful and have larger fins than the females.

LENGTH
Up to about four centimetres.

ACCOMMODATION
These friendly shoaling fish do well in a small aquarium in which the substrate consists of well-washed sand or fine gravel. They like dense vegetation, but make sure the fish have enough room to swim about. Floating plants are advisable.

SOCIAL CHARACTERISTICS
These fish are extremely peaceful and sometimes rather shy. They should therefore only be combined with other

Pseudomugil gertrudae

Pseudomugil gertrudae

small, peaceful and equally good-natured species. Keep these fish in a shoal of at least seven specimens. They are active, and prefer to occupy the middle zone.

TEMPERATURE AND WATER COMPOSITION
P. gertrudae likes a warm environment, so keep the temperature above 26°C. Soft and slightly acidic water is necessary to keep these fish in good health.

FOOD
These fish will eat both small live food and dry food.

BREEDING
Breeding these fish is not easy and should be left to specialists.

Pseudosphromenus dayi

FAMILY
Anabantidae (labyrinth fish)

SUB FAMILY
Macropodinae

HABITAT
Asia.

SEXUAL DIFFERENCES
The males are easy to recognise by their large, tapering fins.

LENGTH
Up to seven centimetres.

These fish will feel at home in a small or medium-sized aquarium with a low water level (no deeper than 25 centimetres), dense, feathery-leafed vegetation, floating plants and a dark substrate. They do not like a current in the water.

SOCIAL CHARACTERISTICS

Like nearly all other labyrinth fish, P. dayi likes peace and quiet and has a ponderous manner. It also quickly becomes disconcerted in the company of boisterous or intolerant fish.
The fish are extremely peaceful and will not trouble the other aquarium dwellers. They are best kept in a pair, and usually occupy the top zone, among the floating plants.

TEMPERATURE AND WATER COMPOSITION

26-28°C. They are not very demanding as regards the water composition.

FOOD

These fish eat both dry food (Sera Vipan, Sera O-Nip) and small live food.

Pseudosphromenus dayi

BREEDING

If you want to breed these fish, put them in a separate breeding tank which does not have to be very large, with water no more than 15 centimetres deep. A substrate is unnecessary, but small floating plants and some larger aquatic plants are necessary. Make sure both parent fish are in peak condition. Once the temperature has been raised gradually (over a period of several days) to 29°C, the parents will build a bubble nest on the water surface. It has been observed that both parents of this species care for their young, in contrast to most other labyrinth fish, where the tending of the spawn is done by the male and the female must be removed quickly from the aquarium after spawning.

SPECIAL REMARKS

This species is a labyrinth fish. Fish in this family have an extra respiratory organ, the so-called labyrinth, in addition to their gills. This organ, which is situated at the back of the fishes heads, allows them to take oxygen directly from the atmosphere. The fish therefore must come to the surface every now and then to take in some

air. A covering is therefore necessary, since there is sometimes a considerable difference between the temperature of the water and the external temperature. This can make the fish seriously ill.

Pseudotropheus lambardoi

FAMILY
Cichlidae (cichlids)

HABITAT
Rocky banks of Lake Malawi in Africa.

SEXUAL DIFFERENCES
There are few fish in which the difference between the sexes is so obvious. The males, with their yellow body colour, appear to belong to a totally different species from the bright blue females.

LENGTH
Up to about 12 centimetres.

ACCOMMODATION
These fish do well in large (at least one metre) aquaria of the "rock" type. They will not leave plants alone, so you are best limiting your layout solely to rock formations. The fish feel at their best if the water is constantly in motion, so a strong current is more than desirable.

SOCIAL CHARACTERISTICS
These Lake Malawi cichlids are extremely aggressive and intolerant. Fights will often take place, especially among several fish of the same species.

The best combination is two females and one male. Do not keep them with smaller or less robust fish. This species forms a territory and defends it vigorously.

TEMPERATURE AND WATER COMPOSITION
23-27°C, 12-25° gH, pH 8-8.3. Regular changes of water and strong filtration are essential, since these fish are sensitive to waste products in the water.

FOOD
These Malawi cichlids are easily pleased,

Pseudotropheus lambardoi

but they do like to be fed more than once a day. Cichlid sticks will go down very well and the fish can remain healthy on them all their lives. They do also enjoy live food and algae now and then.

BREEDING
Breeding these fish is very easy. You do not have to follow any special precautionary measures; the fish will look after their offspring themselves. The females take the fertilised eggs in their mouth (mouth brooders). The fry swim out after about three weeks, but when danger threatens they will still take refuge in their mothers mouth as long as that is possible.

SPECIAL REMARKS
All young fish of this species are blue. The males later turn yellow while the females remain blue.

Pseudotropheus zebra

ZEBRA CICHLID

FAMILY
Cichlidae (cichlids)

HABITAT
Rocky banks of Lake Malawi in Africa.

SEXUAL DIFFERENCES
Males have round white spots on the anal fin (egg spots), which are either completely absent or very indistinct in the females.

LENGTH
Given enough space these fish can reach more than 20 centimetres, but only grow to about half this length in most cases.

ACCOMMODATION
The zebra cichlid will do best in a spacious aquarium without plants, because these fish continuously nibble them. Provide refuges in the form of rock formations. The fish like the water always to be in motion.

SOCIAL CHARACTERISTICS
Zebra cichlids are well-known for their aggressive behaviour. They can be particularly intolerant of their own species.

Pseudotropheus zebra *(variant)*

A male together with two females yields the best results. This species is territorial and mainly occupies the bottom zone. These fish keep moving almost constantly.

TEMPERATURE AND WATER COMPOSITION
22-25°C, hard water, pH 8. Regular water changes and strong filtration are desirable.

FOOD
Zebra cichlids enjoy eating and eat a lot. Dry food (cichlid sticks, Sera San), live food and algae will go down well.

BREEDING
Zebra cichlids are very easy to breed. You hardly have to do anything if the fish are well cared for they will reproduce spontaneously. The fertilised eggs will be taken into the mouth of the mother fish (mouth brooder).

Pseudotropheus zebra

There are several known variants which vary in colour from each other.

Pterophyllum altum

FAMILY
Cichlidae (cichlids)

HABITAT
Mainly in the vicinity of the Orinoco River in Venezuela, in slow-running water in quiet spots among plants.

SEXUAL DIFFERENCES
It is extremely difficult to distinguish any difference between the sexes outside the mating season. During the mating season the sexually mature females are usually fatter and can be recognised by the sexual papilla, which is larger than that of the male of the species.

LENGTH
P. Altum can grow to more than 35 centi-metres high, but stays much smaller in the aquarium.

ACCOMMODATION
Due to the height to which these fish can grow, only a deep aquarium (at least 50 centimetres) will provide suitable accommodation. Plants which will make these altums feel at home include giant vallisneria. These fish will not mind a bit of current, but they certainly do not enjoy too much movement in the water.

SOCIAL CHARACTERISTICS
These stately aquarium dwellers can be kept as a pair, but will also do very well in a small group. They normally form couples spontaneously out of the shoal, which live in harmony together. They rarely cause any problems to other large and quiet fish. Do not keep them with small fish such as the neon tetra, however, since these will certainly be viewed as live food. The fish move very slowly and like to "stand" amongst the aquatic plants.

TEMPERATURE AND WATER COMPOSITION
27-29°C, 4-10 gH, pH 6.5.

Pterophyllum altum

P. altum eats everything. Dry food (S. Discus, Sera San) can serve as a basic staple, but these fish also like to eat live food regularly. Feed the fish on blanched lettuce leaves once a week.

BREEDING

The breeding method is similar to *P. scalare*, but much more difficult.

SPECIAL REMARKS

In the first instance, *P. Altum* seems to be similar to *P. Scalare*, the angel fish. The external difference between the species is in the head: the head of *P. Altum* has an obvious indentation when seen in profile. These fish are not often available for sale because they are very delicate and more difficult to keep than the more popular angel fish.

Pterophyllum scalare

ANGEL FISH

FAMILY
Cichlidae (cichlids)

HABITAT
Amazon region, mainly in quiet areas by slow-flowing waters amongst plants.

SEXUAL DIFFERENCES
The difference between the sexes cannot be distinguished outside the mating season and the same also applies to immature fish. As the fish prepare to lay their eggs, the female fish is recognisable by a larger sexual papilla.

LENGTH
The angel fish can attain a height of more than 25 centimetres.

ACCOMMODATION
When you buy your angel fish, they are usually not much bigger than a large coin, but within a year they will have grown rapidly and you will need to find more suitable accommodation, at least if the fish are to be kept in a medium-sized aquarium. An aquarium at least 50 centimetres high is essential. *Vallisneria* varieties are very good as peripheral vegetation, but the Amazon sword plant can also be considered. The fish like to "stand" among these plants. Too much current in the water will upset their equilibrium, since they like peace and quiet.

SOCIAL CHARACTERISTICS
Angel fish can be kept as a pair or in a small shoal. If you buy a shoal of young angel fish, pairs will form spontaneously. These fish are friendly towards each other, but there are also exceptions. Angel fish do well in a community aquarium, but not with species which are too active and certainly not with tiger barbs because these have a tendency to nibble the fins of angel fish. Small fish such as neon tetras and small long-finned guppies, are also not ideal neighbours because the angel fish will sometimes eat them. Angel fish are stately aquarium dwellers. They move around gracefully and, once fully grown, are usually placid and ponderous.

TEMPERATURE AND WATER COMPOSITION
24°C. This fish does not make many demands on the water composition.

Pterophyllum scalare *(spotted variant)*

Pterophyllum scalare *(veiltailed variant)*

Pterophyllum scalare

Pterophyllum scalare *(original form with fry)*

Pterophyllum scalare *(black-spotted variant)*

spontaneously. If angel fish are kept together in a shoal from when they are fry, they will form one or more pairs. You can transfer one of these pairs into a separate aquarium but this is often not necessary if your aquarium is big enough and is not overcrowded. Gradually increase the water temperature to 28°C. The water hardness should be around 6 to 9° gH and the pH at 6 to 6.5. A compatible breeding pair will choose a strong leaf or another fairly firm surface which is well polished before the hundreds of eggs are deposited on it. The parent fish tend the eggs excellently, and "dead" eggs are removed. When the fry hatch the fry "hang" on the leaf at first – the parent fish care for and protect them as well. The fry can simply stay with the parent fish because their lives will not be at risk. Rear the fry on recently hatched brine shrimps (artemia), which you can breed yourself using eggs available from specialist dealers.

VARIANTS
Over the years many different colours of angel fish have been bred, such as a golden variety and an (almost) black or white angel fish. Spotted and marbled angel fish are also often seen. The original colour of the angel fish is similar to the colour of Pterophyllum altum, often with bright red rings around the eyes. There is also a long-finned variety. The colours of these fish can "disappear" very quickly due to stress or unexpected events.

SPECIAL REMARKS
Angel are part of a select group of fish species which have been popular with aquarists for decades.

Pterygoplichthys gibbiceps

SPOTTED SAILFIN SUCKER CATFISH

FAMILY
Loricariidae (armoured catfish)

SUB FAMILY
Hypostominae

HABITAT
Peru, in running water.

SEXUAL DIFFERENCES
No difference has yet been found.

FOOD
The angel fish is an omnivore. It can be kept perfectly healthy on a varied diet of dry food (cichlid sticks, Sera San and Sera Premium). The fish also enjoy live food such as brine shrimps and water fleas from time to time. These can be either dried or frozen.

BREEDING
It is not very difficult to breed angel fish, as long as you allow the pairs to form

Pterygoplichthys gibbiceps

LENGTH

These fish do not usually exceed 20 centimetres in the aquarium.

ACCOMMODATION

This catfish, with its spectacular markings, can be kept in a small aquarium when young, but the fish grow fast under the right conditions and will then need more space. Provide refuges such as pieces of petrified wood, stone formations and dense peripheral vegetation so that the fish can hide in them during the day. Keep the water moving with a powerful motorised filter, since the fish like this very much.

SOCIAL CHARACTERISTICS

This catfish is a very friendly fish which keeps to itself and leaves other aquarium dwellers alone. They do not chase smaller fish, even when they have grown quite large. If there are plenty of refuges you will not see this fish much during the day. It likes to rest in shady places somewhere under the petrified wood among the dense vegetation, and does not become active until dusk. That is also the best time to feed the fish. These catfish are often kept as individual specimens but, because they swim together in large shoals in the wild, they do also appreciate the company of their own species in the aquarium.

TEMPERATURE AND WATER COMPOSITION

24-27°C. This fish is not very demanding as regards the water composition, but the water should be kept clear and clean.

FOOD

This fish mainly stays on the bottom and clears up anything the other aquarium dwellers have not eaten. Apart from this their diet consists chiefly of vegetable food such as algae, which the fish scrape off plants, stones, petrified wood and aquarium sides with their strong sucker-like mouth. If the aquarium is not full of algae, it is essential to provide the fish with vegetable food every day. Food tablets containing a high percentage of vegetable food are very suitable (Sera Viformo, Sera Premium), but the fish will also eat blanched lettuce leaves.

BREEDING

Nothing is known so far about reproduction.

Above: Rachoviscus crassiceps   *Below:* Rhinogobius wui

Rachoviscus crassiceps

FAMILY
Characidae (characins)

SUB FAMILY
Paragoniatinae

HABITAT
Rio de Janeiro area.

SEXUAL DIFFERENCES
The most significant external difference is very clearly visible on the fins; the males have clear white streaks along their fins.

LENGTH
Up to about five centimetres

ACCOMMODATION
These shoaling fish do very well in a small or medium-sized aquarium with plenty of free space for swimming and dense peripheral vegetation.

A dark substrate and floating plants (to provide the necessary shade) will bring out the colours of these fish much better.

SOCIAL CHARACTERISTICS
This still fairly unknown species is a shoaling fish and can therefore be kept with several others of its kind (at least seven specimens). If these fish are kept as individuals or in too small a shoal, they will experience a lot of stress and may fall sick and die as a result. These good-natured and active fish are friendly towards other aquarium dwellers. They mainly occupy the middle zone.

TEMPERATURE AND WATER COMPOSITION
20-24°C. These fish are not demanding as regards the water composition, but they feel less at home in water which is too hard or too basic.

FOOD
R. Crassiceps is an omnivore. These fish will eat both dry food and small live food with no difficulty.

BREEDING
These fish have not yet been bred in the aquarium.

Rasbora heteromorpha

Rasbora heteromorpha

HARLEQUIN FISH

FAMILY
Cyprinidae (carps and minnows)

SUB FAMILY
Rasborinae

HABITAT
South East Asia in thickly vegetated flood areas in the jungle.

SEXUAL DIFFERENCES
The males are somewhat thinner and the

black spot is larger than that of the females.

LENGTH
Up to about five centimetres.

ACCOMMODATION
Harlequin fish can be accommodated in small or medium-sized aquaria. Make sure there is dense(!) peripheral vegetation and also plenty of space for swimming.

A dark bottom and some floating plants will bring out the colour of these fish at its best.

SOCIAL CHARACTERISTICS
These peaceful shoaling fish are quite active and prefer to occupy the middle or top zone. Keep at least seven of these fish together. They are very well suited to the community aquarium.

TEMPERATURE AND WATER COMPOSITION
24-26°C. Harlequin fish are quite robust fish and can be kept in any water composition, but these fish will feel much better in water which is not too hard and is slightly acidic. Peat filtration, or a substrate consisting partly of peat, is desirable.

FOOD
These popular fish do very well on a diet of nothing but varied dry food, but they will also gladly take small live food such as fruit flies and water fleas now and then.

BREEDING
Harlequin fish do not mate very easily in the aquarium. It is important for the water to be extremely acidic (pH 5.5) and very soft (less than 4° gH). Peat filtration is essential and the water temperature must be rather higher than the fish are used to. The water level should not be too high and there must be plenty of coarse and large-leafed plants such as cryptocorynes, for example, available in the breeding tank. The fish lay their eggs on these.

Choose a good, fully-grown breeding pair. The fish often lay their eggs in the morning when the sun's rays first appear; so it is best to site the breeding tank in a fairly sunny place. The parent fish will eat the eggs, so remove the fish from the breeding tank after spawning.

SPECIAL REMARKS
The harlequin fish has been kept by aquarists since the beginning of this century and has been one of the most popular tropical shoaling fish ever since.

Rasbora maculata

DWARF RASBORA

FAMILY
Cyprinidae (carps and minnows)

SUB FAMILY
Rasborinae

HABITAT
Sumatra, Molucca and parts of Malaysia, mostly in small, stagnant pools and slow-flowing waters.

SEXUAL DIFFERENCES
The female has a fuller belly than the male, which is also smaller.

LENGTH
Dwarf rasboras are one of the smallest aquarium fish we know. Adult fish grow to barely 2.5 centimetres long.

Rasbora maculata

ACCOMMODATION

This dwarf fish does outstandingly well in small aquaria. You can keep a small shoal even in an aquarium only 30 centimetres wide. The colours of these fish show up best against a dark substrate. They feel more secure in a slightly dim and shadowy environment. Floating plants and dense, feathery-leafed vegetation are desirable. Do not keep them together with excessively active or large fish, and certainly not with fish of an intolerant nature.

These small rasbora are absolutely no match for more robust species and are best kept alongside other small – and above all quiet fish.

SOCIAL CHARACTERISTICS

Dwarf rasboras are very lively and good-natured. Always keep them in a shoal of at least five fish; a solitary dwarf rasbora will hide among the vegetation and will fall ill due to stress. The fish mainly occupy the middle zone.

TEMPERATURE AND WATER COMPOSITION

23-26°C. The fish feel most at home in water which is slightly acidic (pH 6-6.5) and not too hard.

FOOD

Dwarf rasboras are omnivores, but the pieces of food must be very small in order for these fish to be able to eat it. They like dry food and take it readily, and suitable types of live food include small water fleas and chopped tubifex; red, white and black mosquito larvae are often too big for them.

BREEDING

Breeding rasboras is not easy, not only because the parent fish do not lay many eggs and are egg-eaters, but also because it is not always easy to find suitably small food for the tiny fry.

If you want these fish to reproduce you will need a separate breeding tank which obviously does not need to be very large. The water must be very soft (definitely no more than 4° gH) and the pH should be around 6. Dwarf rasboras eat their own eggs after they have laid them, so it is best to plant the aquarium with dense fine-leafed vegetation such as myriophyllum and Java moss. A substrate spawner which is attached around two centimetres from the bottom will also help.

Rasbora pauciperforata

Rasbora pauciperforata

FAMILY
Cyprinidae (carps and minnows)

SUB FAMILY
Rasborinae

HABITAT
South East Asia.

SEXUAL DIFFERENCES
The stomach of mature females is fuller and rounder than that of the slimmer males.

LENGTH
Up to about 6.5 centimetres.

ACCOMMODATION
These fish love to swim about and feel most at home in a medium to large aquarium. Plenty of open space for swimming is essential and the fish appreciate dense (feathery-leafed) peripheral vegetation and floating plants. Against a light background the fish are often pale, while a dark substrate will brings out their red stripe much more attractively.

SOCIAL CHARACTERISTICS
These eye-catching rasboras are shoaling fish; they will come into their own if you have at least seven, but they prefer to be kept in even larger groups. They leave both each other and other aquarium dwellers alone, but you should not put them with intolerant fish species. They prefer to occupy the bottom and middle zone, so they combine very well with other shoaling fish which stay in the middle and top zone.

FOOD

This rasbora is a real omnivore. Live food and dry food both go down well. They also eat algae and other vegetable food.

BREEDING

It is extremely difficult to breed these fish because they make such stringent demands on the water composition. The water must certainly not be harder than 3° gH and the pH must be around 6. A good breeding pair is also important. If you have a substantial shoal, choose two fish which are already swimming close together. The breeding tank must be planted with dense feathery-leafed vegetation. The fish eat their own eggs, so they should be removed immediately after spawning.

Rhinogobius wui

FAMILY
Gobiidae (gobies)

SUB FAMILY
Gobiinae

HABITAT
South China

SEXUAL DIFFERENCES

The difference between the sexes is easiest to see from the head – the males have red markings on the lower part of the head.

LENGTH
Up to about five centimetres

ACCOMMODATION

This curious fish has an unusual lifestyle. It maintains its own territory on the bottom, preferably under or near a "covering". If you partly bury a small flowerpot in the gravel, the fish will gladly make use of it but, failing this, it will dig out a hollow for itself under a piece of stone or petrified wood. The bottom should therefore never be sharp. Fine, rounded gravel or well-washed sand is a fine substrate for this fish.

Outside the mating season, the fish will not tolerate any others of its species within its territory and other fish will also have to stay some distance away.

SOCIAL CHARACTERISTICS

Given a large enough aquarium and plenty of refuges, *R. wui* can be kept together

Rhinogobius wui

with several of the same species. Otherwise it is better only to keep one specimen. These fish are usually placid and have a ponderous manner. They should not be kept in an aquarium in which the rest of the inhabitants will constantly interfere with them.

TEMPERATURE AND WATER COMPOSITION
18-26°C. These fish can be kept in an unheated aquarium, as long as it is in a well heated room. The water composition is not very important, but they do appreciate a strong current.

FOOD
These fish mainly eat live food such tubifex and artemia (brine shrimps) and they also enjoy frozen food organisms. They rarely accept dry food.

BREEDING
This unusual aquarium fish is actually quite easy to breed. The only problem is that the intending partners sometimes are not compatible. When temperatures rise in the spring the eggs are laid in the refuge and guarded by the parent fish.
The fry should be reared on small live food.

Rineloriearia fallax

FAMILY
Loricariidae (armoured catfish)

SUB FAMILY
Loricariinae

HABITAT
South America, in fast-flowing streams.

SEXUAL DIFFERENCES
The male fish are recognisable by the row of bristles on the side of the head.

LENGTH
Up to about 16 centimetres.

ACCOMMODATION
This catfish can be kept in medium-sized or large aquaria.
These fish should be kept in flowing and oxygen-rich water; you can keep the water in motion using a strong motorised filter and some airstones.

These fish also need refuges in the form of petrified wood or stones. They prefer an aquarium which is lightly covered in algae.

SOCIAL CHARACTERISTICS
These fish get on well together and leave other aquarium dwellers in peace, tending to keep to themselves.
They hide under a stone or piece of petrified wood during the day, but become active at dusk and go around looking for food.

TEMPERATURE AND WATER COMPOSITION
18-25°C. In warmer climates and in summer, these fish can be kept in unheated aquaria. The water composition is not very important, although they do have a slight preference for slightly acidic and soft to medium-hard water. n any case the aquarium should be kept free of waste material; regular changes of water and powerful filtration are desirable.

FOOD
R. fallax eats almost exclusively vegetable food. They will diligently scrape algae from stones, aquarium windows and petrified wood.
You should also feed these fish with food tablets (Sera Premium), but do this towards dusk, otherwise the food will be eaten by all the other aquarium dwellers before this fish starts actively looking for food.

BREEDING
Breeding is possible, but it is definitely not easy.

Rineloriearia *sp. 'Red'*

FAMILY
Loricariidae (armoured catfish)

SUB FAMILY
Loricariinae

HABITAT
Unknown

SEXUAL DIFFERENCES
The male fish are recognisable by the row of "hairs" along the head.

LENGTH
Up to about 18 centimetres

ACCOMMODATION
This species can be kept in medium-sized or large aquaria. These fish need refuges and shady places, which you can create using floating plants. The fish also like to have a current in the water.

SOCIAL CHARACTERISTICS
Like most catfish, these fish are very peaceful and keep to themselves. Other aquarium dwellers will also be left alone. You can keep them as solitary specimens, as a pair or in a group. They stay in their refuges during the day, but emerge and become active at dusk.

TEMPERATURE AND WATER COMPOSITION
23-26°C. This fish is not very demanding as regards the water composition. They prefer moderately hard water and a neutral pH.

Rineloriearia *'Red'*

Rineloriearia 'Red'

FOOD

This armoured catfish mainly eats algae, blanched lettuce leaves and food tablets for bottom-dwellers.

BREEDING

If you want these fish to breed, put a pair which are already well matched into a separate breeding tank. Obviously, the water conditions in this tank should be the very best. After spawning the males look after the eggs and the female should ideally be removed. An aquarium with a good supply of algae will provide plenty of food for the fry initially, but after a week you will also have to feed them on very small live food.

SPECIAL REMARKS

This fish belongs to the large group of catfish which still have no official scientific name. It is also not known whether this is a separate species or a mutant/variant form. Nevertheless, this fish is fairly popular with aquarists in many countries.

ACCOMMODATION

Like most killifish this species also likes shady areas in the aquarium, and direct sunlight and strong lighting should definitely be avoided. Make sure there are enough refuges such as petrified wood and plenty of feathery-leafed plants. The substrate must be dark and should consist partly of peat dust.

SOCIAL CHARACTERISTICS

These fish are extremely tolerant towards each other, and they leave other aquarium dwellers in peace as well. Due to the vulnerability of this species it cannot be kept in a community aquarium. You can best keep them in a special aquarium with other good-natured killifish. The fish are easily frightened and like peace and quiet. A cover is essential since these fish are very good jumpers.

TEMPERATURE AND WATER COMPOSITION

22-25°C, 6-10° gH, pH 6.5.

FOOD

This killifish is not easy to satisfy because it will rarely – if ever – accept dry food. Small live food, especially artemia and cyclops, will suit this fussy fish very well.

BREEDING

Breeding these fish is a specialist job.

Rivulus xiphidius

FAMILY

Cyprinodontidae (egg-laying tooth carps)

HABITAT

French Guyana and Surinam

SEXUAL DIFFERENCES

The males are eye-catching because they are much more attractively coloured than the females. They are also larger.

LENGTH

Up to 4.5 centimetres

Rivulus xiphidus

Roloffia occidentalis

GOLDEN PHEASANT

FAMILY
Cyprinodontidae (egg-laying tooth carps)

SUB FAMILY
Rivulinae

HABITAT
West Africa, particularly in Sierra Leone

SEXUAL DIFFERENCES
The males are much more colourful than the females. The brown-beige coloured females have transparent fins.

LENGTH
Up to nine centimetres

ACCOMMODATION
These fish should normally be kept in a special aquarium with a substrate consisting of (boiled) peat. The aquarium needs to be about 60-70 centimetres long and there must be enough space for swimming. Plants to use include feathery-leafed and floating varieties. The golden phea-sant prefers to stay in a shadowy environment and therefore will not feel at home in a brightly lit tank. You should also make sure that sunlight never shines directly into the aquarium.

SOCIAL CHARACTERISTICS
The golden pheasant is quite an aggressive fish which is very intolerant towards smaller fish. This fish is therefore usually kept in a special aquarium without any other species. The males are extremely aggressive towards each other, but the females usually leave each other alone.

TEMPERATURE AND WATER COMPOSITION
24°C, 6-8° gH, pH 6.5

FOOD
These fish eat all kinds of live food, including mosquito larvae, tubifex and water fleas. Dry food will be only taken in dribs and drabs or simply refused. They are gluttons and need to be fed several times a day.

BREEDING
Breeding these colourful and interesting fish should be left to specialists.

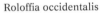
Roloffia occidentalis

Scatophagus argus astromaculatus

LEOPARD OR TIGER SCAT, ARGUS

FAMILY
Scatophagidae (scats)

HABITAT
New Guinea and Australia, mainly in coastal regions in both brackish and sea water.

SEXUAL DIFFERENCES
Unknown

LENGTH
These fish can reach 40 centimetres in length in their natural habitat, but in the aquarium they usually remain much smaller.

ACCOMMODATION
Because of its size, the argus feels more at home in spacious aquaria at least 1.2 metres wide. These fish like to swim around a lot, so there should be plenty of open space for swimming in which the fish will not be hampered by decorative materials.

You can use plants in the aquarium, but only use strong varieties (which can cope with a high salt content in the water) because the fish often nibble at the plants. The water must be particularly well filtered. These fish also like a current.

SOCIAL CHARACTERISTICS
These argus fish (there are several varieties) are shoaling fish and should therefore be kept in a group of five to seven specimens.

These fish are usually kept in a specially designed aquarium, since they are brackish water fish. They will usually occupy the middle zone.

TEMPERATURE AND WATER COMPOSITION
20-28°C. Medium-hard brackish water.

FOOD
When it comes to feeding, these fish are not very demanding. They will eat virtually anything, from algae to plants, live food and dry food.

BREEDING
So far nothing is known about reproduction.

Scatophagus argus astromaculatus

SPECIAL REMARKS
These fish are not easy to keep. Younger fish can usually adapt if the salt content is not quite right, but older fish are not so flexible. This argus fish is not as familiar as *Scatophagus argus argus*, the most popular argus, but its colouring is particularly attractive.

Sphaerichthys osphromenoides

CHOCOLATE GOURAMI

FAMILY
Anabantiidae (labyrinth fish)

Sphaerichthys osphromenoides ♂

Sphaerichthys osphromenoides

SUB FAMILY
Trichogasterinae

HABITAT
Sumatra, Malaysia and Molucca, in shallow pools and streams.

SEXUAL DIFFERENCES
The male is usually more intensely coloured than the female.

LENGTH
Up to about six centimetres.

ACCOMMODATION
Since chocolate gouramis are quiet and also quite small fish, they do very well when kept in a small aquarium. This species is rather shy and likes peace and quiet. A dark substrate, plenty of peripheral vegetation and floating plants are desirable. The fish live in stagnant water in the wild and also prefer not to have a current in the aquarium water.

Since these fish come up to the surface now and then to take in oxygen, it is better for the water level to be no higher than 20 to 25 centimetres. A cover is necessary to regulate the temperature difference between the water and the atmosphere.

SOCIAL CHARACTERISTICS
Chocolate gouramis are quite shy. They should never be kept with boisterous or intolerant fish because they will retreat to the safety of the vegetation and will never be seen again. They prefer to stay among the foliage just below the water surface. You can keep them either as a pair and or with several of the same species.

TEMPERATURE AND WATER COMPOSITION
27-29°C, 2-7° gH, pH 6-6.5. Filter over peat. These fish are extremely sensitive to polluted water and will fall ill very quickly if the water is too hard.

FOOD
Small live food will go down well, as will frozen food organisms and dry food.

BREEDING
There are many conflicting ideas about the way in which these fish breed. Some people say that these labyrinth fish build a nest of bubbles on the surface, that their fry are born alive, that their eggs are laid in hollows on the bottom and that they are mouth-brooders.

Steatocranus tinanti

FAMILY
Cichlidae (cichlids)

HABITAT
Republic of Congo

SEXUAL DIFFERENCES
The males are larger than the females and also have a larger head when fully grown.

LENGTH
Up to about 15 centimetres

ACCOMMODATION
It is best to keep this very unusual species of cichlid in quite a large aquarium. It appreciates plenty of refuges in the form of groups of stones and petrified wood and also plenty of vegetation. A soft substrate is preferable. These fish enjoy a current in the water, which should also be as clean and pure as possible. This can be achieved by using a powerful motorised filter.

SOCIAL CHARACTERISTICS
The fish have a typical way of moving around and mainly occupy the bottom zone, lying on the gravel or sand. They form a territory and defend it against other aquarium dwellers.

There must therefore be enough space and – above all – enough refuges available in the aquarium for all the species. It is best to keep these cichlids alongside other cichlids.

TEMPERATURE AND WATER COMPOSITION
26°C, 4-10°gH, pH 6.5 to 7

FOOD
When it comes to food, these fish are not very demanding. They readily accept dry food and tablets for bottom dwellers, but also like to be given live food regularly.

BREEDING
Breeding these fish is not easy and should be left to specialists.

Steatocranus tinanti

Stigmatogobius sadanundio

Stigmatogobius sadanundio

FAMILY
Gobiidae (gobies)

HABITAT
Borneo, Sumatra, Java and the
Philippines

SEXUAL DIFFERENCES
The difference between the sexes is not
always easy to see. The females often do
not grow as large as the males.

LENGTH
Up to about eight centimetres

ACCOMMODATION
This unusual fish can be accommodated in
a medium-sized aquarium. They prefer to
stay on the bottom or in the bottom zone
and like a soft substrate. The aquarium can
be positioned in a sunny spot, but in that
case the fish must have an opportunity to
hide if they feel the need.

If you do not have any petrified wood or
dense vegetation in the aquarium, provide
another hiding place, for example in the
form of a partly buried flowerpot.

SOCIAL CHARACTERISTICS
You should not have any problems with this
species, either towards others of its kind or
other aquarium dwellers.

TEMPERATURE AND WATER COMPOSITION
21-26°C. They prefer hard water with a neutral pH. Add some sea salt (or iodine free
cooking salt) to the water regularly, because these fish do best in brackish water.

Stigmatogobius sadanundio

FOOD
This species mainly eats live food and cannot easily be tempted by dry food. They
will also eat algae and other vegetable
food occasionally.

BREEDING
Breeding these fish is not very difficult.
They are extremely productive and the fry
respond well to small live food. These fish
are oviparous.

SPECIAL REMARKS
This solitary fish should be kept in a separate aquarium, possibly with some black
mollies for company. These also do well
in brackish water and prefer to occupy the
middle and bottom zone, so they will be
no trouble to *S. sadanundio*.

Sturisoma aureum

GIANT WHIPTAIL CATFISH

FAMILY
Loricariidae (armoured catfish)

SUB FAMILY
Loricariinae

HABITAT
Colombia

SEXUAL DIFFERENCES
With a bit of effort you will be able to spot
the difference between males and females
of this species. The males have small rows
of bristly hairs running along the head.

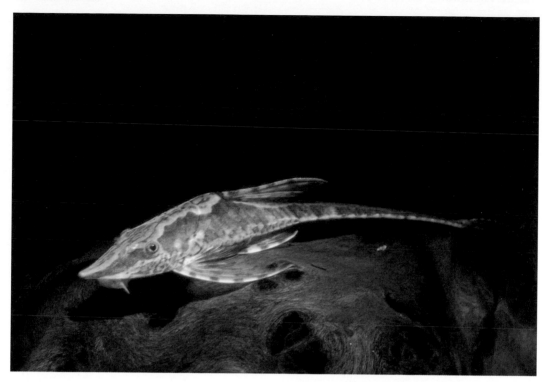

LENGTH
Up to about 20 centimetres

ACCOMMODATION
Due to its size *Sturisoma aureum* is best housed in a largish aquarium. A dark substrate is advisable, as are plenty of stones and petrified wood. Unfortunately this species eats plants; either these should be kept out of the aquarium, or you can let them serve as food for the fish.

In the wild these fish live in fast-flowing rivers and so they also need a similar environment in the aquarium.

The filter must be very powerful, partly because these fish cannot tolerate polluted water either.

SOCIAL CHARACTERISTICS
S. aureum is a very placid fish which starts actively looking for food around dusk. You can keep *S. aureum* as a solitary specimen or with others of its kind. They seldom cause any problems and keep to themselves.

TEMPERATURE AND WATER COMPOSITION
23-26°C, soft to medium-hard water and neutral pH.

Sturisoma aureum

FOOD
This fish is principally an algae eater. It is very good at scraping algae from the windows and petrified wood with its sucker-like mouth. Feed it with extra vegetable food if there is a shortage of algae.

Blanched lettuce leaves and food tablets containing plenty of plant material (Sera Premium) will go down well.

You could also consider raising some fast-growing and cheap waterweed yourself so that you always have a good supply of soft-leafed aquatic plants available for

Sturisoma aureum

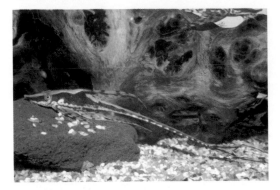

your fish. They will appreciate some live food from time to time.

BREEDING

Breeding these fish is possible, but if you want any of the eggs and fry to survive it is still very wise to transfer a suitable breeding pair into a separate breeding tank. This must have been standing in a sunny spot for some time so that enough algae will have grown to act as food for the fry later on. The filter in this tank must be very powerful and the temperature should be raised gradually to 29°C.

The parent fish do not eat the eggs or the fry, and can therefore stay in the tank with their offspring.

You will have difficulty rearing all the young if the aquarium does not contain sufficient algae.

Symphysodon aequifasciatus *and* Symphysodon discus

DISCUS FISH

FAMILY
Cichlidae (cichlids)

HABITAT
Discus fish are found in the Amazon region, in the Rio Negro and Orinoco rivers among others.

SEXUAL DIFFERENCES
The sexes are very difficult to distinguish except during the mating season, when the sexual papilla of the male fish are more pointed than those of the females.

LENGTH
Up to 20 centimetres

ACCOMMODATION
Keeping or even breeding of these fish is a challenge for experienced aquarists. These are quite delicate fish, and make extremely high demands on the water composition, so they should be kept in a special aquarium. This must be extremely large (at least 1.50 metres wide) to give them enough space. They like a soft (sandy) bottom and plenty of space for swimming. Peace and quiet is important for these fish, so the aquarium must be put in a quiet spot. Too much current in the water will not help.

If the aquarium is near to doors or in a place where lots of people pass by the fish will be highly stressed, which affects their health.

You can put plants around the edges of the aquarium. Floating plants will provide

Symphysodon discus

Symphysodon discus *(variant)*

Symphysodon discus

shaded areas and diffuse the light slightly. This makes the fish feel good.

SOCIAL CHARACTERISTICS
Discus fish are shoaling fish. It is best to keep a number of them in the same aquarium. They feel more at home in an aquarium in which they are not disturbed by other fish. They should therefore usually be kept as the only species in a specially designed aquarium. During the mating season one or more pairs will separate themselves from the rest and form a territory but, since these fish are very choosy, it may also be the case that no pairs will emerge from the shoal. These fish are placid and stately movers. They usually occupy the middle zone.

TEMPERATURE AND WATER COMPOSITION
Discus fish need very warm conditions. The water temperature must be at least 27°C, but it is even better to keep it at around 29-30°C. The water temperature is vitally important for these fish. They require very soft (definitely no higher than 4° gH) and slightly acidic water (pH 6 or 6.5). Peat filtration is essential.

These fish are also very sensitive to polluted water, so you should regularly change part of the water.

FOOD
Discus fish are very fussy eaters. Some species will accept only varied live food such as artemia, tubifex and mosquito larvae. Others will take dry food as well (S. Discus).

BREEDING
Breeding these fish is a job for specialists because of the extreme difficulties which have to be overcome. A lot depends on the pair and the conditions in which they are kept. The fish are good parents, and care for their offspring for a long time.

During the first week the fry eat a skin secretion from their parents' mucous membrane, and afterwards they are able to feed themselves. The fry can be left with the parents without any difficulty until they are large enough to be transferred to other aquaria.

VARIANTS
Both S. *discus* and S. *aequifasciatus* come in a variety of natural colours and patterns, and there are also variants. These fish also cross-breed, which can sometimes make classification virtually impossible.

The S. *discus aequifasciatus* species also includes S. *discus aequifasciatus aequifasciatus* (green discus), S. *discus aequifasciatus axelrodi* (brown discus) and S. *discus aequifasciatus haraldi* (blue discus). The most obvious difference between S. *Aequifasciatus* and S. *discus* is that the latter has a rather shorter body.

SPECIAL REMARKS
This extremely sensitive and expensive species of fish is definitely not recom-

Symphysodon aequifasciatus *'Royal Blue'*

Symphysodon discus

S. *angelicus* likes to search for food on the bottom. It is therefore best not to use coarse or sharp gravel as a substrate, since the fish can injure themselves on it. Fine, rounded gravel or well-washed sand is desirable. This species also needs refuges such as large pieces of petrified wood and dense vegetation.

SOCIAL CHARACTERISTICS
This catfish has a very unusual swimming style. The fish regularly swim upside down through the water, a characteristic which *Synodontis* species share with *S. Angelicus.* These are quiet and rarely seen during the day, but they become active at night and go out looking for food.

They mainly stay in the bottom zone and are best kept as solitary specimens.

TEMPERATURE AND WATER COMPOSITION
23-28°C. The water composition is not very important, but the water must be kept in motion (use a powerful filter).

Synodontis angelicus

mended for beginners; keeping discus fish requires a great deal of knowledge and experience. These fish are extremely demanding as regards the water composition.

Synodontis angelicus

Synodontis angelicus

FAMILY
Mochocidae (naked catfish)

SUB FAMILY
Mochocinae

HABITAT
Cameroon and Republic of Congo, in stagnant and slow-flowing water.

SEXUAL DIFFERENCES
Adult females are larger and their basic colour is rather paler.

LENGTH
Up to about 18 centimetres

S. *angelicus* eats both vegetable food and small live food. If there is not much algae in the aquarium you should give this fish replacement vegetable food, for example plant tablets (Sera Viformo and Sera Premium) or blanched lettuce leaves.

BREEDING

So far breeding these fish in the aquarium has never been successful.

Synodontis nigriventis

UPSIDE-DOWN CATFISH

FAMILY
Mochocidae (naked catfish)

SUB FAMILY
Mochicinae

HABITAT
Republic of Congo

SEXUAL DIFFERENCES

The difference between the sexes is not easy to see, but an experienced eye will recognise the female by her rounder girth. Adult females are larger than males.

LENGTH
Up to 10 centimetres (female)

ACCOMMODATION

S. *nigriventis* can be kept in a medium-sized aquarium, as long as plenty of vegetation and refuges are provided.

Synodontis nigriventis

SOCIAL CHARACTERISTICS

This *Synodontis* species likes to live in a shoal and leaves other species alone. They therefore do very well in community aquaria. The fish always swim with their stomach upwards and their back to the bottom and in this way they search for food under pieces of petrified wood, stones and plant leaves. These fish hide during the day, but become active at dusk and emerge to search for food.

TEMPERATURE AND WATER COMPOSITION

23-26°C. The water composition is not very important, which makes these upside-down swimmers ideal for new hobbyists.

FOOD

These fish are always looking for food. They eat not only food left over by other aquarium dwellers, but also algae and live food.

BREEDING

There have been a few reports of successful breeding. The fish always lay their eggs underneath something (for example under a piece of petrified wood or inside a flowerpot). The fry swim the right way up at first, but gradually take on the same swimming position as their parents until eventually they swim upside down all the time.

Synodontis rebeli

FAMILY
Mochocidae (naked catfish)

Synodontis rebeli

SUB FAMILY
Mochocinae

HABITAT
Cameroon

SEXUAL DIFFERENCES
Unknown

LENGTH
Up to about 20 centimetres, depending on the space available.

ACCOMMODATION
Due to its size, this species belongs in quite large aquaria. Plenty of refuges (petrified wood, stones and vegetation) are necessary because these fish like to hide during the day. If they are not able to do this, it causes them a great deal of stress.

SOCIAL CHARACTERISTICS
These large, peacable naked catfish are very friendly, both towards each other and towards other fish. They are strikingly coloured and will be found among the vegetation or under stones during the day, but they come out at dusk to search for food. These fish very seldom emerge from their hiding place during their rest period, so it is best to feed them at dusk.

TEMPERATURE AND WATER COMPOSITION
23-26°C. These fish are not very demanding as regards the water composition, but they appreciate strong aeration.

FOOD
This species really will eat anything. Dry food, algae, other vegetable food and live food will all be devoured with pleasure. These fish will also eat anything that the other aquarium dwellers leave uneaten.

BREEDING
Not successful so far.

Synodontis schoutedeni

FAMILY
Mochocidae (naked catfish)

SUB FAMILY
Mochicinae

HABITAT
Africa, in the Congo River area

SEXUAL DIFFERENCES
So far none are known

LENGTH
Up to about 15 centimetres

ACCOMMODATION
Since *S. schoutedeni* likes to hide in holes and cracks during the day, you should provide some rock formations or petrified wood. During the evening these fish emerge and show that they are active swimmers, best suited to large aquaria.

SOCIAL CHARACTERISTICS
Schoutedenis are fine if kept as individuals. These fish are seldom seen during the day, but tend to stay in their refuges. At nightfall they become active and move around the bottom searching for something to eat. This species swims both upside-down and the right way up.

TEMPERATURE AND WATER COMPOSITION
22-26°C. This fish is not very demanding as regards the water composition. All it needs is a current in the water, which you can provide by means of a powerful motorised filter or some airstones.

FOOD
Schoutedenis eat soft vegetable food (aquatic plants) and small live food. They also like food tablets for bottom dwellers.

BREEDING
Nothing is known about how these fish reproduce.

Tanichthys albonubes

WHITE CLOUD MOUNTAIN MINNOW

FAMILY
Cyprinidae (carps and minnows)

SUB FAMILY
Rasborinae

HABITAT
South East China, in the Hong Kong area.

SEXUAL DIFFERENCES
It is not difficult to see the difference between the sexes. The males of this species are more slender and usually also more intensely coloured than the females.

LENGTH
Up to 4.5 centimetres.

ACCOMMODATION
The white cloud mountain minnow is an active swimmer, but does not need to be kept in a large aquarium. These fish do, however, like plenty of open space for swimming with dense peripheral vegetation and some floating plants. A bottom consisting partly of sand will give the fish an opportunity to search for food in it now and then.

SOCIAL CHARACTERISTICS
White cloud mountain minnows are good-natured fish which will leave all the other aquarium dwellers alone. Always keep them in a shoal of at least five and preferably more, of the same species, otherwise they will feel insecure and suffer from stress. These fish mainly stay in the middle zone and they are extremely active.
Due to their toughness, white cloud mountain minnows are good fish for beginners.

TEMPERATURE AND WATER COMPOSITION
16-23°C. White cloud mountain minnows are almost insensitive to the water composition, but the water must be very clear and clean. They can easily survive in garden ponds during the summer. In heated rooms they can be kept in un-heated aquaria. They can pass the winter at a temperature of 17°C.

Trichogaster trichopterus

Tanichthys albonubes

FOOD
The white cloud mountain minnow is an omnivore. It will stay healthy on an exclusive diet of varied dry food.
It will also enjoy some small water fleas and tubifex.

BREEDING
This fish is quite easy to breed. It is productive and the young are not particularly sensitive. After a winter period at lower temperatures, you can slowly raise the water temperature in a separate breeding tank to 22-23°C (definitely no higher).
The fish are free layers and notorious egg-eaters, so the breeding tank must contain plenty of feathery-leafed plants. You can also attach a substrate spawner a few centimetres above the bottom to prevent the parent fish from eating the eggs. The parent fish can be removed after

spawning. The fry can be raised on fine powdered food.

There is a long-finned variant of this small shoaling fish, but these are not available for sale anywhere near as often as the original form.

Tateurndina ocellicauda

FAMILY
Eleotridae (sleeper gobies)

HABITAT
New Guinea, in both flowing and stagnant water.

SEXUAL DIFFERENCES
It is easy to tell the differences between the sexes in adult fish. The females have a fat, round stomach while the male's body

is straight. Above all, the males are much colourful, especially on the fins.

LENGTH
Up to about seven centimetres.

ACCOMMODATION
Since these fish are not particularly active, you can very easily keep them in a small aquarium. They prefer to stay near the bottom and like to hide. These very much like refuges in the form of dense vegetation, plenty of roots and stones. Because of their lifestyle, a substrate of well-washed sand or very fine rounded gravel is ideal.

SOCIAL CHARACTERISTICS
These unusual fish can be kept alone or in a group. The fish normally leave other aquarium dwellers in peace, but they can be rather more intimidating during the mating season, since they are territorial during that period.

TEMPERATURE AND WATER COMPOSITION
23-26°C. Medium-hard water and neutral pH (7).

Tateurndina ocellicauda

FOOD

These fish mainly eat live food such as tubifex, water fleas and artemia.

BREEDING

If you want to breed these fish you should transfer them to a specially designed aquarium. Put several males and females together: a suitable breeding pair will soon split off from them. In order to get the fish in the right frame of mind you should gradually lower the water hardness to around 5-7°gH and increase the temperature by one or two degrees. You can remove the female after spawning. The male will guard and care for the eggs. When they hatch it is time to remove the male as well.

The fry can be fed with very small live food.

Telmatherina ladigesi

CELEBES SAILFISH, CELEBES RAINBOW FISH

FAMILY
Atherinidae (silversides)

HABITAT
Celebes

SEXUAL DIFFERENCES
The males are more colourful than the females, and they also have remarkably long fin rays.

LENGTH
Up to about 7.5 centimetres

ACCOMMODATION
Since these shoaling fish are lively swimmers, they should be kept in an aquarium about 80 centimetres long (or larger), in which their swimming will not be excessively hampered by plants. Celebes sailfish, like most Atherinidae species, particularly like a soft bottom, although this is not absolutely essential.

SOCIAL CHARACTERISTICS
Celebes sailfish must be kept in a shoal of at least six fish. The ratio of males to females should be 1: 2. They are peaceful fish which will leave even their smallest neighbours alone. They mainly occupy the middle zone.

Telmatherina ladigesi

Telmatherina ladigesi

TEMPERATURE AND WATER COMPOSITION
24-28°C. Add two teaspoonfuls of iodine-free cooking salt for every 10 litres of aquarium water. Soft to medium-hard water is preferable.

FOOD
The Celebes sailfish is an omnivore which will enjoy some small live food as well as good quality dry food. These fish will never, or very rarely, take any food from the bottom.

BREEDING
In a separate breeding tank, and under ideal conditions, these fish will lay their eggs on feathery-leafed plants and amongst the roots of floating plants. They are stimulated by direct sunlight, so the breeding tank should not be put in a dark place.

The parent fish are egg-eaters and must be removed from the breeding tank after spawning. The young can then be reared on small live and powdered food (Sera Micron).

Tetragonopterus argenteus

FAMILY
Characidae (characins)

SUB FAMILY
Tetragonopterinae

HABITAT
South America, especially in Peru and Brazil.

SEXUAL DIFFERENCES
The males have a longer dorsal fin than the females.

LENGTH
Up to about seven centimetres

ACCOMMODATION
These shoaling fish belong in a medium-sized or large aquarium in which there is sufficient swimming space available. The edges of the aquarium must contain plenty of strong plants, preferably varieties which partly cover the surface (vallisneria).

These fish enjoy a strong current in the water.

SOCIAL CHARACTERISTICS
This species is a shoaling fish and should therefore always be kept in a shoal of at least seven fish. Due to their robust and lively nature, they are excellent company for a number of cichlids. They prefer to occupy the middle zone.

TEMPERATURE AND WATER COMPOSITION
22-26°C. These fish hardly make any demands on the water composition. They do, however, prefer clear water which is always kept in motion.

FOOD
These fish are omnivores. Various types of dry food (Sera Flora) and live food all go down very well.

Tetragonopterus argenteus

This species is easy to breed. Put a shoal in a separate breeding tank with plenty of feathery-leafed vegetation. They are free layers and happily eat their eggs. The parent fish cannot find all the eggs in a breeding tank with dense vegetation, but it is even better to attach a substrate spawner through which the eggs can fall after spawning, a few centimetres above the bottom. The fry can be easily be reared on fine powdered food.

Tetraodon biocellatus
(syn. Tetraodon steindachneri)

FIGURE EIGHT PUFFERFISH

FAMILY
Tetraodontidae (pufferfish)

HABITAT
Thailand, Malaysia, Sumatra and Borneo

SEXUAL DIFFERENCES
The difference between the sexes is very difficult to see. The females are probably larger and fatter than the males.

LENGTH
Up to six centimetres

ACCOMMODATION
These pufferfish can be accommodated in smaller aquaria. Because of their unusual, ponderous way of moving they do not need much space to swim. They mainly stay among plants, looking for food.

SOCIAL CHARACTERISTICS
As long as there is enough food (in the form of snails) available in the aquarium, this fish will not trouble anyone, but if there is any shortage they do tend to take "bites" out of their neighbours. In any case, keep only one specimen at a time and do not put them with fish which are extremely delicate or timid.

TEMPERATURE AND WATER COMPOSITION
22-26°C. These puffer fish are not very sensitive to the water composition.

FOOD
Puffer fish have a strong predilection for snails, which is what they are looking for

Tetraodon biocellatus

all day amongst the feathery-leafed plants. They crack the shells with their strong beak before devouring the contents. They are ideal fish for aquarists struggling with a surplus of snails but, after polishing off these unwelcome neighbours in record time, the puffer fish will quickly become predatory and will reduce your fish stocks unless they are offered anything better. There are only a few aquarium dwellers which are a match to the strong jaws of this fish; therefore these fish are very difficult to keep in the long-term. A daily supplement of snails and mussels is essential. They will also sometimes eat small pieces of beef heart.

BREEDING
Breeding these fish in captivity has not yet been successful. It is, however, known that the males care for the eggs.

SPECIAL REMARKS
Although most puffer fish prefer to live in brackish water and therefore need added sea salt, this species lives only in fresh water in the wild. *T. biocellatus* therefore does not need any extra sea salt.

Thayeria boehlkei

BOEHLKE'S PENGUIN FISH

FAMILY
Characidae (characins)

SUB FAMILY
Tetragonopterinae

Amazon region, along densely overgrown banks.

SEXUAL DIFFERENCES
The females are rather larger than the males and also have a rather fuller stomach.

LENGTH
Up to six centimetres.

ACCOMMODATION
These shoaling fish, which are American characins, can be kept in an aquarium 60 centimetres long. Penguin fish will do best in an aquarium with a dark substrate and some floating plants. Space for swimming in the centre of the aquarium and dense peripheral vegetation with large long-leafed plants which partly cover the water surface is ideal. A cover is needed because these fish are inclined to jump above the water surface.

SOCIAL CHARACTERISTICS
Most importantly these peaceful fish belong in a shoal of at least six fish because otherwise they will hide in the foliage. Their unusual markings will also come out better in a shoal. Penguin fish are quiet fish and have a characteristic way of swimming; they always hang at a slight angle in the water. Do not put them with boisterous, excessively large or predatory fish. They mainly occupy the middle and bottom zone.

TEMPERATURE AND WATER COMPOSITION
22-27°C. These fish are not very demanding as regards the water composition.

FOOD
Alternate good quality dry food with some small live food. These fish very much appreciate fruit flies and water fleas.

BREEDING
It is very difficult to get these fish to breed, but once they do it they are very productive. Put a shoal of penguin fish in quite a large aquarium with a substrate spawner so that these free spawning fish cannot eat their eggs after spawning.

Thoracocharax securis

FAMILY
Gasteropelecidae (hatchet fish)

SUB FAMILY
Gasteropelecinae

HABITAT
South America

SEXUAL DIFFERENCES
Unknown

LENGTH
Up to nine centimetres

ACCOMMODATION
A spacious aquarium at least 80 centimetres long will accommodate these large hatchet fish well. Floating plants or overhanging plants will filter the light, but the water surface should certainly not be too densely overgrown, because the fish usually stay just below the surface of the water.

Thayeria boehlkei

Thoracocharax securis

These can jump enormous distances, and a cover is absolutely essential in order to prevent this.

SOCIAL CHARACTERISTICS
Hatchet fish are problem-free and fairly peaceful fish which are very good for keeping in a community aquarium. They are also good company for smaller, peaceful cichlid species. Always keep them in a shoal of at least seven fish.

TEMPERATURE AND WATER COMPOSITION
24-27°C. The water composition is not very important, but the fish do prefer soft water.

FOOD
These fish mainly eat insects and their larvae in the wild, but in the aquarium they will eat dry food just as readily. You can give them insects (mosquitoes and fruit flies) and mosquito larvae every now and then.

BREEDING
There have not yet been any reports of successful breeding.

SPECIAL REMARKS
There are many different types of hatchet fish. *T. securis* is one of the largest.

Trichogaster leeri

PEARL GOURAMI

FAMILY
Anabantidae (labyrinth fish)

SUB FAMILY
Trichogasterinae

HABITAT
Thailand, Sumatra, Borneo and Molucca

SEXUAL DIFFERENCES
The males have a longer dorsal fin and also have a bright red chest and belly during the mating season.

LENGTH
Up to about 12 centimetres.

ACCOMMODATION
The pearl gourami can be kept in small

Trigogaster leeri

aquaria (60 centimetres wide), since these fish are usually quiet. They do not like bright lights, so it is best to have duckweed or crystalwort floating on the surface of the water. Since these fish regularly take oxygen directly from the atmosphere, the water level must not be too high (no more than 30 centimetres). If the room temperature differs from the temperature in the aquarium, a cover must be placed on top of the aquarium to reduce the difference in temperature between the air and water, since this can cause the fish to fall ill. A strong current in the water is not good for the fish.

SOCIAL CHARACTERISTICS
The males of the pearl gourami can be intolerant and constantly chase each other. It is best to keep only one pair in an aquarium. These fish are very peaceful and will leave even fish which are much smaller than itself in peace. Do not put them in an aquarium with active swimmers or very aggressive species, because they do like peace and quiet. Tiger barbs are also not suitable companions, because these fish have a tendency to nibble the gouramis' long antennae. Pearl gouramis tend to stay in the top zone.

TEMPERATURE AND WATER COMPOSITION
25-28°C. The water composition is not very important.

FOOD
These placid and very decorative fish are omnivores and do very well on a varied diet of dry food (Sera Vipan, Sera O-Nip). You can also give them some mosquito larvae and tubifex from time to time.

Diamond gouramis very seldom reproduce if they are in the company of other fish species. Put an adult pair in a separate breeding tank in which the water level is no higher than 25 centimetres. The lighting must be slightly subdued. Make sure there are floating plants (crystalwort) on the surface as well. The males build a bubble nest and look after the eggs and larvae until the young begin to swim around freely. The female must be removed after spawning. The young can be reared on fine powdered food and very small live food.

Trichogaster trichopterus

THREE SPOT GOURAMI

FAMILY
Anabantidae (labyrinth fish)

SUB FAMILY
Trichogasterinae

HABITAT
Vietnam, Thailand, Burma and Malaysia

SEXUAL DIFFERENCES
The males of this species have a more pointed dorsal fin.

LENGTH
Up to 11 centimetres.

ACCOMMODATION
Despite its size the three spot gourami can be kept in smaller aquaria, since it is a placid swimmer. It is a labyrinth fish, so it will not only filter oxygen out of the water, but will also take in air from the surface, so the water level should not be too high. The three spot gourami does best in a dim environment and will not feel at home in a brightly lit tank, which can clearly be seen from its behaviour and the paler colouring of the fish. To create a shaded environment you can allow duckweed or crystalwort to float on the surface. You should put a cover on the aquarium if the room temperature is significantly different from the temperature in the aquarium. A powerful filter is not necessary; the fish are actually disturbed by water which is constantly in motion.

SOCIAL CHARACTERISTICS
It is best to keep these fish as a pair, since the males can be intolerant of each other. The three spot gourami is a peaceful and very quiet fish which gets on very well with smaller species. It certainly will not feel at home in an aquarium with excessively boisterous and obtrusive fish. It is also not advisable to put them together with tiger barbs, because these will chew off their long antennae.

TEMPERATURE AND WATER COMPOSITION
26-28°C. These fish are not difficult to please, and they feel at home in the most diverse water conditions.

FOOD
This popular labyrinth fish is an omnivore which does well on a diet of assorted types of dry food. It also likes live food occasionally such as mosquito larvae, tubifex and water fleas.

BREEDING
Three spot gouramis very rarely mate if they are in the company of other fish. The pair should therefore be transferred to a separate aquarium with floating plants and water 20 centimetres deep or less. Get the fish into the right frame of mind by raising the water temperature (slowly!) to 29-30°C. The male builds a bubble nest on the surface. The female is best removed after mating because the male will carry on chasing her. You can leave the male with the larvae until they can swim around freely.

The young fish should be reared on recently hatched brine shrimps, fine powdered food and small live food.

Trichogaster trichopterus *(variant)*

Trichogaster trichopterus 'Cosby'

There are various known forms of the three spot gourami, of which the "Cosby" (marbled gourami) and the "Gold" (golden gourami) are the best-known and most popular. Both the original forms and the variants are robust and can grow to a ripe old age if well cared for.

Uaru amphiacanthoides

FAMILY
Cichlidae (cichlids)

HABITAT
South America

SEXUAL DIFFERENCES
It is very difficult to tell the difference between the sexes in this cichlid species. Outside the mating season it is completely impossible. The male's genital papillae are visible for a few days before and during the reproductive cycle.

LENGTH
Up to 30 centimetres, but these fish often remain smaller in the aquarium.

ACCOMMODATION
Uarus should be kept in a spacious aquarium at least 1.20 metres long, but they prefer it to be even larger. These fish burrow around in the bottom and like to nibble soft-leafed plants. They need hollows and other refuges. Make sure the decorative material is well stuck down so that these fish do not undermine it with their excavations. Uarus absolutely hate bright lighting. Shadowy spots can be created by using floating plants. These fish enjoy a gentle current in the water.

SOCIAL CHARACTERISTICS
These remarkable cichlids get on fine both with their own kind and with other larger cichlids, such as discus fish, which have the same requirements. Largish catfish have nothing to fear from these fish. Be careful with smaller species, since the Uaru will see these as food. They form pairs during the mating season but otherwise they live in a small shoal.

TEMPERATURE AND WATER COMPOSITION
27-29°C, 2-6° gH, pH 6-6.5. The water should be kept as pure as possible and must be free from waste products. This can be achieved by not giving the fish more food than they can eat, siphoning the waste from the bottom regularly and using a powerful filter. Peat filtration is necessary.

FOOD
Depending on the size of the fish, you can give them mosquito larvae and water fleas, as well as earthworms and pieces of beef heart or fish. Uarus also need vegetable food. Dry food is only accepted in small quantities (S. Discus).

BREEDING
Breeding Uarus is not easy: it is a challenge even for more specialised and experienced aquarists. It is broadly similar to breeding discus fish. The fry of this fish initially feed on skin secretions from their parents' bodies.

SPECIAL REMARKS
Uarus are not easy to keep in good condition and are therefore only suitable for specialists.

Uaru amphiacanthoides

Above: Xiphophorus helleri *(♂)*   *Below:* Xiphophorus maculatus *(♂)*

Xiphophorus helleri

SWORDTAILS

FAMILY
Poeciliidae (egg-laying tooth carps)

HABITAT
Mexico, Guatemala and Honduras

SEXUAL DIFFERENCES
Swordtails owe their name to the elongated lower fin ray which forms the typical "sword" in the male fish. In addition, the males, just like all other (ovo)viviparous fish, are recognisable by their gonopodium. The female's body is larger and fuller with a rounded tail.

LENGTH
Swordtails do not usually grow to more than 10 to 12 centimetres long in the aquarium, but larger fish have been reported in the wild.

ACCOMMODATION
Swordtails can be kept in an aquarium about 60 centimetres long but, because the males need quite a lot of space for their mating ritual, which takes place all year round, it is best to give them more space than this. The aquarium should not be too thickly planted so that the fish have enough swimming space.

SOCIAL CHARACTERISTICS
These fish (with a few exceptions) are peaceful towards other aquarium dwellers, which makes them very suitable for a community aquarium. In most cases even the males get on well with each other. Since the males are very active in their attempts to mate, it is much better to keep them with several females. These fish occupy the whole tank, but prefer the top zone. Swordtails are very active.

TEMPERATURE AND WATER COMPOSITION
Swordtails are not very demanding as regards the quality of the water. They thrive well in a water temperature of around 24°C, but they will also mate in water which is a few degrees warmer or cooler.

FOOD
These ovoviparous fish are genuine omnivores and thrive well on good quality dry

Xiphophorus helleri *(♂) (rare albino)*

Xiphophorus helleri ♂

food. Algae, either fresh or in the form of dried flakes, should definitely be on the menu.

They also very much like mosquito larvae and water fleas.

Swordtails to tend to eat their own young when they are still extremely small.

241

BREEDING

These robust fish are also very productive. A batch contains between ten and fifty or more fry, which can all take care of themselves immediately. Since the swordtails themselves and other aquarium dwellers may also eat these fry, it is wise to rear them in a separate aquarium or to ensure that the aquarium has enough refuges for them, such as Java moss and plenty of floating plants with roots. The strongest fish will survive with no difficulty. Feed the fry on fine powdered food (Sera Micron) and also make sure there is enough algae available for them.

VARIANTS

Over time many different variants of the swordtail have been developed. The so-called "green" swordtail is the original form from which the red, black, spotted, and yellowish-orange coloured fish have all been bred. There are also particularly attractive high-finned ("Simpson") and long-finned varieties. The males of the lat-

ter type frequently have problems with mating. Sometimes they cannot manage it at all because not only the external fin ray of their tail fin, but also the gonopodium (reproductive organ) is extremely elongated. The albino form has become extremely rare nowadays.

SPECIAL REMARKS

There is a lot of discussion about the so-called sexual change which is said to happen frequently in swordtails. Adult females which have borne several clusters of fry are said to be suddenly transformed into males and begin to display the corresponding characteristics (such as a gonopodium and sword). This does sometimes happen, but it is usually old or barren females that are involved. So far there is no proof – and it is very improbable – that the transformed fish actually reproduce. Reports of sudden sexual changes usually refer to males whose sexual characteristics develop late. Before they develop a sword and a gonopodium,

Xiphophorus helleri *(♀) (long-finned variant)*

Xiphophorus helleri ♂

Xiphophorus helleri ♂

these fish appear to be living as females, but this is not the case.

Xiphophorus maculatus

PLATY

FAMILY
Poeciliidae (egg-laying tooth carps)

HABITAT
Mexico, Guatemala and Honduras

SEXUAL DIFFERENCES
The male is recognisable by the anal fin which has been transformed into a reproductive organ (gonopodium). The females are rather larger than the males and also have a fuller stomach.

LENGTH
Female platys can reach about six centimetres in length, but males remain smaller.

ACCOMMODATION
Platys are easy fish to keep and feel very much at home even in very small aquaria. They do, however, like an aquarium with some vegetation.

SOCIAL CHARACTERISTICS
Platys are very peaceful, active fish which live throughout the aquarium. They are extremely suitable for the community aquarium. They should not be kept with large or predatory fish because these are much too aggressive for their friendlier neighbours. Since platys enjoy the company of their own spe-

cies, it is best to keep a number of specimens together (take care that you have more females than males in the aquarium).

TEMPERATURE AND WATER COMPOSITION
22-25°C. Platys are not very demanding and feel at home in nearly any water type.

FOOD
Platys are omnivores. They like dry food and can live their whole life on it with no difficulty, but they will very much appreciate live mosquito larvae, artemia and water fleas as a delicacy. Platys also need a lot of vegetable food. They graze algae from plants and stones.
If there is no algae available in the aquarium, you must provide the fish with some food flakes for plant eaters (Sera Flora, Sera Premium).

BREEDING
Platys are ovoviparous fish which have a fairly simple reproductive method. The size of the batch, as with a number of similar species of fish, depends on the age and condition of the parents, but there are usually about ten to fifty young.
The young are relatively small and do not grow as fast as, for example, young swordtails. You can rear them on either small algae or fine powdered food (Sera Micron). The strongest fry will survive in a spacious community aquarium with plenty of refuges (which can be created using floating plants and Java moss), but you can also choose to set up a separate aquarium for them.

VARIANTS
Countless different attractive colours and

variants have been developed in the course of time by selective breeding, but platys are also found in a very diverse range of colours in their natural habitat.

They come, for example, in yellow, red (coral platy), black, blue and spotted.

There are also varieties in various colours with a high dorsal fin.

SPECIAL REMARKS
These fish are extremely suitable for beginners.

Xiphophorus maculatus ♀

Xiphophorus variatus

FAMILY
Poeciliidae (ovoviparous tooth carps)

HABITAT
Mexico

SEXUAL DIFFERENCES
The males can be recognised by the anal fin which has been transformed into a reproductive organ, the so-called gonopodium.

LENGTH
Up to seven centimetres.

ACCOMMODATION

Xiphophorus variatus is a quiet fish which can be kept in a smaller aquarium with plenty of vegetation. In the wild these fish prefer stagnant water.

SOCIAL CHARACTERISTICS

These lively and colourful fish not only get on well with their own kind, but they will leave other aquarium dwellers in peace as well. Do not keep them with predatory or intolerant species. They are extremely at home in a community aquarium or in an aquarium with other (ovo)viviparous fish. Although they are not real shoaling fish, like neon tetras, for example, they are very happy with the company of others of their kind. The number of females should always be greater than the number of males. These fish swim all day long and occupy the whole aquarium.

TEMPERATURE AND WATER COMPOSITION

X. variatus is a strong fish which will reproduce in water of varying quality, but medium-hard to hard water is ideal. The water temperature should ideally be between 21 and 25°C.

FOOD

This platy species needs good quality dry food and also algae, which you can offer in fresh or dried form. Food tablets (such as Sera O-Nip and Sera Premium) will go down well, as will small live food.

BREEDING

This species is an ovoviparous fish and is very productive. The young can look after themselves immediately after birth and will eat algae and fine powdered food. Some females eat their young, but others do not. This appears to depend on how much space is available.

Fry which can hide will naturally have a greater chance of survival. You can provide floating plants and Java moss for this purpose in a community aquarium.

VARIANTS

X. variatus comes in various colours. The fish shown here displays the colour pattern most frequently seen. All varieties are undemanding and therefore very suitable for beginners.

Xiphophorus variatus ♂

Zoogeneticus quitzeoensis

FAMILY
Goodeidae

HABITAT
Mountain streams and lakes in Mexico.

SEXUAL DIFFERENCES
The males are different from the females because of the anal fin which has been transformed into an andropodium (reproductive organ). They are also more colourful.

LENGTH
Up to about 5.5 centimetres.

ACCOMMODATION
This small highland carp can be kept in a small or medium-sized community aquarium with fish species which require the same water conditions as itself. It appreciates peripheral vegetation.

SOCIAL CHARACTERISTICS
These fish get on well both with each other and with other fish. The males do not fight.

TEMPERATURE AND WATER COMPOSITION
25-28°C, pH neutral. The water hardness is not important. These fish need very pure, nitrogen-free water so you must siphon the waste from the bottom regularly and provide extra aeration.

FOOD
This fish is an omnivore and it is not usually difficult for the aquarist to put a good menu together. They readily eat dry food and also small live food.

BREEDING
This is a viviparous species. Under the right conditions the females will regularly produce live young which can look after themselves immediately. These fish are not known for eating their own offspring, but in smaller aquaria it may be better if there are sufficient refuges for the fry in the form of feathery-leafed plants.

Zoogeneticus quitzeoensis

Register

C

D

E

F

G

H

M

N

O

S

T

X

V

W

Photographic acknowledgements

Acknowledgements

Most transparencies were made by Reinhard Lütje and Norbert Dadaniak, Düsseldorf (D).

Additional material has been produced or provided by:

Archief Sera GmbH, Heinsberg (D):
6; 12 above left; 13 below right; 15; 24 above left; 25 above right; 27; 33 below left, above right; 42; 46; 47 above right; 57 below right; 58 below left; 72 below left; 81 below left; 86 above left; 87 above left; 90 above left; 97 above left; 130 above right; 168 below right; 176 right; 182 above left; 194 above right; 207; 208 above left; 224 above left; 225; 226 above left; 227 above left; 233 above right; 235; 239 below right; 244 above

Gerd Schrieber, Lüdenscheidt (D):
28 below right; 29 below; 56, 63 below right; 64 above left; 119; 146

Aqua Fauna, Vught (NL):
12 below left; 17 above right; 62; 83 below right; 85

Esther Verhoef:
8 top; 9 above left, below left, right; 10 right; 13 above left, below left; 16 above left; 18; 28 below left; 31; 84; 185; 241 above

The publisher and author wish to thank the following people and organisations for their co-operation:

Uwe Harms, Gerd Schreiber, Van Riel Distripet in Waalwijk and Aquarium-vereniging Aqua Fauna (Aqua Fauna Aquarium Association).

Publisher and photographers Reinhard Lütje and Norbert Dadaniak, Düsseldorf (D) wish to thank Bernhard Lücke, Essen (D) for the friendly co-operation and the provision of first class aquarium fish and Zoofachmarkt Verheyen & Schiffer, Bergheim (D) for supplying ornamental fish and aquatic plants free of charge. Special thanks go to Mr. Peter Merz (ornamental fish wholesaler), Heinsberg (D), who has constantly provided a limitless supply of valuable aquarium fish free of charge. Finally our thanks go to Uwe Harms (biologist), Heinsberg (D) for the friendly support and help with the development of this book.

Special thanks are due to the company Sera GmbH of Heinsberg (D); without their kind assistance this encyclopaedia would not have come about.